Presents

Victor Headley's

Fetish

Published by
THE X PRESS, 55 BROADWAY MARKET, LONDON E8 4PH.
TEL: 0171 729 1199   FAX: 0171 729 1771

© Victor Headley 1995.

Distributed by Turnaround, 27 Horsell Road, London N5 1XL
Tel: 0171 609 7836

Printed by BPC Paperbacks Ltd, Aylesbury, Bucks.
ISBN 1-874509-20-4

THE STORM

Visibility nil. The downpour made driving the little Suzuki perilous. With the angry roar of the thunderstorm and the sudden streaks of lightning, this was no night to hang around the country road where each pothole represented a threat to the long-suffering suspension. Although overcome with gratefulness that my friend's uncle had offered to let me use the car, I had since found out that it took a certain type of man to drive this particular vehicle. Once you had learnt to deal with such contingencies as a persistently faulty starter motor and a tendency to overheat, there was the roof leak directly above the driver's lap to come to terms with. As I turned off the main road at the bend, the light car spun into a dance on the dirt track and began the mile long drive through the bush in total darkness. The thought crossed my mind that the car would succumb to the heavy rain as it had done the previous week.

In this part of the African coast, long spells of humidity can, without warning, unleash the elements. I had driven a friend back to town and was on my way back to the house we stayed in a few miles out. Keeping to the middle of the narrow track, I slipped into first gear to avoid the rain-filled potholes and winced at the strangled sound of the engine. 'Hold on, don't stall on me, not here!' As if by spite, the engine spluttered, once, twice, three times and then nothing. The car rolled to a stop.

I knew from experience that I might be in for a long wait, so it was with genuine relief that within only a couple minutes I saw in the distance the double headlights of an oncoming vehicle. I watched the Land Rover get closer until it was close enough to turn half-circle so that it's tailgate almost touched the front of the broken down Suzuki. I climbed out to greet the driver who was already hurrying through the rain towards me.

"I knew this would happen... Let's tow it!" Uncle Ekedi said.

We hooked the tow bar to the Land Rover with a cable and within fifteen minutes, we were safely back inside the house. Uncle Ekedi, who knew his car better than anyone else, had rightly assumed it would give up on me in the storm and driven out looking for me. Though I had seen him come to the house on a few occasions since we arrived, this was the first one on one conversation he and I had had. He was a really easy, open man with a laugh to match his protruding stomach, and an English with a pacific drawl to it. A policeman by profession, he was my friend's maternal uncle. I think we hit it off real nice, so nice in fact that before he left for home, with the storm outside finally abating, he asked me if I like fishing.

"Fishing?" I said. "Yeah, sure..."

"OK, I'm taking you fishing. Be ready about five o'clock."

Uncle Ekedi explained that invariably on his free Saturday mornings, he went fishing and I could see he was doing me an honour inviting me along on one of his trips.

At dawn I found myself driving to the yard where his small motor boat was moored and pretty soon we were all loaded and out in the lagoon headed for the open sea. Breathing the clean morning air, I relaxed as Uncle Ekedi swerved effortlessly in and out of the waves. About two miles out, he cast his lines and after a brief prayer in the Douala language, he began to circle an area as large as a football pitch, waiting.

"They always come..." he told me with a confident grin.

And they did this time too. Within fifteen minutes he had a fish firmly pulling on the rod. I steered a half-circle before Uncle Ekedi could draw the catch in. At over four feet long, the barracuda seemed to be all teeth and menacing even out of water. Our relatively short time at sea brought in two more barracudas plus a couple of smaller fish. Later as we shared a meal in one of the numerous roadside restaurants in town, Uncle Ekedi confirmed that he had spent a little time studying in the States, UCLA no less, when he was younger. We talked for while. He seemed pleased to hear how the black community in Britain had come out in support of the Cameroon team in the 1990 world cup. I told him Roger Milla and the boys had done us proud.

"A lot is still missing, money mainly, but we're getting better," Uncle Ekedi nodded, while munching on his cassava-based 'nyondo'.

"Everybody's talking about Africa," I said. "We're all watching, you know."

He finished swallowing.

"How do you feel here?" he asked me.

"Here ? I feel alright," I told him. "I feel...home."

Uncle Ekedi smiled.

"This is home. Africa is big enough for all of us. Tell your friends."

I nodded and smiled, but he added very seriously:

"What Africa needs is not just money, Africa needs her people from outside, those that were taken away."

"That would be the greatest thing," I agreed.

Uncle Ekedi sounded confident about it.

"That is what will save all of us. Those who went as captives have become the powerful ones. We must all get back together now."

Uncle Ekedi proved to be the first policeman I really got to know and he seemed genuinely sad to see me go when the time came. By then we had done some more fishing and I'd gotten quite successful at it. Who knows. I could have enjoyed living off it...

Victor Headley
Douala, Cameroon. Winter 1994.

FETISH

This tale is for my children; 'You make it all worthwhile!'

"Then said the woman; Whom shall I bring up
unto thee?
And he said; Bring me up Samuel."

I Samuel 28. v.11

CHAPTER ONE

The big engine spluttered and shook and finally stalled once more. It took ten more minutes of fiddling with the carburettor before Jaimie finally lifted his head from under the bonnet. He had a strong feeling that two hours of work were about to be rewarded at last. Wiping his greasy hands on the rag hanging out of his boiler suit pocket, Jaimie sat behind the wheel, taking care to keep the plastic seat cover in place. One turn of the key, a light tap of his foot on the gas pedal and the six cylinders came to life, thundering as Jaimie increased the pressure. He smiled and released the gas pedal, leaving the engine to purr at low regime. 6.43 pm. It had taken him longer than he thought to sort out this one. Now it only needed a few adjustments and the car would be ready for its anxious owner to collect. Jaimie thought about giving it a test run but realised he'd had enough for the day. The week had been pretty busy, right now he felt for a nice shower and long drink. Beyond the half-raised shutter, the drizzle was still coming down. So much for spring time! Jaimie closed the bonnet.

"Hey, Paul...I've got it ticking...I'm outta here!"

From the small office at the back of the garage where he was having yet another cup of tea, the boss mumbled:

"Alright son, see yah tomorrow."

Paul would probably be here for most of the evening, having tea, eyes staring at the portable TV on top of the filing cabinet. He had mentioned to Jaimie that he was having 'bother' at home, which explained why he had arrived at work late in the last couple of weeks. Jaimie usually opened the place up anyway, but Paul normally arrived shortly after. He was a good boss to work for and Jaimie sympathised with him but there wasn't much he could do. In the last six months that he'd been working there, Paul had treated him well, even advancing him part of his wages on two occasions. Jaimie wiped off the grime from his fingers before washing his hands. He took off his overalls and cap, stretched and started out past the row of Chevrolets and Buicks lined up to the shutter, some already fixed, some awaiting work to be done on them. The Dodge pick-up truck last in line was next on Jaimie's list. Paul's place was one of the few garages that dealt exclusively with American cars in

1

London, so Jaimie and the two other mechanics were usually fairly busy.

The street was wet, grey clouds were bringing down an early darkness and people with and without umbrellas were heading for dryer places. Jaimie crossed over the green of the nearby low rise apartments and climbed into his jeep. Inside, he picked up his baseball cap from the dashboard, adjusted it on his near-shaven head then turned on the stereo.

A reassuringly familiar hip hop beat blasted out of the large speakers at the back. Before switching on the engine, Jaimie turned down the volume a little; early in the morning he needed the high intensity of the loud beat, after a hard day's work he felt for a little less punch. He switched on his road lights, put the car in gear and the Renegade jeep eased out of parking. Whether it was the fine, persistent rain of the day or something else, Jaimie wasn't quite sure how he felt. No major problems to sully his usual relaxed attitude but he had felt strange all day, like something was on his mind but what, he couldn't tell. Before hitting the high street, he ejected the cassette and dug in the glove compartment for something else, something more mellow. He pushed another cassette in the stereo, neatly slipped into a gap in the traffic as the Jodeci track poured out of the speakers. He turned it up, letting the synchronised harmonies and throbbing bass fill the cabin space.

Caught in the slow moving flow of vehicles, Jaimie surveyed the familiar rush hour scenes on Kilburn High Street until, humming to himself, he saw his escape route on the right, by McDonald's. He manoeuvred himself into position and crossed over, took a few more back streets to avoid the busy spots. After almost a year of living in London, he knew most of the shortcuts in this part of town now. Traffic could get real bad over here he had found out, though not quite as bad as in New York. But considering the relative sizes of both cities, London held its own. Down Ladbroke Grove, it took Jaimie fifteen minutes bumper to bumper in a tight stream of vehicles just to get over the bridge. After that, he hitched right at the roundabout and made it home without any further delays. Someone, probably one of the neighbours' numerous visitors, had parked right in front of the house so he left the jeep around the corner.

Inside the corridor, the smell of food was strong and the state of the kitchen confirmed that someone had just finished having dinner. Junior was in, or so Jaimie thought. He shouted but got no reply. Probably his younger brother had just left. These days, with Junior out every night minicabbing and Jaimie working sometimes until late in the evening, they rarely saw each other.

While his bath was running upstairs, Jaimie selected a station on the hi-fi. Invariably, Junior had it on the heaviest ragga station; Jaimie dialled until he could find something more suited to his mood. He loved reggae music but right now he felt like something warm and slow to linger in a hot tub. Immersed to his chin in the perfumed water, Jaimie relaxed and let his mind free-wheel in no particular direction. All day he had been feeling like today was Friday, but he was one day too fast, there was still one day to go to the weekend. Unless there was an emergency at the garage, he liked to keep his Saturdays free, so he could take care of the other things he enjoyed in life. Jaimie picked up a wet rag and rubbed it over his head and face, mentally going through his agenda up to the audition date. It was a long shot but he had to try it. Ever since arriving in Britain, he had been up and down, knocking at doors, calling numbers, trying to get a part, any part in a film. He would even do a play, anything that would give him a chance to show what he could do, to get noticed by the elusive and almighty executive producers who controlled this heartbreaking business. Jaimie knew only too well how hard it was to get on the inside but, despite having had little luck so far and seeing his personal approaches politely turned down over a dozen times, he still persevered. There had to be a break somewhere out there for a versatile, six foot three, young, black American actor with limited experience but huge potential!

The tub was too short for Jaimie to stretch fully, so he lifted himself up and extended his legs over the taps. As he massaged his aching muscles, he realised he hadn't worked out since last Sunday. Sure, he got some exercise coaching the local youth club's junior basketball team on Saturdays, but that was no real sweat. He usually managed two workouts a week, sometimes with Junior, but his brother was lazy, preferring clubs to gyms.

It was only when he had finished dressing and was on his way down to the kitchen that Jaimie remembered his date. He had no real desire to call Brenda. They had been out on a couple of dates in the last two weeks. Things were fine between them, she was fun but Jaimie knew deep inside him that he wasn't really interested. He

3

couldn't feel any real excitement about Brenda, didn't look forward to seeing her again, all telltale signs that he shouldn't push the situation any further. He started fixing himself some dinner instead, reflecting with amusement that a couple of years back, he never bothered to check out his real feelings towards a woman until after he had 'touched down' with her. He smiled to himself, thinking:

'I must be getting good!'

The more he thought about it, the less he felt like spending the evening with Brenda. She had been doing all the calling and Jaimie had gone along but maybe now was the time to slow it down. He knew Brenda was interested in him, had said so and was visibly looking for a relationship, with a big 'R'. He wasn't. Sitting at the kitchen table, munching on his omelette, Jaimie decided he wouldn't call, and if she did, he would simply have to be tactful. At least, she couldn't say he had used her...

His dinner over, Jaimie stretched on the sofa and took in the TV news. More accidents, killings and disasters. From the States, England always seemed a safe, quiet little place, but no more apparently. It was becoming more and more like back home. He got up and went to check the stack of videos piled up against the wall unit. He'd seen all of them several times over but he learned something new from the movies every time. That was part of his training too. Back in New York, his drama teacher had always said there is at least a dozen ways to watch a movie. And he was right! Going over his collection of films, Jaimie had learned to pick them apart, carefully studying dialogue, angles, body movement, lighting, etc. Eventually he hoped he would one day be a director himself but for the time being he would settle for being in front of the camera. By now, he could play entire scenes from his favourite films, almost perfectly. Halfway through the pile, he picked up *Once Upon A Time In America*, a classic. With a three hours running time, it should take care of the evening...

Friday was a nice day, as it always is. A timid sun had hovered over the town all afternoon, no grey clouds were in sight and people on the main street looked more relaxed. Jaimie was strolling around the market stalls, a sandwich in one hand, a can of Pepsi in the other. He wasn't really looking for anything in particular, so once he'd taken a tour of the stalls he just leaned against the street railing and watched the comings and goings around him. With the

4

smell of springtime in the air, business wasn't bad for the shops. Two police officers crossed over from the other side of the road and stopped by a flower stall. While her colleague exchanged a few words with the trader, the policewoman smiled to Jaimie as their eyes met. 'Definitely springtime!' he thought to himself as he tossed the empty can in a nearby bin. Leisurely, he walked back up the road. At the garage, there was only Paul and himself today, the other two had both taken the day off. Jaimie went back to the truck he'd started on before lunch. The afternoon passed quickly enough. By 4.30 Jaimie decided to call it a day. As he climbed inside his car, he resolved to pass by Tony's house in nearby Cricklewood before going home. Tony was the first friend he had made on arriving in this country the previous year. They had met at a West End club and got on well. Jaimie found out that Tony had family in New York whom he visited regularly. And he even knew some of the neighbourhoods where Jaimie had grown up.

When he got to the house, Jaimie scanned the street but there was no sign of Tony's BMW. Just to be sure, he parked and went to ring the bell but Tony wasn't home. Shrugging, Jaimie walked back to his car and drove out. Knowing Tony, he had probably driven to Leicester where his girlfriend lived, straight after leaving the travel agency where he worked. The best thing Jaimie could think of now was to chill until later when he would go down to the radio station for his weekly spot. He stopped at the intersection, got the car into first gear and started to turn right to get back on the main road when it suddenly appeared out of nowhere; small, fast and cutting the corner much too sharp. Jaimie's reflexes were good: the jeep stopped at once, but the little blue car was too far gone and no amount of breaking from the driver prevented the inevitable. The right side caught the front bumper of the jeep at the back, just hard enough to make an ugly, crushed metal sound. Swearing, Jaimie pulled his handbrake, switched off and got out of the jeep. The blue Renault Clio had stopped against the sidewalk. The voice reached Jaimie just as he was checking the damage.

"Can't you look where you're going?!"

Startled, Jaimie looked up.

"Excuse me?"

He found himself facing a young woman with a furious look on her brown-skinned face. Dressed in a designer suit, she was standing by her car, hands on her hips.

5

"Didn't you see me turning?"

The woman was implying Jaimie was in the wrong. He frowned.

"Wait a minute, I think you've got it all wrong. You were the one who cut the corner, and at speed too!"

The woman was inspecting the back of her car and in particular the rear wheel arch where there was a long scrape.

"Look what you've done to my new car!"

The woman lamented accusingly, throwing a dark look at Jaimie. He sighed and decided to straighten her out.

"Look lady, you were going much too fast to turn into a small street like this, and you cut right across the corner. You're lucky I managed to stop, you could have been hurt..."

The woman squared up to him.

"I'm lucky? I suppose I should thank you too?!"

Jaimie was not a man to easily lose his temper but all the same, right is right, and she was definitely wrong.

"Listen, this is getting nowhere. Let's exchange particulars so the insurance can deal with it. We could call the police if you want to, but maybe..."

"I can't give you my 'particulars'," the woman cut in, stressing the last word.

"Why not?"

She sighed.

"I just got the car today, it's not insured yet."

"I'm sorry to hear that, it's unlucky I guess..."

"Yes, and you're the one to bring me bad luck."

That was rich!

"I told you, you were going too fast!"

The woman stared at Jaimie as if she wanted to hit him, then turned around, got back inside her car and slammed the door. He followed her, and leaned his head in her window as she kicked up the engine.

"Listen, maybe I could help you. I work in a garage, come down and we'll work something out. It's only a small job..."

The woman looked up at him, her features closed up, her dark hair neatly tied back by a golden clip.

"No, thank you, you've done quite enough. You have ruined my weekend."

With that, she put the car in gear and drove off at speed, leaving a puzzled Jaimie standing by the kerb.

"Can you believe this?" he said out loud. Shaking his head, he got back inside his car after a cursory glance at his bumper. He was still pondering the incident when he opened the door of the house. The smell of fried food and the loud, pumping ragga beat told him immediately Junior was home. The kitchen was empty but two eggs were about to turn dark in the frying pan. Sighing, Jaimie turned off the stove just as the sound of running feet came down the stairs.

"Hey Toddy, what's up man?"

Jaimie started.

"Quit calling me..."

But Junior went on, while scooping his dark brown eggs into a plate.

"Guess what happened to me last night?"

He sat at the kitchen table

"What now?" Jaimie asked, ready for anything.

"I got arrested...spent the night in the can!"

"What? Again?"

Junior seemed amused rather than distressed.

"Yeah, again. And you know what for?"

"Let me guess..." Jaimie cut in, opening the fridge. "No insurance? Drink driving? Speeding maybe?"

With Junior's record there was scope for choice.

Between two bites from his egg sandwich, Junior said:

"Offensive weapon, can you believe it?"

Jaimie took a swig from the juice he'd just poured into a glass.

"What weapon?" he asked, expecting the worst.

Chewing hard, Junior looked at him, shook his head.

"Spanner," he managed to say.

"A spanner?" Jaimie repeated, sitting on the other side of the table. He had to wait until his brother had satisfied his hunger to get the full story. Incredibly, Junior always seemed to get into the worst troubles through no fault of his own.

"Remember I told you how some of the guys at the office got robbed dropping off people in South London in the last few weeks?" Junior started once his plate was empty.

"So I took this big spanner, you know, like a monkey wrench, from my boot and put it under my seat, just in case, right?"

Jaimie nodded. Junior emptied his glass.

"So last night I came in around midnight, had some food..."

"Yeah, I heard you," Jaimie remarked, remembering being

7

awakened by Junior rambling through the house.

"Alright, I was going to get some sleep but around two-thirty, I decided to go and do a few more runs. Anyway, I get this fare to Wembley, two girls, nice. So here I am, driving down, not speeding or anything. All of a sudden, this police car comes right behind me, flashing me to stop. So I stop and these two cops start to question me, asking for my papers, you know, the usual hassle. So one of them starts to search the car, finds the spanner. The next thing I know, they decide to take me in, leave my car around some corner and the two girls out on a limb in the middle of the night. Can you believe it?"

Junior looked up at his brother with the face of a man who has just suffered a grave miscarriage of justice.

"What can I say, man?" Jaimie shrugged. He had to admit, for once he couldn't blame Junior. "Didn't you explain to them what you had the thing for?"

Junior let out a short, bitter laugh.

"You bet I did, but apparently they were more concerned about me hurting a guy who would rob me than him hurting me. Might as well try talking to a wall, man."

Jaimie knew the feeling. He got up.

"So, what now?"

"They'll take me to court, soon probably."

"Here we go again..." Jaimie quipped, walking out of the kitchen.

In the year he had lived with his brother, Jaimie had seen him go to court three times already, for various small offences. He'd got off each time with a fine. As far back as Jaimie could remember, his younger and only brother had always attracted trouble. Both boys had attended the same primary school back in Brooklyn, before their mother took Junior to England with her when she left, and even then Jaimie had many fights because of him.

Upstairs, the bathroom was a mess. Jaimie leaned over the stairwell, shouting above the music.

"Yo! Come and clean up this place, man. I need to shower."

CHAPTER TWO

The lady at the reception thanked Jaimie as he gave her back the keys to the lockers and wished him a good weekend. Outside the Centre, a few of the team players were still hanging around, loudly discussing their respective scores in the game they had just finished.

"Did you watch my wicked dunk at the last minute?" a teenager with a screechy voice and round glasses asked another.

"Yeah, I saw it," Jaimie answered while walking past them towards his car. "If you worked harder at your stamina you'd probably score more of them too!"

The youngster turned towards him, some of his team mates sneered.

"I'm gonna work on it," he promised.

"That goes for all of you. Have a nice weekend now..."

As Jaimie was opening his car door, someone called.

"Jaimie!"

Richie was running towards him, his large shirt flapping about him. He was a promising player, almost six feet tall at barely fifteen years of age, but still too skinny.

"Remember you said you'd run some tracks for me?"

Jaimie took the blank cassettes Richie was handing him.

"No problem."

"I want the same kind of tunes you played last night." Richie specified.

"You got it. And I want you to do me a favour."

Jaimie looked at the youth as he switched on his engine.

"What's that?"

Jaimie closed his door, broke into a grin.

"Go and eat some food!"

Richie laughed, Jaimie drove off, the other players waved as the jeep moved past the gates. The result of the weekly practice game had been hotly disputed today. Whether it was the good weather or whether the kids were getting better, Jaimie had enjoyed the session. He usually had a good time every Saturday, and the youths responded well to his coaching. They liked Jaimie, who was always there if any of them had problems they might not want to talk about to their parents. Also they all listened regularly to the hip hop show

9

he played on Friday nights on a local community station. That was a definite bonus in getting their trust. Most of those kids were very involved with hip hop music and culture so to have Jaimie, an original rap DJ from the States, as a basketball coach was the coolest thing possible.

Six thirty on a warm, breezy Saturday early evening...Jaimie felt nice within himself. The cold shower after the sweat of the game had refreshed him. He looked forward to a big dinner and maybe a couple of beers. The pager in his jeans pocket went off: beep...beep...beep. Louder each time. Jaimie checked it, holding the wheel with one hand. The message wasn't really a surprise: 'CALL BRENDA. I'M AT HOME NOW'.

Sighing but smiling, Jaimie dropped back in second gear as he entered his road. He just didn't feel like answering that call. The KRS1 track was blasting from the speakers behind him. He switched off the engine and sat listening to the end of the record, then picked up his bag and walked up to the house. Junior wasn't in, he had still been in bed about midday when Jaimie had left.

Dropping his bag upstairs, Jaimie realised he didn't feel like staying inside and cooking dinner. The weather was much too nice outside, he would rather buy himself a spicy meal at the local Indian restaurant. He picked up his wallet and left the house. Ten minutes of leisurely walking later, Jaimie walked inside the restaurant on Ladbroke Road. He ordered, paid, then went back out to buy a drink. The big bottle of Perrier water was more then half empty by the time he picked up the food. Walking back in the slowly descending night, Jaimie could smell the curry flavour of his meal tickling his nostrils. The shout hit him just as he was turning the corner of his road.

"Yo! Jaimie!"

He stopped and turned at the sound of his brother's voice. Dodging the traffic on the main road, Junior grinned as he caught up with Jaimie.

"Hey, what's up?"

"You finally woke up!"

"Yeah, I had a hard night... That smells nice!" Junior remarked.

"Don't even think about it! That's my food, no deal." Jaimie warned him. He knew only too well his brother's insatiable appetite.

"Oh come on, Jaimie man! I ain't eaten all day...and I'm broke..."

10

"Broke, so what happened to your money, you're still working, ain't you?"

Junior kissed his teeth dismissively.

"I ain't going back, it's not worth the hassles."

Today Jaimie wasn't gonna let himself soften so easily.

"Oh no; you're unemployed again!" he quipped, fearing what that meant for him. "And you've got no savings, am I right?"

A sad shake of the head from Junior.

"I did, but Lorraine caught me last night. It's all gone."

"Lorraine, uh-uh!"

Any time Junior mentioned the mother of his two-year-old daughter, it had to be trouble. Jaimie knew once again he was likely to hear a long story. Shaking his head, he dipped into his pocket.

"OK, OK, go and buy yourself some food...and it's the last time!" he said, knowing full well it wouldn't be.

Junior smiled and took the £10 note.

"Thanks, I appreciate that Toddy," he said, scampering away.

"Hey, I told you quit calling me that," Jaimie pointed at him. "And get me a beer too!"

Junior knew his brother didn't like his childhood nickname, but enjoyed teasing him with it from time to time.

Jaimie resumed his walk home, reflecting that Junior would probably never change his ways. He loved his only brother from whom he'd been separated since he was twelve. When their mother had decided to leave home in New York and return to England where she was born, Jaimie's world had been totally upset. As the oldest of the three children, he had felt for some time that things weren't right between their parents. Yet, with childhood innocence and trust in happy endings, he had always believed things would somehow get back to the way they were before. The day their parents sat him, Amanda and Wilfred (named after the father) down and told them the news, would always remain etched deeply in his memory. The worst was when Junior realised what the split meant for him. He went crazy, cried for days. But with all the pain of the break up, their mother just couldn't leave her youngest child behind and eventually it was agreed that Junior would come back to spend every summer in New York until he finished secondary school. For Jaimie, the first two years of separation were hurtful. He missed his mother yet couldn't leave his father whom he felt very close to. Most of all he missed Junior, three years younger than him

11

and already a partner and 'accomplice' in their childhood games as much as a brother.

Curiously enough, Amanda took the separation better than anyone else, at least it seemed that way at the time. By that time, she was already totally submerged in her school environment and friends, and she found in their aunt Madeline, their father's sister, a kind of surrogate mother. Amanda agreed to visit her mother and brother in London for the holidays once a year. She never cried, at least not openly. So life went on. Their father raised Jaimie and Amanda on his own. He soon got himself another woman but didn't involve her in their family life and never remarried.

Jaimie was halfway through his meal, enjoying every bit of it, when Junior came through the door and handed him a Budweiser. Emptying his food container onto a plate, he sat across from his brother and got busy with it. Once he had satisfied his immediate hunger, Junior looked at Jaimie.

"You'll never guess what happened to me last night..." he started.

Jaimie swallowed a piece of curried cauliflower, held up one hand in front of him:

"Stop! I don't wanna hear it."

"No man, check it out, you ain't gonna believe it!"

Jaimie resigned himself and tried to keep as detached as possible while Junior gave him the story. He said he had decided to attend a ragga session the previous night with some friends, in order to cool out after his bad experience with the police the night before.

"The place was 'ram' solid, man, especially like it's getting hot now; excess amount of girls. Anyway, I'm chilling out in a corner, talking to this criss browning, you know, just discussing and things...all of a sudden, who do I see circling through the crowd?" Junior said the name before Jaimie spelt it out.

"That's right: Lorraine! I don't know how she found me down there, man. It freaked me out. So, I try to slip away but she's seen me already so there's no way out. I didn't want her to start in the place, you know what I'm saying, so I tried to get her outside. But she wanted to kick up some shit with the girl, imagine—and I'd just met her! I'm telling you man, it was rough. In the end I got her out with a little help from two of my spars. Then she got mad, talking about I'm hiding from her from last week..."

"Yeah, well, you are."

12

"Sure I am, that girl's crazy, man. It's like she owns me and shit. Every time I try to break up with her she freaks out. I can't take the embarrassment, Jaimie, serious! Anyway, I had to leave my friends and take her home. I left there this morning..."

"Break up to make up, uh?"

"This is no joke. I'm getting away from that girl, trust me!"

Jaimie finished his last mouthful, opened his beer.

"So, what about Keesha?"

Junior winced, shook his head.

"Keesha's cool, I love her, man, but I can't take the mother."

The Budweiser tasted chilled and smooth.

"Yeah, but that's the way it goes: you do the crime you do the time." Jaimie grinned, before adding, "I think you and Lorraine better get married."

Junior chewed some of his food, glanced coldly at his brother.

"I'd rather join the army, I'd have an easier life, you know what I mean?"

"Then tell her you don't want her."

"I tried, once, believe me. Man, that girl ain't gonna leave me alone as long as I'm alive."

"Fatally hooked, uh?"

"Yeah, you make jokes but this is a serious problem. I mean, I need some space. I can't get cooped up with her like she wants me to. Last night I had to give her all the money I had to cool things down."

Junior's plight sounded desperate. Jaimie just sighed.

"Well homeboy, you just gonna have to work this one out. I'm afraid I'm no wiser than you when it comes to that sort of thing."

"But you been through that kinda shit, you could talk to her. She listens to you!"

Jaimie put his beer back down on the table, looked at his brother.

"Me? Oh no, sorry; I want nothing to do with that deal. And like I said: "I can't do nothin' for you, man, I've got problems of my own."

"Come on, homes; at least you could say a word or two, straighten her up..."

"Straighten her up? How?"

"Explain to her that I'm under pressure, she's got to ease up or I'm gonna run."

"Run? Run where?"

13

"What's with you, man? Just tell her that, like you wanna help her, she'll pay attention to you, I know that."

Somehow Jaimie didn't think that his intervention could really help out but then again it didn't cost anything to try.

"Alright, but remember; this is a one-off. Don't ask me again."

Junior's smile came back.

"Thanks, I'll owe you one," he assured Jaimie as he got up with his plate. The two cleaned up the kitchen then went to relax in the living room.

Jaimie checked out the TV channels but there wasn't much worth watching, as usual. He switched to cable TV which he had recently had installed and settled in his chair.

"Oh yeah, Brenda called for you earlier," Junior said, stretched out on the sofa.

Jaimie looked at him, they both laughed.

"I don't know what you did to her, but she's been calling a lot." Junior grinned maliciously.

"That's just the point, I didn't do nothing, man. And I prefer to keep it that way."

"What's wrong with her? She looks fit to me."

Jaimie smiled at his brother's simple logic.

"She is, but I'd rather pass on that."

Junior probably found it hard to understand how he could refuse a 'play' off the nice-looking girl he'd brought home one evening the previous week. Jaimie had learned it was sometimes better not to start unless he was really taken in. And he wasn't.

"So what's happening later?"

Jaimie had no plans, nothing special except to relax.

"So what d'you say we go out, you and me? I didn't even get to rave last night, with all that hassle."

It wasn't a bad idea.

"I don't know, maybe. Where you thinking of going?"

"We could check out the Emerald..."

Jaimie thought about it for a moment. He hadn't been there in three months, since he had stopped working there in fact. Shortly after arriving in London, he was taken to the West End club by Junior and introduced to the manager. Jaimie ended up doing a stint as a DJ for a while.

"Why not? OK, you're on!"

"Alright. You should go out more, Jaimie man, enjoy yourself.

14

Summer's here."

"You could be right; maybe I should go out a little more," Jaimie agreed, stretching in his chair. He could feel the muscles in his back and legs pulling now that he had relaxed. "I better get a little sleep before we move."

Purple rays from the laser lights reflected against the big aluminium, multi-faceted ball spinning from the ceiling, shooting bright arrows all over the dance floor. It was barely two o'clock but a sizeable crowd of dancers were furiously keeping up with the techno beat out of the column speakers. The Emerald opened six nights a week and hosted various live events, bands and PAs. Because it was situated at the heart of the West End, near Piccadilly, many tourists ended up spending at least one of their London nights there. The selection of music was geared to cater for a wide enough range of tastes. Jaimie, however, who had spent the best part of the last hour sipping a beer at one of the small tables near the back, felt rather bored with the music so far. Freestyle, hardcore rap and swingbeat were more familiar to him. As an early experimenter with hip hop rhythms back in New York, Jaimie usually grew impatient with the bland house-type music mainstream clubs played. Junior wasn't that fussy. Though he was a ragga and hip hop man by orientation, he would dance to anything when it came to impressing a leggy girl like the one he had met tonight. Jaimie watched his brother for a while then decided to go and talk with the DJ. The small control room overlooked the dancefloor and the bar. Jaimie introduced himself to the large bearded white guy behind the mixing desk and they started talking music. Meanwhile the DJ was keeping things going on the floor, gradually blending in some heavier tunes, probably to impress his visitor. From where he stood, Jaimie could see Junior, now seated at their table with his new girl. More people were arriving, milling around the bar area, making their way through to the dancefloor. Most were white, with some Chinese and a few oriental-looking young women. Only about a half dozen black faces could be seen. It wasn't openly acknowledged that a club like the Emerald discriminated as to who could come in, but subtle and erratically applied practices like the 'couples only' rule and an even more arbitrary dress code check at the door, sufficed to keep out the unwelcomed. As an ex-DJ, Jaimie had no problem. Ironically, he got

15

his job despite his colour because he was American. An overseas origin and accent strangely worked some way against discrimination at times.

The group of people coming in from the entrance into the brighter area around the bar attracted Jaimie's attention, especially so because two out of the three couples were black. A tall, broad-shouldered, middle-aged white man, sporting a smart suit, was smiling at something one of the black men was saying in his ear. He tapped him on the shoulder and nodded. A waiter appeared and led the little group to a table behind the dancefloor, right across from Jaimie's elevated vantage point. The white woman, permed up and over-dressed in an expensive-looking, off the shoulder evening dress seemed slightly out of place. They each filed past the gesticulating crowd on the dancefloor.

"Hey, you want to spin for me? I've got to pop downstairs for a minute."

Jaimie took his eyes off the woman who had just sat down at the table amongst her friends and turned away from the glass opening.

"Sure, I don't mind."

He got into the seat the DJ had just vacated and started going through the stack of records on the benchtop next to him.

"I won't be long," the DJ said as he stepped out.

"Take your time."

Quickly, Jaimie lined up half a dozen tracks which he found closer to his tastes and still suitable for the audience. He put on the headphones, checked some of the tunes, then by habit slightly shifted some of the knobs and sliding control buttons on the mixer, going for a harder edged sound. The track was finishing so Jaimie swiftly switched to the second turntable and pushed the volume up just a little bit. Then he selected a new record for the first deck. Through the glass in front of him he could barely make out the faces at the back of the dancefloor, getting glimpses as they intermittently caught the rays of the laser lights. The one he was peering through to catch sight of had features that made him want to see more. It was only after a few more minutes of waiting for the bright dancing rays to fall upon the woman that something in his mind clicked. It could have been the hairstyle, or the profile, but something told him he knew that face. But from where? While changing records, checking tracks to be played in advance, Jaimie was searching his memory, the 'deja vu' feeling wouldn't leave him alone. Then it

16

came to him as he was mechanically nodding to a tune pumping through the headphone: it was *that* woman. He was almost sure, it had to be! Checking that the record playing still had some way to run, Jaimie got up and went right behind the glass, his eyes staring hard across the semi-darkness of the room below. At the edge of the dancefloor, a man moved closer towards his partner; the woman's head appeared in the gap, only briefly, but long enough for Jaimie to smile to himself knowingly.

"Yes," he said aloud, satisfied to have been proven right.

It was her, the woman with the car. Jaimie was sure of that now. The very same woman who had been so unkind to him after throwing her precious little car in his jeep's way, was now sitting down below in the crowded club. Coincidence, that's how most people called things like that, but Jaimie always saw more in those little signs in life. He preferred to believe in some sort of law of action-reaction, something of a more subtle nature to explain it. He returned to the DJ booth and got busy for a little while, sending hot rhythms that had his public rocking then he took out Naughty By Nature's *OPP* out of the jacket and placed it on the first deck. As the previous record ended, the heavy beat of the popular tune hit the floor, Jaimie expertly fiddling with the mixer for additional effects. Feeling good, he opened up the mike, smiled.

"Yo! For all of you sneaking out tonight with somebody's property. Naughty...but nice."

Satisfied with his gimmick, Jaimie was bobbing to the track when the DJ came back in.

"Alright, you've got them hot!" the man smiled.

"You bet. Here, take over."

Jaimie thanked the DJ for the beer he'd brought him. Down on the floor below, more people had joined in the partying so that the space was now packed with bodies. Some people were doing their thing in the aisles between the tables. But the subject of Jaimie's attention had not moved. She was almost completely out of sight behind the swaying wall of dancers.

Jaimie took a gulp from his beer, rocked to the last few beats of *OPP* and decided it was time to stir things up. He took leave of the DJ, promising he'd come back to see him some other night, then stepped out. Downstairs was hot. At the edge of the dancefloor, Junior was demonstrating his very own style, totally immersed in the track. His girl too, was dancing wildly, real close to him. Jaimie made his way to the bar, cooled out with his beer while surveying the scene. The slap on the shoulder almost knocked the bottle out of his hand.

"Jaimie, old son!"

Jaimie turned to face Doug, the big Scot who managed the Emerald. As tall as Jaimie but fatter, he was smiling broadly.

"Hey Doug, how is it going?"

"Oh not too bad, mate. Where have you been?"

"Here and there, trying to do my own thing, you know..."

Signalling to one of the bartenders, Dougie insisted on buying Jaimie another beer. They had got on fine when Jaimie used to work at the club. Dougie always had a story to tell and Jaimie enjoyed the colourful tales of the man, even though some of them sounded a little far fetched at times. All the same, from the start Jaimie couldn't help but feeling that Doug's past was somewhat shady. They talked for a while, people passing to and fro around them. Usually the Emerald closed around six am. It was now around four o'clock and the place was lively. A group of elegantly dressed women came in, Doug caught sight of them and looked puzzled for a second or two.

"Have another beer on me, son. I'll be back."

Doug left Jaimie to go and check out something. Sipping from his bottle, Jaimie decided that two beers were enough for now, he didn't really need another one. He felt relaxed, moving easy to the beats the DJ was throwing down. He might not have remembered the object of his earlier attention for a while if the same woman had not passed right by him on her way to the bathroom with a friend. Jaimie watched them. Tonight, the woman was wearing a dark-coloured sleeveless dress, which looked really fine on her. Jaimie smiled to himself, nodded and swallowed another gulp of cold beer. He knew he had to say something, wasn't sure exactly what but felt confident his natural wit would surface at the right time. Around him, the atmosphere was warm, most of the customers under the effect of drinks and having a great time. Soon, the two women came out of the bathroom, walking towards the bar, talking. Jaimie slid forward to find himself in the right position. Almost time...a hand grabbed his left arm.

"Yo, Toddy! Where you been, man?"

Jaimie turned frowning and found Junior's wide grin, his girl right behind him, also smiling. The woman and her friend had passed by now, Jaimie saw them walking away towards the dancefloor. With a dark glance to his brother, he took off after them. Trust Junior to mess things up! A smooth little set up was now turning into a light pursuit through a thick crowd. The woman Jaimie wanted to get to was leading the way, her friend close behind as they walked alongside the rows of tables. Jaimie pushed his way past a few more people and finally caught up with them. He passed the friend and lightly touched the woman's bare shoulder. She turned around, looked up at him, surprised. Jaimie composed himself, flashed his most engaging smile.

"Hi," he said above the noise level.

"Pardon?" Two dark elongated eyes were staring at him. The friend had stopped and was watching him too. He got a little closer, leaned forward.

"I said 'Hi'. D'you remember me?"

Judging from her puzzled look, the young woman didn't. Her fine eyebrows were knitted in concentration. She looked at her friend then back at Jaimie.

"I'm the man with the jeep...you know, the accident yesterday."

He waited for her to recall. It took a few seconds as they stood facing each other in the crowded space. Then she said:

"Yes, you are..."

The tone of her voice wasn't really friendly. Jaimie raised his eyebrows. She asked: "Are you following me?"

What could he say? He felt out of sync, unbalanced by the woman's unfriendly attitude. Her friend was observing him closely with one of those 'I know what you want' kind of looks women can use so well. Jaimie could see this was getting nowhere.

"Look, I'm just saying 'Hello'. Take it easy..."

The friend whispered something in the woman's ear then stepped forward and continued towards the dancefloor. The woman threw Jaimie another deep, almost hostile glance, turned and followed the other one. Jaimie watched her disappear through the crowd then turned back and made his way back to the bar. His approach had been less than successful. Junior was still there, talking into his girl's ear. He stopped to smile at Jaimie.

"You're getting busy, homie!"

Jaimie didn't even bother to answer him. He turned and signalled to the bartender; he could use another beer after all...

CHAPTER THREE

It wasn't the right move, Tony could feel it. But there weren't many more to choose from. He'd already lost two games and if he could help it, was determined to avenge himself. Once again he took his hand off the bishop, sighed, looked up at Jaimie sipping his beer. Though he appeared unconcerned about Tony's next move, slowly nodding in time with the bass of the Billie Holiday CD playing, Tony knew his friend was watching him closely, waiting for him to make the fatal mistake that would give him the third game. Tony rubbed his chin, winced, then got hold of the bishop, again. After that, it took Jaimie exactly three moves to defeat his friend. He smiled modestly, finished his beer can.

"Another one, daddy?"

Tony shook his head, leaned back in the chair.

"It's not funny, man."

"Get used to it, it's on!"

Tony had arrived after work with the big news and Jaimie'd been teasing him ever since. Three straight defeats at chess had done nothing to make Tony feel better. Jaimie got up and stretched, went to the small ice box by the window and took out two more chilled beers.

"Here you go."

The beginning of the week had been heavy at work, with new vehicles coming in for the last three days and Jaimie had finished late, except today. Tony's call in the afternoon had made him realise he needed to ease up a little. Made no sense trying to keep up with the work, he told himself. Tonight, a few beers with his friend felt just right. In fact, it seemed as if Tony needed to chill out even more than him.

"You told your mother?"

Jaimie had met Tony's mother a few times, a sweet but very emotional, middle-aged woman who absolutely adored her youngest child and only son.

"I'm just getting used to the idea myself, I'm not ready for that part yet."

"She's gonna love it, don't worry."

"Yeah? She ain't never even met Charlene! I wanted to wait first, see if things were serious with her."

Jaimie swallowed some of his drink, laughed.

"Well, they'd better be now!"

"You're enjoying it, I can tell."

Tony's pitiful face was a sight.

"Come on, Tony, it's not that bad. You'll feel good about it when the baby's born."

Tony took a large gulp of his beer.

"I guess you're right, it's just that it's a big surprise, you know what I mean?"

"Yeah, I know. But why you wanna get married right away? I mean, are you under pressure?"

"No, not really..."

Tony's face said the opposite.

"OK, you are under pressure," Jaimie nodded.

"It's just that...Charlene's mother is a Christian and all that, she's her only child..."

"So...is Charlene a Christian too?"

Tony frowned.

"No, well...she don't go to church."

"I see..."

Jaimie's little smile spelled what he really thought, but he wasn't one to tell his friend what to do. Yet Tony seemed in need of advice.

"You don't think I should get married, right?"

Jaimie raised his eyebrows.

"How could I tell you that, Tony? There's nothing wrong with marriage."

It was Tony's turn to smile.

"That's not what you said last time..."

"I didn't say it was bad, only that it's a vastly overrated experience. Then again, it was only because mine didn't work. Everybody is different."

He could see there wasn't much he could do to cheer Tony up.

"Relax, Tony. A few of months from now, you'll feel much better about it." Jaimie added mischievously: "Besides, it's too late to worry now, the dice are cast."

Tony shook his head.

"You're right, it's too late." With that, he took a long swig of his Brew. "Let's talk about something else; any luck with that audition you told me about?"

21

"Nothing, man. It's probably rigged up for all I know. I think they advertise but already have their own choices."

"Keep at it, something will come through."

"Oh yeah, I can't quit. I'm also working on some ideas for scripts. Maybe I'll get a break that way."

Tony seemed interested. "I didn't know you could write."

"I don't know if I can, but I'm gonna have a damn good try. When I did my training back in New York, they used to make us draft scenes. I'm working on that at the moment."

"So, what have you got so far?"

Jaimie shrugged, got up to change the CD.

"Nothing much, just a few ideas..."

He selected a classic: Sam Cook. He felt in that kind of mood tonight. Tony was finishing his beer.

"So what d'you say, Tony, you wanna go and shoot some pool?"

Tony thought about it but declined eventually. Apart from the fact that Jaimie usually beat him at that too, he wanted to go and visit his mother, maybe break the news to her. He got up.

"Don't forget the job I told you about. You have the number?"

"Yeah, I wrote it down in my book."

"The man is a good customer of mine, always books flights with us for him and his family. Give him a call tomorrow, he'll explain what's wrong with the car."

Jaimie followed his friend outside, walked him up to his car. The night was warm, perfumed with spring fragrance.

"Say 'Hi' to your mother for me, OK?"

"I will. Call me Friday."

"You got it, daddy!"

Jaimie couldn't help a last little friendly jibe. The comical frown on Tony's face spelt his state of mind. He slipped the BMW in gear and drove off. Jaimie walked back slowly to the house, stretched and yawned. He had a fleeting thought for Junior whom he hadn't seen since Monday, hoped he hadn't gotten himself into some new trouble. As he entered the bedroom, the silky voice greeted him:

...And I know that if you loved me too,
What a wonderful world it would be.

Even with the map, the place wasn't easy to find and Jaimie wasn't familiar with Hendon. He stopped the truck for the second time, checked the A to Z for the street he was in. Five minutes and one more wrong turn later, he found the road and the number, parked just past the tall wrought-iron double gate. He had told the man he'd come for the car around three, it was now almost five. Jaimie didn't like being late but Friday at the garage was usually busy. There was always one or two rich suburban-type guys who would have suddenly noticed something suspect with their cars and wanted it fixed for the weekend. That morning it had been a middle-class, visibly shaken woman who had smashed the front of her husband's Trans Am against a bus. She was extremely concerned that the car should be fixed before he came back from a business trip on Saturday. She was at the garage early, had practically begged Paul to finish the car, offering to pay him extra. So Jaimie had kept at it all day, without lunch, and eventually finished the job. He thought the woman was going to kiss him, the way she was happy. Fortunately, she didn't but slipped him a £20 bonus. Then away she went, ready to welcome hubby home without fear.

Beyond the gate, a gravel pathway between two grass expanses led to a two storey, red brick mansion with slated roof. A lush trail of thick fern bordered the second floor windows to the right; at the back, a smaller building stood behind large rose bushes. Jaimie pressed the bell twice and waited. Nothing happened, but the gate was open so he decided to walk in and try the main door further up the path. He was about to climb the steps when from the left corner of the house he saw something that froze him. Two healthy-looking Doberman dogs were running his way, silently, effortlessly sprinting on the gravel. Jaimie knew he was too far from the gate to retreat, and the door of the house was closed. He climbed up the entrance steps quickly, backed against the thick wooden panel. One of the dogs came to a stop barely a yard from him, barked twice, then his companion joined him and the two stood growling on the concrete steps, staring at a very still Jaimie. Before he had time to dwell on his precarious situation, there was a whistling sound and from around the corner appeared two men, walking his way. The first thing Jaimie noticed was the size of the one at the back. If he was six three, the man had to be at least six foot six—and bigger built than him. With a shaven head and dark complexion, he was dressed in loose trousers and tee shirt and seemed unconcerned about the intruder. He whistled then patted the two dogs as they obeyed his call and came to him. The other man, of more average size and sporting a moustache, wore a blue suit and had a small revolver in his right hand which hung loosely by his side.

"Turn and face the wall."

Jaimie frowned, gasped:

"What?"

The gun in the man's hand was pointing his way now.

"Turn around, hands against the door."

The tone was insistent, the accent somewhat familiar. The giant and his black dogs were watching. Jaimie did as he was told. The man stepped up and frisked him quickly, then made him turn around to face him.

"Who are you? What is your business here?"

"I'm a mechanic...I'm supposed to pick up a car. Mr Heywoode?"

The man with the suit studied him briefly, he said:

"You're American. Where you from?"

"Brooklyn...New York."

Somehow that seemed to relax the atmosphere. The man had some kind of American accent too but Jaimie was still too puzzled to inquire.

"Follow me, please."

Slipping back the revolver inside his jacket, the man walked down the steps and started towards the left side of the house. Jaimie followed, feeling three watchful pairs of eyes on him. The man led the way inside the house, through a side door and into a large room. With its high ceiling, chandelier and large wooden desk, it looked like the study of a nineteenth century stately home from a period movie.

"Have a seat."

The man waited until Jaimie had sunk into one of the large leather armchairs then disappeared. Still under the shock of the incident, Jaimie breathed deep and calmed his mind. He wasn't easily shaken, but this was unexpected to say the least. Gang-banging for most of his teens back in NYC, he had learned to be ready for anything at anytime but he was a mechanic now; he was here to pick up a car not steal one! On either side of the tall window in front of him, he could see two framed paintings which, judging by the look of the place, were probably quite valuable. He got up and walked up to the well-furnished book cabinet against the back wall, read through the polished glass some of the classical names on

24

the volumes. A few of these had been part of his early reading during his daily trip to the prison library back then...

A clear voice behind him took Jaimie away from his literary thoughts.

"I'm sorry about the misunderst..."

As Jaimie turned, the sentence remained unfinished. The woman who'd just entered the room stopped, squinted at him.

"You...again!"

Jaimie was no less surprised but couldn't repress a smile.

"Can you believe it?!" he said, walking slowly towards her.

The baggy jeans and sweater she was wearing made her look even younger than the last time, but it was the same face, now harbouring the same haughty expression as at the club.

"I'm here to see Mister Heywoode," Jaimie declared nonchalantly.

This was definitely a day full of surprises. The young woman answered coldly:

"You're late."

Jaimie shrugged.

"Yeah, well...that's probably why your dogs nearly ate me..."

She didn't see the joke.

"They're well trained, they don't bite unless you try to run."

"What's with the gunman?"

The woman didn't flinch.

"He is our caretaker, he was only doing his job. You shouldn't have walked in like that."

"The gate was open..."

"The maid probably didn't close it. My father had to leave early. I'll show you to the car."

Jaimie followed the young woman out and to the back of the house. One of the two garages was open, a grey Oldsmobile parked inside.

"He explained the problem to you, I think."

Jaimie nodded.

"Yeah, the transmission. How long has it been parked?"

"A couple of months. My father has been too busy travelling to look for a garage."

"That's me, that's what I do. I think I told you that before," he smiled.

It seemed as if the woman was determined to ignore Jaimie's

25

humour.

Still he asked:

"By the way, did you get your car fixed?"

There was a very slight pause before she answered:

"Yes, thank you."

"You know you were in the wrong, right?"

She sighed, stood his gaze for a second.

"Let's not get back into that. Are you going to tow it?"

"I've got a truck outside."

"Fine, let me call some help to get it out."

She left Jaimie, went back towards the front of the house. The concrete area extended from the garages to the back fence, forming a wide sort of playground divided in two by a badminton net. Nearer the fence stood an official size basketball hoop. An expanse of cultivated ground spread to the left, with neat rows of various vegetables and herbs.

"Here are the keys. They will help you to push the car."

The woman came back with the well-dressed gunman and the giant dog man, without his dogs. She added, with an uncharacteristic hint of mischievousness:

"I think you've met Eddie and Luke already..."

"Briefly," Jaimie answered, trying one of the two keys in the car doorlock. Inside smelt of leather and perfume. He turned the key in the ignition and got a feeble red light on the dashboard as the battery was too low to start up. On the phone, Mr Heywoode had said the gearbox needed seeing to. Jaimie released the handbrake. Luke was already at the back of the car pushing, when Eddie joined him. Jaimie steered out and they got the car onto the sloping driveway leading to the gate. Jaimie went to back up his truck onto the entrance and, with efficient help from the two other men, managed to hook the big car onto the truck towing ramp without too much difficulty. A little way aside, hands in the pockets of her jeans, the woman was watching the operation. Jaimie jumped down from the truck platform, made one last check.

"It'll be OK, it's more or less a straight run."

"How long d'you think it will take you to fix it?" she asked.

Jaimie wiped his hands on the rag from his overall, shrugged.

"I'm gonna strip everything down, check it out. If you call me next week I'll let you know."

He dug up his wallet, took a card from it and handed it to the

26

woman.

She took it, handed Jaimie an envelope from her pocket.

"My father said to give you this as an advance, for parts?"

"Yeah, we discussed that. Thanks, I'll get you a receipt."

He went to the truck, wrote the receipt and gave it her. She said: "You're not from England..."

Jaimie laughed.

"Neither are you." He suddenly realised he had not introduced himself, with all the excitement.

"I'm Jaimie, from Brooklyn, New York."

He extended his right hand, she hesitated slightly but eventually took it and shook it lightly, once.

"Tania," she said simply, then added: "I'm from Liberia."

"Liberia? In Africa?" Jaimie exclaimed. "I understand the accent now." He laughed.

They were standing outside the gate, near the truck. Eddie and Luke had walked back inside.

"So, what d'you do? Are you a student?" Jaimie asked.

"I'm finishing a law degree."

"A lawyer. Yeah, it suits you."

Tania almost smiled for the first time.

"You think so?" Then she turned serious again. "OK, so I'll call in the week about the car. Tuesday?"

"Say Wednesday."

Tania nodded.

"Fine. See you later."

She started to walk back slowly, Jaimie hadn't moved. His rag in one hand, he was watching her. She stopped.

"What is it?"

He smiled.

"Nothing. You have a nice weekend."

"You too," she answered, though less warmly than him.

When she passed the gate and closed it, Jaimie was still standing there. He started to move to the truck, called out as he climbed inside:

"And drive carefully now!"

He was sure she pulled a face at his snide remark, before turning around and walking off towards the house. The trip back to the garage in the Friday evening traffic was slow but Jaimie hardly noticed.

CHAPTER FOUR

"Nothing like home cooking!" Junior said, helping himself to some more roast potatoes. Sitting across from him, Lorraine finished feeding a spoonful of rice to their daughter before stating calmly:

"You have to have a home, to get home cooking..."

Jaimie swallowed and refrained a smile. These two had been sparking the meal with lively exchanges, as always, but he didn't mind. Lorraine had been nice to offer to cook the Sunday meal and it tasted really good. The fact that she used the occasion to keep pinpointing what she saw as Junior's shortcomings was fine with Jaimie, in fact, he enjoyed it. He found it ironic that someone as troublesome as his younger brother should have found his match in a little woman like Lorraine. Personally, Jaimie got on fine with her. She complained to him about Junior and he, in turn, told her childhood stories about his younger brother. To be truthful, he had to admit that the girl was a handful though.

"I have a home," said Junior.

Lorraine took a drink, looked at him.

"Me too, and you better take up your space while it's still there."

Veiled threats, no doubt, which Jaimie could relate to something Junior had told him about earlier. For several months now, the pressure on Junior to finally move in with Lorraine and his child had intensified. Ever since she had gotten her own flat earlier the previous month, Lorraine had relentlessly pushed to get her way. As long as she was still by her mother, things were more or less alright for Junior. He would be there regularly, and as soon as Lorraine started getting 'heavy' he could still slip out and go home. Now things had changed and even Lorraine's mother, who loved Junior as her own, was lecturing him whenever she saw him about the beauty of family life.

"Lorraine man, why you have to talk to me like that all the time?" Junior paused, his chicken leg in his hand. "This is a serious step, I need to think about it. Don't pressure me, alright?"

Lorraine's eyes shot two darts straight at him. He got back to his chicken leg. Jaimie pushed back his empty plate, sighed contentedly.

"It's such a nice day, why don't you take a little stroll through the park, work this thing out? I'll keep Keesha."

The suggestion was apparently not welcomed by Junior who squinted threateningly at his treacherous brother.

"Him? You ever see him walk in the park with me?" Lorraine countered, throwing an accusing look to Junior across the table. He ignored her, reflecting how he hated when she sounded just like her mother.

"Well, you must have done something like that at some point," Jaimie laughed suggestively. He got up and walked to Keesha, still throwing food around in her obstinate attempts to feed herself with a big fork.

"Ohhh, look at that, you messed up the place."

He laughed. The little girl smiled with all her four front teeth as he picked her up.

"Come on, homegirl, let's leave those two crazies."

Lorraine got up and started to clear the table. As she passed Junior on her way to the kitchen, he heard her say:

"My job's done, this is yours."

He kissed his teeth, got up and went to join Jaimie and Keesha by the open window. Outside, a bright sun shone over peaceful Sunday afternoon scenes.

"I can't take her vibes sometimes..."

Junior sounded depressed.

"The woman loves you, man."

"Love?! She only loves to pressure me!"

Jaimie laughed. Playfully, he bit Keesha's ear, teasing the little girl until she giggled.

"So, you ain't gonna move in with her?"

The look on Junior's face was pure frustration.

"I can't. You know I can't. I like things the way they are now."

"Yeah, I know you do, but I guess Lorraine wants you to face your responsibilities. She feels you should be there with your family, you can't blame her."

Junior asked:

"So you're working for her now!"

"Come on, man, I'm just explaining to you why she's being nasty right now."

Junior sighed.

"Yeah, I know, but I just can't do it. I need time..."

Keesha grabbed Jaimie's face with both hands, pulling on his cheeks.

"Hey! What's up?" he clowned.

The little girl laughed, then went at it again. Her mother joined them. She wasn't looking at Junior until she stopped right by him, took his arm.

"Would you like some ice-cream?" she asked nicely.

Junior's squint was comical. He didn't answer but didn't draw back his arm all the same.

"Yes please," Jaimie answered.

"Keesh, ice-cream?" Lorraine asked her child, knowing full well the answer.

The smile and nod meant 'yes', definitely. Lorraine let go of Junior's arm and said before turning around:

"I hope you like strawberry."

Junior watched her walk away, shook his head.

"Jaimie man, you got to help me...talk to her."

"Uh-uh, I can't do that, homeboy. The girl wants a life, with you. Nothing to do with me, you're on your own."

"Thanks, I appreciate your support," Junior said.

"Be cool, Will, this is your life. It happens to all of us." The philosophical comment did nothing for Junior, neither did the tease of being addressed by his first name, Wilfred. Lorraine came back with a tray and they all sat down to enjoy the ice-cream. Keesha insisted on eating hers with her uncle and managed to spill some onto his beach shorts, but he didn't mind. Lorraine picked up the empty bowls, Junior got up and stretched.

"How about throwing a few balls over the park?"

"No, it's too hot for that. And I'm still stiff from yesterday."

Jaimie had spent the evening coaching the youth basketball team. Today, he needed to relax totally. Junior picked up a cigarette from his pack, lit it near the window, knowing neither Lorraine nor Jaimie appreciated the smell of tobacco. She was still pressuring him to quit from time to time.

"Hey, that's your girl coming over."

Jaimie looked at his brother, wondering what he was talking about.

"I ain't got no girl," he said, smiling, then blew in Keesha's soft neck.

"You're my girl, ain't you? Ain't you?"

30

Keesha laughed, showing her few teeth, grinning mischievously.

"Well, you better think again, homie." Junior seemed to be enjoying it. He waved.

"Hi Brenda!"

That got Jaimie's attention. He frowned.

"Quit bugging, man."

Yet, when he looked down the road, he realised it was no joke. The tall and slim young woman walking towards the house was, indeed, Brenda. Jaimie gasped:

"Oooh shit!"

Junior laughed:

"She's determined to get you."

Jaimie found it less funny. He gently put down Keesha, scratched his head and sighed:

"I can't believe it..."

All he felt for was a long, quiet, lonely afternoon.

"Didn't you have a date with her yesterday?"

"I didn't show up, man," Jaimie shrugged. "I stopped by Tony and ended up moving with him instead. Look, tell her I'm not in."

Junior smiled broadly.

"Well, the tables have turned. Are you asking for my help now?"

"Don't be like that, Junior. 'Am I my brother's keeper?' " Jaimie flashed a little *New Jack City* impersonation on his brother. Junior laughed.

"Yes I am! Here she comes, Nino," he answered in kind.

Jaimie started to move away from the window.

"Yo! I'm not here, OK?"

"Forget it, man, your car's parked right in front!"

"Damn..."

Lorraine came in the room, picked up Keesha. She immediately noticed Jaimie 's 'intense concentration' look.

"What's happening?"

Junior was still grinning, he was finding the whole thing quite amusing.

"His girl's coming down and he's trying to run."

"Why? What have you done?" Lorraine enquired.

"She ain't my girl, OK? And it's more about what I ain't done."

Jaimie was thinking fast. No matter how hard he tried, he didn't feel like spending this glorious Sunday afternoon with Brenda. An idea came up. He was trapped more or less but there was still a way

31

to limit the damage, keep Brenda in check...

"Check this out: I had an accident!"

"What?" Junior raised his eyebrows.

The bell rang twice. Jaimie whispered, scampering up the stairs:

"I damaged my knee yesterday, I'm hurt, remember. Let her in, I'll be down in a minute."

He disappeared. Lorraine looked at Junior.

"What's wrong with this girl?" she asked.

"Nothing. He's just playing hard to get."

Lorraine smiled, shook her head and went to open the door. She came back in with Brenda.

"Hey, Brenda, what's happening?"

"Hi!" she smiled back. She was wearing cycling shorts with a multicolour vest on top, her hair short and tightly curled on top. From behind, Junior caught Lorraine's puzzled look.

"Have a seat, I'll get Jaimie." Junior went for the stairs.

"Would you like something to drink?" Lorraine asked.

Jaimie was sitting on his bed, wrapping a length of bandage around his knee, securing it with a clip. It looked genuine enough, felt a little tight but bearable when he got up and took a few limping steps. Junior shook his head in wonder.

"You're going all the way!"

Jaimie stopped and grinned:

"A true artist always does," he declared with a mockingly pompous tone, then added: "I never thought I'd run from it, you know what I'm saying?!"

"Wait 'til you see that honey today, man. Either you're a holy man or you're crazy. You want me to send her up?"

"Oh no! I'd better see her downstairs."

He took a few steps towards the door, stopped abruptly as the approaching voice called from the stairs.

"Jaimie, it's me. Are you OK?"

It looked like Lorraine had done her bit and told Brenda about the accident. Brenda had been to his room once before, she knew the way.

"Hm hm!"

Junior grinned that foolish, suggestive grin. Jaimie couldn't share his fun unfortunately, not at that precise moment. He sighed, sat back on the bed, left leg outstretched in front of him. There was a knock on the door before it opened.

32

"Hi Brenda," Jaimie said as heartily as he could.

She entered.

"What happened to you?"

A fatalistic wince from the 'artist'.

"Just a little mishap playing ball yesterday."

She came closer, looking down at the bandage with concern.

"Is it bad?"

Jaimie had time to catch a flicker of a smile in Junior's eyes. He shook his head and said with understated bravery:

"Hurt like hell yesterday, but I'll be back by next week."

To Brenda, Junior's nod was one of sympathy. Jaimie read it as 'You bare-faced liar, you'.

"He's tough, he'll survive," Junior said lightly before walking off and out of the door. Pre-empting Brenda's likely question, Jaimie asked:

"How was the show yesterday?"

"Brilliant, you missed it. Why didn't you call to let me know?"

Jaimie sighed.

"I was in pain...I forgot everything else."

Brenda gave him a sideways look but didn't insist.

"Would you like me to get you something?"

"No, I'm fine. I had some lunch, I was just about to get a nap. Where you going?"

"Nowhere, since I didn't hear from you I decided to pop over."

She wasn't going anywhere, ' "Pop over" she calls it,' Jaimie thought to himself. He was trying to be nice, yet he couldn't help wishing she hadn't come. He got up, hopped to the stereo and picked up a couple of CDs from one of the shelves. It was essential to select something appropriate to the situation at hand, nothing too smooth and nothing that would stir Brenda's passion. Jaimie settled on Kool G Rap, sure that Brenda wouldn't appreciate it. As he sat back on the bed, she said kind of matter-of-factly:

"You know Jaimie, I feel like I'm doing the chasing."

"The chasing?" he repeated in a puzzled tone of voice.

But he knew only too well that the time for the critical 'moment of truth' was fast approaching.

"You know what I mean: I'm running after you but you don't seem interested, not really..."

"Why d'you say that?" he asked, but it was hard to sound innocent. She was right. Yet how could Jaimie admit it to a woman like Brenda who liked him a lot.

"I'm just saying it, because I get the impression you've been avoiding me."

Jaimie was starting to feel bad now. What could he say?

"I've got a lot on..." he began rather lamely. "A lot of things on my mind lately." His voice had the necessary hint of gravity to make it sound genuine. Brenda sat not too far away from him, on the bed. She stared at him for a short while, looked away, then came back with:

"You've got a woman already, ain't it?"

"Uh-uh, I said I didn't."

A word of truth at last...

"I'm just not ready to get involved in anything right now, can you relate to that?" he asked.

"Why is that?" she asked, interested.

Through the wide open window, noises and voices were coming in from the neighbouring gardens, the sounds of summer barbecues. Jaimie paused before answering.

"I have this...attitude, towards relationships...I tend to actively avoid getting involved."

"I can see that," Brenda said a little coldly.

"It's nothing personal, I wouldn't like you to think that. I mean, you're a nice woman..."

It wasn't meant to be patronising, yet she cut in.

"OK, just say what you want to say."

Jaimie sensed irritation in her voice. He was deeply reluctant to get involved in that type of discussion, but Brenda's insistent gaze was awaiting his excuse.

"Alright, remember I mentioned I used to be married?"

"Yeah."

"Well, it's got to do with that. The whole thing is still kinda recent and since the breakup, I've kept away from problems, you understand?"

Brenda took it in.

"Was it that bad?" she asked.

There was no need for play-acting for that part. Despite himself, any mention of that period in his life still automatically brought up the bitter taste of painful memories.

"Put it this way: it has cured me of women up to now. I got cynical, I can't help it."

Brenda was silent for a while, then she asked:

"So, you're planning on staying single?"

Jaimie let out a short laugh, shifted slightly on the bed, carefully moving his left leg.

"I can't say that, but it's gonna take the time it's gonna take."

That sounded definite enough. Brenda nodded.

"Well, what can I say? I just thought me and you could, you know, see each other."

"Sure, I'm not saying I can't see you. But I don't want to waste your time, it's not gonna happen."

"I understand."

He asked quickly:

"Would you like a drink?"

"No thanks."

He stood up, taking his time.

"Excuse me a minute."

"You shouldn't move too much, with your leg. I'll get it for you."

"No. it's OK. I need to exercise it."

The bandage kept his knee tight, the limping was difficult to fake. Once out of the room, Jaimie let out a deep sigh, started down the stairs, one at a time. Outside was such a nice day, through the open front door he saw Lorraine and Keesha sitting on the concrete steps. In the kitchen, he found Junior leaning against the fridge, leisurely rolling a spliff. He motioned to the small herb bag on the table.

"Want a little touch, man?"

Jaimie shook his head, moved his brother from the fridge door to get a drink.

"I gave up blunts years ago, you know that."

He opened the can, downed half of it in one go. Junior laughed.

"Dry throat, uh? Too much lyrics."

"It ain't easy saying 'no', trust me!"

"What's with you, anyway. The girl comes to give you a little flavour and you're dissin' her..."

Jaimie smiled.

"Yeah, in fact she wants to give me a lot of flavour. That's why I can't afford to start it up, I gotta pass."

Junior's mind worked differently, he found this 'passing' thing strange. But then again, he wasn't Jaimie.

35

"I never thought I'd see the day when you went straight. You might as well be a monk, man," Junior commented before striking his lighter for the spliff.

"It happened to me, could happen to you," Jaimie answered as he left the kitchen, can in hand. Behind him, Junior said:

"I'm facing my responsibilities, like you said. I'm taking the family for a spin. Behave yourself up there, homes!"

Jaimie climbed back up the stairs, one by one, conscientiously. He pushed the door open. Inside the beat was still pumping, Brenda had kicked off her sandals and was half-stretched on the bed. She threw him a quizzical look.

"Play that cassette you played last time."

Jaimie tried not to focus too long on the dark, shapely legs neatly filling the cycling shorts. He hobbled over to the music rack.

As they say: it seemed like a good idea at the time. Now, listening to the bespectacled, self-assured, thirty-something executive in the Gucci tee shirt, Jaimie was getting increasingly impatient with the whole thing. But he kept cool, in keeping with the plush office.

"What we're looking for is a big but friendly type of guy, someone threatening but...harmless, if you know what I mean. Someone close to the product..."

Jaimie nodded, apparently paying attention while his mind drifted out of the room towards the bullshit-free air beyond the window. Deep inside, he felt close to telling that harebrain snob what he could do with his jolly green giant.

"I realise that's not the kind of work you're looking for, I'm sure Alison will dig up something more suitable very soon."

The rejection Jaimie could accept, but not the condescending attitude.

"Yeah, well, thanks for your time anyway."

Jaimie got up, eager to leave the whole depressing experience behind. He couldn't blame Alison at the agency; she had told him that he might not want to bother with commercials, as it was hardly what he was looking for, but he decided to try it once anyway. She knew the guy and had recommended Jaimie, but he soon found out how soul-rending it all was to lower his professional expectations for the sake of that elusive break. Only now he felt something close to discouragement. He left the building quickly, took a deep breath

36

on the pavement outside, in the midday sun, and walked back to his car. 'Anyway', he told himself to help shake out the bad feeling, 'Wednesday is always a weird day.' Determined as he was to land a part, however small, in some production, his lack of success made him feel a little down at times. But he still stuck to his ambition, no matter how slow things were in this country and how much harder he had to try. Despite all the frustration, Jaimie still held fast to the promise he had made to himself during his time in confinement.

The jeep rejoined the lunchtime traffic on Kensington High Street. Jaimie was distractedly watching the shoppers and idlers alongside the storefronts. Cycles and motorbikes darted in and out of the slow line of vehicles, pedestrians crossed over between the bumpers. Jaimie changed cassette as he sat out a red light, inserted a rough mix of some sampling he had been working on the previous night. He forwarded the track to where he wanted it. A 'phat' bass boomed out. Floating on top came a double sample mix, short vocal phrases colouring the atmospheric beat. By nature, Jaimie applied himself to everything he did but when it came to music, he was downright obsessive. He would hear something in the recesses of his mind, some undefined sound fragment and from then on, doggedly, would spend whatever time it took to obtain the exact rendition of it on track. It was that love of his work and wide musical grounding which had made him one of the earliest innovators in hip hop back in the early days, and for years afterwards up and coming DJs would come and learn from him whenever he and the crew would rock the venues in and out of East New York.

Jaimie drove on, listening carefully to the track, rewinding it to the beginning to take it in again. Something was still missing but he knew a few more hours on it and he'd get what he wanted. He had been thinking of the station's big anniversary show to be held in August. All the DJs would be performing for the occasion and the competition would be friendly but serious all the same. Jaimie felt confident that clever mixes like the one playing now would get the huge crowd expected at the event, slamming. He stopped at a newsagent before reaching Kilburn and got himself a soft drink and some peanuts. Having sacrificed his lunch hour, he could feel hunger teasing his stomach, but there were a few hours more to spend on the car he'd left behind and he decided that food would have to wait until afterwards. He parked and walked through towards the garage, munching a mouthful of roasted peanuts.

It was a little after two. Inside the garage, the roaring of a big engine drowned everything. As the din eased out, Henry's head emerged from behind the van he was working on.

"Jaimie, they delivered your stuff. It's down at the back."

"Thanks, man. How's it going down there?"

Henry lit up the cigarette butt hanging from his lip.

"Almost there, but I'm gonna break up for food."

"Alright."

Jaimie finished his drink, crushed the carton and made a long throw for the big plastic bin by the back wall...close, but he missed. The sealed box on the floor behind the car contained the parts he had been waiting for, now he could finish the job. He took off his white Sox cap, placed it safely on the dashboard, put on his overalls and tied up his working bandanna over his head. Next, Jaimie picked up his walkman, and slipped the headphones on. A couple of spanners in hand, he slid under the chassis and started working. The transmission problem wasn't major, he had fixed worse cases. As far as Jaimie could remember, he had always been fixing things. Growing up, it quickly became clear to his parents that nothing in the house was safe from his inquisitive mind. No amount of 'shake down' by Pop could discourage Jaimie from exploring mechanical and electrical appliances, not for long anyway. Later on, when he started messing with cars, and other self-taught mechanics, it served him well and he quickly became known for his expertise. Looking back, it could be said that his first illegal 'borrowing' of a car, at fourteen, was for educational purposes...he sure couldn't afford one at the time! By the time he ended up doing his three-year stint in the Army, Jaimie's very first formal mechanical training became more of a specialisation.

Now he was ready. Jaimie slid back out to change cassettes. Remembering something, he went inside the car and opened the glove compartment; the track was what he had thought it was. It had been some years since Jaimie had heard Nancy Wilson. He slipped the pre-recorded cassette inside the walkman and pressed 'PLAY'. The first few bars immediately made him smile despite himself, struck his eardrums like an echo. The world could change and life go up and down, but after all these years, Nancy Wilson's voice, warm and creamy, brought home a feeling of timelessness. Picking up the melody as it flowed over punchy horn riffs, he nodded in time with the drop on the hi-hat. He could sense things coming up, the stream of buried pictures slowly surfacing, pictures of lazy summer Sunday mornings back then when Pop got in the mood to spin a record from his jazz collection.

His heart tip-toeing over the rhythm, Jaimie slid back under the car. It took him around another hour but he was almost there when a sudden and brutal sound exploded through the mellow vibes in the headphones. Jaimie cursed, slid back out and took off the earplugs. He caught sight of the legs first, looked up and asked:

"What's up with the horn-blowing?"

He got up, containing his initial displeasure.

"I called out, you didn't answer."

It sure sounded logical! The woman was looking at Jaimie from behind dark glasses. She asked:

"D'you always work with music?"

"I do, as a matter of fact."

Jaimie was standing by the car, looking at the young woman in leggings and sleeveless jersey, bag over her shoulder. Summertime stroller style. She said:

"I called several times."

He knew that, but no point calling back until the car was ready, he told her.

"Is it ready now?"

Jaimie wiped some grease from his fingers before answering.

"Not yet, almost."

"When will it be?"

There was something about her, something Jaimie had noticed before which made her sound haughty, something in the tone of her voice or her phrasing, or both. The Oldsmobile needed about a half-hour more work on it.

"Soon. Why, is your father back from his trip?"

She paused, as if surprised at his directness.

"No."

Jaimie raised his eyebrows, pried further.

"Don't tell me you're gonna drive it?!"

This remark, she didn't appreciate, he could see that. She looked away. Then, after taking off her glasses, she asked coldly:

"What has it got to do with you?"

Unfriendly tone, unfriendly look from her elongated eyes.

For all his trying, he couldn't remember her name. He shrugged.

"Just curious."

"Are you saying I can't drive?" she asked with a hint of defiance.

Jaimie's innocent grin was not the right answer. He said:

"Take it easy, it's just a little joke. Can't you take a little joke?"

"How much more time do you need?" she asked.

"Excuse me, I forgot your name..."

"Heywoode."

"I got that, your first name..."

"Why?"

"Just to know," he added, "I'm curious, remember?"

"Tania... How much longer?"

Tough woman, Jaimie thought.

"Look, I had to send for the parts. I only started on it yesterday. It's almost done now, but I need to give it a check. This is an expensive car, it deserves attention, you know what I'm saying?"

Whether Tania shared Jaimie's love of cars was doubtful. Leaning his back against the car, Jaimie studied her.

"Can I ask you a question?" he asked.

Strangely enough, she smiled for the first time.

"If I say 'no', you're still going to ask, aren't you?"

Jaimie turned his palms upwards, raised his shoulders.

"It's part of my job," he drawled in his best Colombo accent.

Tania wasn't impressed, shook her head.

"When were you born?" he asked.

"You mean 'how old am I?' "

"No, no, I know how old you are. What month?"

"November, why?" Then she asked: "What do you mean, you know how old I am?"

That interested her. With a satisfied side grin, Jaimie explained:

"It's easy: you're driving, so you're over eighteen. You're not married, you're living at home, still studying...I'd say twenty-five but you act a little older than your age. You must be twenty-three."

He waited, watching her face for any reaction. For a few seconds she said nothing, her eyes hard into his, then:

"What are you: a policeman?"

Jaimie laughed, that was funny!

"OK, against the car...assume the position," he clowned.

Tania wasn't laughing. Jaimie said:

"I got to tell you, it's the first time anyone figured me for a cop...I guess you're hiding your age too."

40

"I just don't like people to know too much about me."

"Why?" Jaimie asked. "You famous or something?"

"Look, can you just tell me when I can come for the car?"

Jaimie straightened up, smiled.

"You've got to lighten up the attitude, Miss, loosen up a little bit. OK, check me back at four-thirty. I'll have it ready, how's that?"

"Four thirty?" Tania looked at her watch. "I'll try."

With that, she slipped her sunglasses back on and walked off. Jaimie wondered why the woman always seemed so uptight. Maybe it was him, he reflected. Not that he felt attracted to her or anything, but his naturally inquisitive nature always tried to figure out what made people 'tick'. His throat felt dry, and a little walk in the sun would do him good. He called out:

"Yo, H!"

'H', as Jaimie called Henry, appeared near the office.

"Yo!"

Jaimie had converted the garage staff to his speech style within a few short months. As he had told them jokingly, "you all got to be down with it from now on, or soon you'll have language problems in this country."

Still, it gave him non-ending kicks to jive talk white people and have them try too.

"I'm out at the store. Want a drink? It's on me."

"Cheers, son. I'll have whatever you have."

"Paul?"

"He went out," Henry answered.

Jaimie stepped outside, strolled to the high street. On his return, refreshed, the work didn't take him long to finish. He moved a pick-up truck at the front and drove the Oldsmobile outside, then took off his overalls. Henry came back from a trip to the shops with some more beer, so he and Jaimie sat outside on some crates, talking and taking in the descending sun. Paul came back, still reddish rather than sun-tanned from his weekend in Brighton the previous week. From what he had told Jaimie, it sounded like a whole lot of drinking with a bunch of friends. He declined Henry's offer of a beer and retreated to the shade of the office. Shortly after four-thirty, Henry winked at Jaimie, motioning ahead of him.

"Looks like you're in business, mate..."

Jaimie turned. She'd come back after all.

"She's a customer, H," Jaimie pointed out.

41

The man laughed.

"Is that what you call it?"

Jaimie got up, shaking his head.

" 'Naughty H' I'm gonna have to call you. Be cool, I'll see you tomorrow."

Henry got up, slapped Jaimie on the shoulder and went inside, beer still in hand. Jaimie waited for Tania to come up. She looked towards the parked car.

"Is it working alright now?"

"Sounds good. We're gonna test it out. Gimme a minute."

Jaimie left her there and went inside to let Paul know he might not be back. Tania was still standing by the car when he came out.

"Come on, get in."

He sat at the wheel.

"Where are we going?"

She climbed into the Oldsmobile and eased herself down on the cream leather.

"For a test drive. Get strapped and leave it to me."

Jaimie turned the key in the ignition, firing up the powerhouse under the long gleaming bonnet. Tania observed him quietly as he slipped the car into reverse and manoeuvred neatly to exit onto the road. The car was large inside with enough room at the front for three. Jaimie expertly steered through the intersection, headed down Maida Vale. The afternoon sun with its oblique rays shone through the windscreen, cool air flowing in the open sun roof. Along Edgware Road and then around Marble Arch, Jaimie was making conversation, driving easy.

On the radio, a drive-time show was in progress, playing mellow tunes to match the late afternoon mood. They were driving down Notting Hill now.

"How long have you been here?"

"I was born here."

He looked at her.

"Really? I thought you said..."

"My parents are from Liberia. I left England as a young child, came back ten years ago."

"What's Liberia like?"

Tania paused.

"Like the States, in many ways."

"Yeah?"

42

Jaimie remembered from his varied readings that Liberia was a West African country founded by returning black Americans after emancipation. Tania explained that everything there was set up after the American pattern, descendants of the first settlers from the US having ruled the country up to 1979. That was when her family had moved to Britain.

"I think I read about that, they had a revolution..."

"It was a coup, actually," Tania pointed out.

"A coup, alright." Then he asked: "So, you been to the States?"

"Sure, we fly to Miami to visit family every year or so."

"What about New York?"

"I've only been there twice with my mother to do some shopping," she said.

"Shopping, uh? You been to Brooklyn?"

She shook her head. "No, we don't know anyone there."

Jaimie smiled. "Well, now you do. That's my hometown."

Tania didn't seem impressed. Jaimie realised she was unlikely to know his part of town. After all, East New York was hardly a tourist spot. They were approaching Shepherds Bush now. She asked:

"Don't you think we ought to be getting back? The car seems to be working fine..."

"Sure, I fixed it. Don't you enjoy the ride? It's a nice evening..."

She didn't answer. He asked:

"So, you sure you wanna drive this car?"

Her look was a sufficient answer.

"I'm not referring to your driving, it's just that you got to practise before you get on the road. It's a big car."

"Thank you for your concern but I can handle it."

Tania sounded confident.

"What does your father do?" Jaimie asked.

"Why?"

"I'm just inquisitive, remember?"

"He's into import-export," she said vaguely.

"Would you like to go for a drink? Are you hungry?"

"No thanks." She threw him a quick sideways glance. Jaimie waited a little, then asked:

"Are you an only child?"

This time she turned to him, frowning.

"Don't you think you're getting a little personal here?"

He laughed.

43

"No, not really; I'm just asking a few innocent questions, in a friendly manner, you know."

He asked again:

"Are you?"

She sighed.

"If you must know, I am not. I have a younger brother, he's seventeen. Anything else?"

"Not if you resent me asking."

"I'm not used to discussing my private life with strangers."

That sounded very discouraging. Undeterred, Jaimie grinned.

"I can understand that, but I thought maybe we could be friends. After all, we' re almost cousins in a way."

She clearly didn't agree with that, but she said nothing. Jaimie was finding the woman totally different from the ones he'd grown used to. Compared to the open attitude of native New York females, Tania was distant. Even in the short time he'd been in the country, he couldn't recall meeting anyone so reserved. Whatever the reason, she didn't seem inclined to socialise, not with him anyway. Maybe it was just the way some women are...

Jaimie was getting a little tired of the clubbish type of sounds coming out of the radio. He remembered the two cassettes in his pouch, took them out. He tried the first one. An insistent hip hop track punched its way through the speakers. The look on Tania's face said it all.

"I guess you don't like rap music, uh?" Jaimie quipped.

"And I guess you do."

"Sure, I been into that since day one. It's my life. So what's your thing: classical?"

He tried the other cassette. This time the expression on Tania's face was different. A little flicker of recognition showed on her face as the first few bars of the R. Kelly track filled the space. Jaimie laughed suggestively.

"Hhum-hummm, that's more your kinda style. I bet you're one of those girls who let loose at his shows!"

She chose to ignore the innuendo.

"I just like the music."

"Swing beat is cool, I play some too. What about jazz, you like jazz?"

She seemed a little surprised.

44

"Do you?"

"I grew up with it."

Tania was taking the initiative now.

"I thought you were one of those 'hardcore' rappers." She stressed the adjective. Jaimie nodded.

"Yeah, that's me. But jazz is the ancestor of rap too."

"How's that?"

"You ever heard jazz singers do 'scatting'? That was how it started. Then the kids started talking ad-lib without music in the sixties, kinda freestyle. After that, the Jamaican DJs brought their own styles in the seventies. That's how rap music was born."

Tania seemed interested for once. They were back in Kilburn now.

"So, what do you do...I mean, socially?" Jaimie asked.

"Socially?"

"Yeah, you know, social life. You go out?"

"Not really, I usually keep myself to myself."

"Right, you only go clubbing once in a while," he smiled mischievously.

She knew what he was referring to and corrected him.

"Actually, I wasn't clubbing. I had to take some of my father's foreign clients out."

"Oh, public relations, I understand..."

He saw her looking at him suspiciously.

"Why d'you look at me like that?"

"You always sound so sarcastic."

"I just enjoy teasing people," Jaimie shrugged.

"Have you been working here long?" she asked as they turned into the street leading to the garage.

"No, I started about a year ago, shortly after arriving over here."

"Oh, you haven't been here long." Then she enquired: "Why did you leave New York?"

"I had to come and bury my mother. I ended up staying."

"I'm sorry."

"It's OK."

Jaimie slowed down the car, parked facing out.

"Here you are, Miss, safely..."

"Thank you for the drive. Let's talk about the bill," Tania said, picking up her handbag.

"Not with me. See Paul in the office, he's the man."

"Alright." She opened the door.

"Why don't you pass by sometime, gimme a check. Maybe we could hang out or something," he suggested.

There was a slight pause as she looked him in the eye, as if trying to read his thoughts.

"I don't think so, but thanks anyway."

Jaimie smiled.

"You know, I love the way you speak. It's so...neat."

Tania squinted a little, weighing up his latest remark, but he insisted:

"No, I mean it. It's nice." Then he asked: "You sure you can drive this thing?"

"Yes, I'm sure."

"OK, have a nice evening then."

"And you too."

With that she stepped out of the car. Jaimie watched her walk to the garage, then followed, leaving the key in the ignition. He went to pick up the bag with his dirty overalls.

"See you in the morning, Paul," he called out as he passed the office on the way out.

"Alright, son."

Tania was sitting, back to him. She didn't turn. Outside, Jaimie stretched and walked leisurely to the Renegade parked in the small courtyard in front. He rolled back the top, opened both side windows. As he kicked the engine alive, he saw Tania climb into the Oldsmobile. The urgent braking after the first few yards made him smile. Just as he suspected, Tania was likely to have some problems getting her daddy's car home. He watched as the big black car lurched forward again before coming to a halt again. Laughing to himself, Jaimie switched off his engine, got out and walked back slowly towards the garage. At her third attempt, Tania got the car almost onto the main road, a little too far forward in fact, causing a passing motorist to blow his horn at her. Eventually, Tania gave up and climbed out. The first thing she saw was Jaimie leaning against the garage wall, arms crossed on his chest, shaking his head slowly from side to side.

"Excuse me!" she called out.

Jaimie didn't move. She eventually started walking towards him. He could see the frustrated look on her face as she approached.

"I forgot your name..." she said first.

CHAPTER FIVE

Jaimie knew why he had taken today off, today especially. Sure enough he wanted a little time to himself, felt tired from the weekend too. Apart from the relative physical exertion of coaching the team at the Centre and doing a little extra on a friend's car on Saturday, he'd spent the whole of Sunday afternoon lifting heavy boxes with Junior. Almost three weeks after eventually moving in with Lorraine, on a trial basis as he said, Junior had decided it was now time to move the rest of his stuff. That included a weighty record box and other such items which the two of them struggled to hoist up to the second floor flat on the estate. Trust Junior to drag him into that on a warm Sunday afternoon! Yet the real reason for taking the day off had to do with the date. Today marked a year to the day since their mother's funeral. Jaimie couldn't help but count time, and today served as a kind of reference point.

Jaimie put down his pen, knowing very well he was unlikely to further the story he'd been trying to write until his head had cleared. It felt like something hanging over him, something he didn't want to think about but which he know, sooner or later, he'd have to face. He got up and walked to the bedroom window, opened it wider. Not much sun today, but a heavy heat with low clouds pregnant with rain. A storm was brewing, Jaimie thought. The cassette in the stereo had stopped long ago, as he sat at the desk, eyes staring down at the blank sheet of his open notepad as if it was a screen. Re-surfacing memories held him there for some time, as if in a trance. Now the room was in near darkness, the house was silent and he felt thirsty. Picking up the empty glass, he went downstairs.

Junior still came up sometimes in the evening but it felt strange now not to expect him anymore. Jaimie had experienced solitude and even enforced confinement, but in the year he had lived with his younger brother he had gotten used to a kind of family warmth, a feeling of closeness, something he used to know and had missed. The two of them were getting on as if they'd never been parted. Jaimie had learned that Junior had felt bad about leaving his brother behind in the United States, for years afterwards. He didn't hold any feelings against their mother about that though, nor loved her less. Of all of them it was Junior, the one she chose to take with her who had felt the immediate loss most deeply. Jaimie cried for his mother too. For all his toughness and previous experience of seeing loved ones depart, the grief reached him more than he had thought it would. Though he had learned to love her at a distance, he always felt she was there. Now the two brothers had found new strength from the reunion which their mother's death brought.

But it wasn't his mother's shadow Jaimie had felt hovering around him all day. Pop, Jaimie could never call him anything but that, had announced the news to Jaimie following Junior's phone call. Jaimie was back at the house then, after the disastrous second try with Loretta. When he came home, Pop was sitting on the living room floor shifting busily through a pile of old records. He had looked up at his eldest son and said three words in a monotone voice.

"Your mother's dead."

That was it, all that Jaimie was able to get out of him until later in the evening. Though he knew his mother was ill and the doctors gave her little hope, the words hit Jaimie like a cold slap. He had left Pop there with his records and gone to call London but no one answered the phone. He didn't get through to Junior until later that night. The next day, Pop had sat with Jaimie at the kitchen table. Neither of them said much.

The two of them had grown to know each other better than father and son usually do and became partners in loss, as it were, to survive the pain and go on living without their dearly departed.

"I can't go," Pop had said repeatedly. There was no changing his mind. So Jaimie took the plane at JFK airport alone the next day and after an overnight flight, landed in London to bury a mother he hadn't seen for fifteen years, without the father who couldn't forgive.

How he ended up staying, he couldn't quite explain but looking back, it seemed logical in a sense. New York, his old stomping ground, had become heavy and oppressive to him in a way he had never felt before. Moving back in the house with Pop after five years away had felt right at first. Jaimie did what he promised himself to do after his first year in the pen. He enrolled on a drama course downtown and started working seriously at his ambition. Together with the part-time job he managed to get in a nearby garage, he had kept quite busy. He soon ran into some of his

48

homies, those still alive and free, as he knew he would. Of those, he only still felt close to two or three but by the time Jaimie explained what his interests were now, they quickly realised he wasn't down with gang banging no more. That was cool with them though, and he knew they would always be there for him if he needed them. Jaimie had rolled with the set for longer than most, he was one of the few OGs and everybody gave him the props due for his part in avenging Twist. So he kept himself occupied, focused on drama and cinema and he even started playing music again. That, he could never give up. Mostly he was content with mixing and kicking about with the DAT and desks, working on tracks with up and coming young DJs from the neighbourhood eager to learn what they could from him. Only occasionally would he accept an invitation from an old friend of his who'd want him to play at one of the numerous hip hop mixing contests held all over Brooklyn. There, for a short time, Jaimie would recapture some of the old magic touch, feel the juice flowing within and wreck the venue with some out of this world crazy mixing like back in the day. For almost a year, he immersed himself in images and sounds so completely that he forgot about everything else, or almost...

All that changed after he met Loretta. Looking back, Jaimie had since realised that his earnest desire to make up for lost time had played as much a part in his infatuation with her. Three months after their first meeting, they were married. Barely eighteen after leaving the Army, Jaimie found himself with a wife and a baby well on the way. It felt good at the time, strong and vibrant like a new lease of life under the sun.

Outside, some of the low clouds had started bursting. The tapping of fat drops of water on the window brought Jaimie back from his thoughts. He sipped some of the drink. 'No use dwelling on the past', he told himself resolutely. He realised he hadn't had much to eat since the morning; his supposed writing had kept him upstairs most of the day. From the fridge, Jaimie picked up a cabbage, tomatoes, corn, some rice, a tin of corned beef from the wall cupboard. After switching on the portable TV above the fridge, he got cooking. Rain was pouring down outside now, a real summer storm with lightning illuminating the approaching darkness at regular intervals. Jaimie covered the rice, turned the fire low. He switched channels on the TV but there wasn't much to choose from. The wide choice of programmes was one of the things he missed the most from back home. Back to the fridge, Jaimie picked up a lettuce, washed it, drained it. He was mixing some olive oil, malt vinegar and black pepper in a bowl when the sound of a key in the front door distracted him. The door slammed and a soaked Junior stepped in.

"Hey, homie! Did you smell the food or what?" Jaimie quipped.

But Junior, uncharacteristically serious, barely acknowledged the joke and after hanging up his wet jacket, sat at the table.

"How come you all wet, what's up with your car?"

"I just come from work, I go by train."

"Alright, you got the job!" Jaimie smiled.

He recalled Junior mentioning an interview he had on Monday. Jaimie wiped his hand on the kitchen towel then placed the salad bowl in the fridge. Junior looked up at him, serious.

"I need to talk to you."

The tone of the voice alerted Jaimie, he sat down at the table, across from his brother.

"Please, don't say that you kicked up with Lorraine already?"

But Junior shook his head; it wasn't Lorraine.

"I had some problems with some guy on the estate."

Jaimie raised his eyebrows.

"What? But you've just moved in!"

"Yeah, I know but I had no choice."

"Oh shit, talk to me."

Jaimie waited, ready for anything. Junior let out a sigh, then started:

"OK, you know you left me Sunday night, I went to bed, got up the next morning to go to the interview. I get downstairs, find my two front tyres cut up."

"Your tyres? Cut up?" Jaimie exclaimed, incredulous.

"That's right, that's the way it hit me! You can imagine how mad I was, man...but I still went to the interview and things. Anyway, when I get back now, I'm starting to turn the place upside down to find out who did it. I ask some black kids I always see hanging out by the block. Now check this out..."

Junior paused to sigh one more time.

"They tell me that the space I park my car in on Sunday night 'belongs' to some white guy from across the green. Jaimie, do you hear that?"

It sounded crazy to Junior even as he recounted it. Jaimie was waiting, frowning already.

"I'm talking to these three kids, right? And they're telling me how things run on the estate. There's only a few black people down there, so it's kind of strange, you know? I didn't notice at first but there's hardly anybody that talks to you or even looks at you straight. You know like I always talk to people, anybody, right? Well down there, they're not sociable, but it's only when those kids told me that I got the lowdown. So they're saying that this white guy, Chas they call him, that was his parking. That's why he got my tyres cut up."

Jaimie shook his head sombrely. Sounded like some crazy story.

"What did you do?" he asked.

His brother looked at him straight. Jaimie waited. After such an insult, he expected anything, almost. Junior leaned back in his chair. For the first time since his arrival, his hard face relaxed a little.

"What would you have done?"

Tricky question...

"Come on, just tell me how bad it is first..."

Junior cut him:

"No, no...I wanna know: what would you have done?"

Jaimie shook his head with a heavy and genuine sigh.

"Why? I mean, why do things always happen to you?"

Junior jumped up. Opening his two hands in front of him in a gesture of innocence, he told Jaimie:

"You see! Whatever happens to me, it's always got to be my fault. It's the same thing all the time."

Junior apparently felt strongly about being blamed for the incident.

"Take it easy, I didn't say it was your fault. Alright, so what happened? What did you do?"

"I went home."

"You went home? Right, then what?" Jaimie asked, still awaiting the outcome.

"OK, so the kids gave me the door number of the guy. Apparently, he's hustling stuff or something. So, I went down there, man."

"Yeah?"

"Yeah, I knock on the guy's door, he opens up, asks me what do I want. I say I've come to ask him about my tyres. He don't know

51

what I'm talking about..."

Jaimie waited.

"I ask him again, the guy's telling me he knows nothing about that and to fuck off from his door. Some other white guy comes up to the door and starts to join in, telling me to move."

Jaimie's face was a mask of concentration, his eyes frozen in a squint.

"What would you have done?" Junior asked him.

"What's up with you?" Jaimie said, annoyed at the delay. "What did *you* do?"

Jaimie wasn't sure of the answer to his brother's question and didn't care to discuss it until he found out what Junior had done. But Junior insisted. He had a point and he knew it, a chance to confront Jaimie who was always warning him against reacting rashly.

"I want you to turn it around, like you always say. What if that happened to you?"

Jaimie could see his brother had taken his exhortations to stay out of trouble to heart. Yet something this bad had come up.

"Right, so the guy's lying, right?" Jaimie started, to get Junior back onto the story, and avoid having to answer.

It worked. Junior's face showed his feelings clearly.

"Lying? The guy's smirking, man! And his fat friend tries to get smart and tries to edge me on. Then listen to this: the guy insults me and slams the door in my face like he's thinking I'm gonna go for them. Through the door he's shouting, 'by the way, move your car out of my space by tonight or I'm gonna burn it down'."

Junior stopped, watched for his brother's reaction.

"That guy is a madman!" Jaimie declared with a dark look in his eyes.

"You're right, but I'm more mad than him, he don't know that!"

"I know that. What did you do?"

Junior opened up his eyes wide.

"The motherfucker cuts up my tyres, insults me and slams the door in my face. What do I do?"

"I wouldn't like to bet on that. Now, stop toying with me and tell me what went down."

Junior shrugged.

"What went down? I went down, went home."

"You went home," Jaimie repeated.

Junior nodded.

"I felt like getting wrecked on that white fucker, ya know that!"

"I do know that!"

"But I got my family to think of, right? So I sat down at home, trying to figure it out. I was so upset, I couldn't even talk to Lorraine. Anyway, I called my boys and we moved my car."

Jaimie knew it had taken a lot of self-control for Junior to control his notoriously hot temper. He was impressed. But he knew his brother was no 'turn-the-other-cheek' kind of man.

"Then?"

"Then, early next morning we went out with Markie and T-Man and got two new tyres."

Jaimie gave his brother a knowing glance.

"That's all you did?"

A slight grin formed on Junior's face now.

"Yeah man. The rest of the morning, we stayed in the flat, taking turns at the window, waiting for that fool to come out."

"And?"

"Motherfucker made us wait until almost one o'clock. So he comes down to his parking space, gets inside the Jag, starts out like he's in a hurry."

The grin on Junior's face was getting wider as he went on.

"He drives out, right, almost fifty yards or so before he realises something's wrong. He gets out of the car. Me and the bwoys, we nearly died laughing upstairs, I'm telling you."

Jaimie couldn't help but smile at the description of the incident.

"The guy gets out of the car, man, you should have seen the look on his face! Red, like he was gonna blow up."

"What happened to the car?" Jaimie asked.

"Me and T-Man did a wicked job on his tyres. We cut them up but inside, against the rim, just enough so they stay solid until you start to drive the car. Then the inside walls split, dropping the car on its wheels."

Sounded like a real technical job. Junior added:

"You can imagine how mad he was..."

"Where was your car?" Jaimie asked.

"Parked by Lorraine's mother's."

'Not so crazy, Junior!' Jaimie reflected.

"So the guy leaves his car there, runs home," Junior continued. "A little after that, we see a car coming for him. Him and two more white guys are coming up to the flat..."

"Lorraine was at work?"

Junior nodded.

"Yeah, it's just me and the crew. So they come up and start banging on the door, shouting. I open the door and they try to rush in on me, so I back in. Next thing they know, they're looking down Markie's double barrel. They got real quiet."

"You had a shotgun in there?"

Junior looked at his brother like he had lost his senses.

"You don't think I was gonna let them murder me in there?! We searched them and picked up two knives and a revolver. Anyway, we pressured them a little, explained to them that they shouldn't mess with me, then we let them go."

Jaimie was silent, taking it all in. He couldn't really fault his brother, but the mention of guns gave him a bad feeling about the whole incident.

"Took him all afternoon to get new tyres on..." Junior added, laughing.

"I don't find it funny, man. What you think's gonna happen now?"

Junior shrugged.

"That's up to him, but I'm gonna make sure I get ready for him if he tries anything."

"You told Lorraine?" Jaimie asked him.

"I had to. She don't know many people on the estate yet. I told her to watch out."

Jaimie sighed. He still had a bad feeling about everything. It was unlikely to stop here.

"What you gonna do?"

Junior made a fatalistic gesture.

"I'm gonna wait and see. But I just want you to know, before anything else happens. 'Cause if the guy tries anything, it's on!"

"Oh, so you're ready to smoke him?"

"I don't want it to go that far, but I'm gonna keep my insurance close to me."

"Your insurance? You're out to get strapped?"

"That's what I came for. Markie don't live with us, I got to have my own."

Jaimie kept quiet for a minute, then looked at his brother.

"That's what you came for? You mean you already got a gun?

54

Since when?"

Junior had gotten up and started exploring the food cupboard.

"Since...since last year."

He sounded natural about it. Jaimie sounded unhappy.

"Yo! Sit down, man. Talk to me... You've kept a piece, in this house, since last year?"

"Yeah..." Junior answered lightly.

Jaimie couldn't believe it.

"What's wrong with you, man? You trying to send me down over here?"

"What are you talking about, Jaimie man?"

Apparently, Junior couldn't see what the big fuss was about.

Jaimie was downright serious.

"Look man, you wanna take your chances, it's down to you. But don't ever get me involved like that. One thing I learned on coming up here: they find you with even one bullet, you're going down, mandatory. This place is worse than California for that. And you're telling me today you been keeping a piece in this house since last year?"

There was silence after Jaimie spoke. Junior could see on his brother's face how he felt about it. Then Jaimie asked:

"Where is it?"

"In my room. It's only a small gun."

Junior sounded almost comical. Jaimie got up, shaking his head, went to the window. The storm was over but the rain was beating down heavy in the darkness of the garden.

"OK," Jaimie started. "He comes for you at the flat, you got your gun, he got his. One way or another, someone's gonna drop. Then you have your wife and baby there. What d'you think?"

The pertinent question hung in the silence between them for a short while.

"What else can I do?" Junior asked.

"You and this guy gotta talk."

"Talk?! It's too late for that!"

"It's not too late. So far it's only property, nobody got hurt yet."

Junior doubted very much that his brother really understood the situation.

"You can't talk to these guys, they're fucked up. Racist motherfuckers..."

"I say let's try to talk, there's still time. Come on, let's go!"

55

Junior looked at his brother.

"Now?"

Jaimie was already switching the gas off under his pots. He stood over the table.

"Let's go, man. Come on! My dinner's off."

The way Jaimie sounded determined, Junior had no choice. He got up. As he followed his brother through the lounge, he asked:

"Maybe we better take my thing with us, just in case."

"What's up with you and that shit?" Jaimie seemed concerned. "Look," he said firmly, "I'm about to do something I don't want to, but you're my brother so I got no choice. But don't start bugging out like you feel to get strapped, OK? It's not life or death, we gonna talk."

"Sure, OK, I just hope you're right."

Jaimie didn't answer. He already had his jacket on and was out of the door. Junior followed him, running through the rain to get to the jeep down the road.

The estate was wet, dark already but for the areas under the lamp posts. The few people still outside were scurrying home, away from the downpour.

"That is his car, there."

Junior pointed it out, as they turned right to get to the other side of the green. Jaimie found an empty space and parked before switching ignition and lights off. He didn't really want to be involved in this, especially not tonight, but here he was. He heard Junior say:

"So, you just wanna go knock on his door, just like that?"

"Where's the place?" Jaimie asked quietly.

"First flat on the right, ground floor."

Junior was motioning towards the lit entrance of one of the blocks to their left.

"What if the guy pulls something on us?"

Jaimie looked at his brother in the semi-darkness of the car, the rain beating over the metal around them. He asked:

"You afraid?"

No way Junior was ever going to admit a thing like that.

Jaimie opened his door, eased his long frame out of the car, apparently oblivious to the pounding rain falling on his head. Junior climbed out of the passenger side and followed him quickly. By the time they reached the entrance to the block they were soaked.

"That door?" Jaimie asked.

"Yeah."

He pressed the bell once. The light melody sounded weird in the circumstances. Jaimie, who was standing right in front of the peephole, could hear the shuffling of feet behind the door. A few seconds later the door opened. The white man's eyes bulged out of their sockets at the sight of Junior. He looked late twenties, medium height, with short blond hair and an earring. He wore a hostile expression that bent his mouth sideways.

"You got a fucking nerve coming back here."

Jaimie ignored the man's hostility. He said:

"I understand you and my brother had a little problem, so I came to see if we could talk about it, to avoid it going any further. You know what I'm saying?"

Jaimie's tone was polite enough but coming from a six foot three, one hundred and eighty five pound shaven-headed black man, it sounded like a request hard to ignore, angry or not. The white man said:

"You're brother pulled a gun on me. He's dead, that's it."

"He told me, but he says you had one too, and he said he didn't start no trouble. What d'you say we talk and sort it out before it gets out of control?"

There was a heavy pause on the doorstep until the arrival from inside of a bulky-looking, shortish guy.

"Chas! What you doing out there?" He froze on seeing Junior, a beer can in his right hand. His eyes narrowed and his puffy face tensed up.

"You should have run away while you had the chance," he spat. "We gonna do you, you cunt!"

The tension was thick, the four men facing each other a couple of feet either side of the doormat. Junior said defiantly:

"You're the ones who fucked with me in the first place..."

Jaimie cut in quickly, that wasn't exactly the approach he favoured.

"Hold on, hold on." He told Chas: "Look man, can we settle this whole thing peacefully? I don't think we've got anything to gain from getting angry."

Chas turned to Jaimie:

"First of all, your brother better pay for my tyres."

57

At least there was scope for negotiation here. But once again, it was the fat boy who turned up the heat. He was standing by Chas' side, hands on his hips now, with a bad smirk across his face.

"You think you can get away with pulling a shooter on us? You black bastard!"

The insult echoed, Jaimie looked at the man straight. Shaking his head, he said in a normal tone of voice:

"I didn't realise this was a racial problem, maybe it was a mistake to try to act civilised with you guys."

"We don't like your kind around here," Chas said.

"And I don't like white motherfuckers like you!" Junior had been itching to get involved. He didn't see why they should be diplomatic with fools like these two. The remark hit home...

"You're asking for it, nigga!" the fat boy hissed, looking redder in the face.

"I'm outta here bro', I got no time for these honkies," Junior kissed his teeth derisively, waving a dismissive hand and turning to walk away.

He didn't see the man's move. The next thing Jaimie knew, the fat boy was standing with a small shiny handgun pointed at his brother's back, just out of his reach. Then the gun switched his way.

Junior turned, froze, eyes fixed on the fat man. In the heavy silence, the man with the gun said:

"Two dead niggas, you are."

He pointed the gun at Jaimie's head. Jaimie noticed the thin line of perspiration above the man's upper lip. It wasn't the first time he had been jacked up, but it had been a long time since and right now, something had to be done quickly to solve the perilous situation they were in. Glancing briefly at Junior, Jaimie could have sworn he read "I told you so..." in his eyes. Suddenly, loudly in the relative silence of the evening hour, Jaimie's voice rose.

"Awww shit, Junior, man, look what you got us into! I told you! Didn't I tell you? I asked you not to cause any trouble. You know you shoulda come to me before you start messing with them. This is their turf, man, this is the white man's country. Now they gonna kill us and I didn't even have nothing to do with it! What the fuck is wrong with you, nigga? Them white boys always looking for an excuse to kill us, why you had to go and do a thing like that?"

Jaimie was loud enough to be heard all the way upstairs, his plaintive voice echoing through the entrance hall. Junior glared at his brother, about to erupt with anger.

"What the fuck's wrong with you?" he asked.

Jaimie shifted uneasily, his back to the two white men he was unsettling.

"What's wrong? What's wrong?!" he repeated, louder the second time, his eyes opening wide. "Some white guy I've never seen before wants to blow my head off, you asking what's wrong?!!"

The gun was still trained on him, but the man on the trigger seemed less intent on shooting now.

"Shut the fuck up!" he told Jaimie firmly.

Jaimie turned halfway to face him.

"Look man, you do what you wanna do, but until then I'm gonna tell this nigga here what I feel, OK. Don't get involved, it's between me and my brother."

With that, he started on Junior again.

"All your life, you always got me into some fucked-up situation, 'cause you're always too smart to listen. What you gonna do now, uh? What you gonna do to get us out alive? You're so smart, any ideas?" As he gesticulated towards Junior, Jaimie noticed Chas looking increasingly uncomfortable on the doorstep and the fat boy holding his silver gun low. Neither man was fast enough to see the move that followed. In a blur, Jaimie jabbed the fat boy in the eyes while his right hand grabbed the man's right wrist, neutralising the gun hand in a vice-like grip. In the same flowing movement, his right hand twisted the man's wrist while the left applied pressure on the elbow. There was a cry of pain, then the dull noise of the gun dropping on the doormat. Chas had no time to react either as he received the weight of his friend in the midriff as Jaimie pushed him forward. The two white men, crashed against the door and fell to the ground in a bundle. While they struggled to their feet, Jaimie picked up the gun and removed the clip.

"You can have that back," he said, throwing the handgun at the fat boy, still moaning with pain alongside Chas. Jaimie looked the two men straight in the eyes, one then the other. His voice was back to normal now.

"Listen carefully: this thing stops here. I don't care who did what to who no more. You don't like niggas, but that's cool 'cause niggas don't like cave boys like you. But you don't want to go all the way with me, so keep away from my family and we'll be happy

59

ever after, OK?"

Chas and his bruised fat friend were unlikely to argue, even if hatred was burning them inside.

"We're leaving you guys now. Have a nice evening."

Jaimie turned and left them there and headed out of the flats followed by Junior, a bemused look on his face. The rain had practically stopped. Junior climbed in the jeep as Jaimie turned the ignition.

"You wanna go for your car now?" Jaimie asked, driving out of the parking lot.

"No, I don't need it for now."

Jaimie drove around the communal gardens and braked the car to a halt in front of Junior's block of flats.

"You wanna come up, get some food or something?"

"I got my dinner at home, remember? You go home to your family. Forget about it, you be cool. A'ight?"

Junior looked at his older brother, knowing he wouldn't want to talk anymore for tonight.

"A'ight. Later," he answered, opening his door and stepping in.

Jaimie drove away slowly, left the estate and took his time to get home. As he turned onto the 'Grove' he stopped by a large rubbish skip beside a building site. Taking the clip from inside his waist, he pushed it deep underneath the pile of refuse and got back in the car. It was getting late and he started to feel hungry now. Today had been a long day.

The next morning, early, Jaimie went for a light jog. The sun was just about rising over the town, the streets were still fairly calm. He ran for a while then did some stretching, the physical strain clearing up his mind. Sure enough, the events of the previous evening were hanging at the back of his mind but it was nothing to stress about too much. As far as Jaimie was concerned, it was over. Back home, he showered and put on some clothes, not much though, as the heat seemed to be back after the storm the previous evening. A light breakfast, then Jaimie left the house for the garage. The day off had done him good, he realised. Backtracking over the last few years was something he had needed to do since coming to England. It worked like some kind of therapy, helped him to come to terms with things past and to feel stronger for things to come. Once he had opened the garage, he hung around for a while, got talking with the old black man who walked past every morning with his little dog, regular as clockwork. At first, Jaimie had simply said "good morning" to the man, then one day they started exchanging words until it had become a habit. The old man lived in one of the houses across the main road. He told Jaimie his wife had died two years earlier, that he came from the Caribbean thirty years ago and had worked for British Rail until his retirement recently. He was a kind person, short in stature with a twinkle in his eyes that belied his years. Jaimie always enjoyed their conversations. They were still talking when Paul arrived, looking like a bear with a sore head. He mumbled a greeting before disappearing in the office. Apparently, his home situation had not improved. Eventually, Jaimie let the old man continue his morning dog-walk and went to tackle the timing problem on the car he'd left from Tuesday. The day stretched lazily, the heat from outside making everyone sweaty and slow. Jaimie was passing the office on his way to lunch when Paul called him. The ventilator in the small room was blowing on full, the small TV on the filing cabinet showing one of those cricket test matches Paul was so fond of. To Jaimie, the game was a total mystery.

"How is it hanging, Paulie?" Jaimie smiled at his boss.

"It's still there, I think," Paul picked up on the joke.

He seemed a little more alive than earlier on, his shirt opened on a hairy chest, feet stretched on one of the office chairs. He fumbled on the desk for something.

"Here, that's for you."

Paul handed Jaimie a printed card, the name *Jefferson & Stone* printed black on gold in the middle. Jaimie frowned, until he turned the card over and read the scribbled writing at the back: T.S. Heywoode. Paul was looking up at him with a kind of smile.

"Seems you're moving up in the world, son!" he said.

"She's the woman with the Oldsmobile, you remember her."

"Is she? I wasn't there, she left that with Henry."

"I wonder what's happened to her now..."

"You want to call?" Paul pointed to the phone, buried under a pile of bills and letters.

Jaimie shook his head.

"Not right now, anyway. I'm out for lunch. Can I get you anything?"

"No thanks, I'm alright."

"OK, later."

61

Jaimie left the garage and walked up to the high street. It was hot, bright and busy. Sitting near the shopping centre, munching on his sandwich, he wondered briefly what 'Ms Heywoode' wanted now. It was unlikely to be a social call. From what Jaimie knew of her, she was the kind of woman too conscious of herself to be friendly and too straight to hang out with someone like him. It had been three weeks since Jaimie had obligingly driven her back home in her daddy's car. She had probably felt embarrassed at her inability to handle the vehicle and, true to himself, Jaimie had not been able to resist teasing her about it. He thought he might call her later.

Two very shapely teenagers in 'minimal' summer clothes came out of the supermarket and smiled at him as they passed. Jaimie returned the smile but kept cool. He felt relaxed, couldn't even bother to start picking up on hints like that. All in all, he had been pretty laid-back since coming over. He had spent a couple of months dating a woman Tony had introduced to him, or rather pushed onto him, the previous winter, but eventually couldn't keep it up. When he realised he wasn't motivated in any way, Jaimie had let her know and they had remained friends. Then there was Brenda whom he had, up to now, managed to keep ahead of, but otherwise he was easy. He got up to go, there was still a few more hours' work left before going home. He thought about giving Alison at the agency a check, if he finished early enough.

Back at the garage, Jaimie found Henry all greasy and visibly in need of some help. Jaimie slipped on his overalls and gave him a hand to replace the propshaft on a Landcruiser. Once that was done, he got back to his own work. The time was coming up to four when he went to wash his hands at the little basin at the back. He felt in need of a shower, a cold one. Taking a swig from a litre bottle of water, he got ready to leave. He would pass by the agency, put a little pressure on Alison; there had to be something she could come up with for him. Deep inside, Jaimie was sure he was going to get a break, get on the screen, some day.

The Renegade was hot inside and in need of a wash too. Jaimie took the roof off and adjusted the mean-looking shades he had on, before pushing a 'phat' Death Row label track and slipping the jeep into gear. The West Coast beat was totally in sync with the weather, hot and bouncy with some 'freaky' lyrics casually dropping in. He was pulling out when he caught sight of someone coming his way, waving. His foot touched the brake and through the shades he watched her walking towards him. It was Tania, in three-quarter shorts and white printed tee shirt. Jaimie almost didn't recognise her, her long wavy hair made her look very different. She reached the jeep. Jaimie turned down the volume a little.

"Hey, Miss Heywoode! What a nice surprise."

As usual, she wasn't smiling but nevertheless seemed friendly enough for once.

"Hi," she said, "How are you?"

"I'm good. Is that hair all yours?"

"Of course, why?"

"It's usually extensions women wear nowadays. Very nice..."

"Thank you. I have a little problem...with the car," she said.

Jaimie laughed, shook his head.

"Somehow I knew it wasn't a social call!" Jaimie said, studying her closely behind his dark shades. He asked: "You been driving it again? Stubborn, uh?"

She didn't answer, but stood there under the sun looking like a child who's just broken the house vase. Jaimie was enjoying it.

"Don't tell me you wrecked the transmission; took me a lot of work..."

"No, I just had a small crash," Tania shrugged.

"A small crash!?" Jaimie repeated. "I told you you shouldn't drive that car, but I guess you don't listen to anyone, ever. OK, ain't nobody hurt, I hope."

"No, no, but I...got hit by a bus."

She sounded embarrassed to say it, the way she averted her eyes for a moment. It sounded funny to Jaimie though.

"Hit by a bus! Damn, you don't play!" He stopped before asking: "Was the bus' fault I bet..."

"Well, not really; it was parked..."

This time Jaimie had to burst out laughing.

"You hit a parked bus!!!"

Tension was etched on Tania's face.

"Alright, alright, I know. Now, can you help me?"

"Where's the car now?" he asked.

"At home. It's only a small scratch."

"Good."

She said in a serious tone of voice:

"But my father's coming back on Saturday. I need to get it fixed

63

before that."

Jaimie looked at her.

"Is he gonna beat you up?"

She frowned at him.

"Don't be silly. I just don't want him to see it, that's all."

Jaimie smiled at her.

"You know what I think, I think your father told you not to drive his car but you decided to drive it anyway. It was too tempting, wasn't it? He knows you can't handle the car, forbids you to touch it but you had to do it. Am I right?"

Tania disliked being found out, you could read it in her eyes. She sighed then said:

"You really think you're smart, don't you?"

But Jaimie had the upper hand today and wasn't prepared to pass on it just like that.

"Uh-uh! I wanna know: did your father expressly tell you not to drive his car? Yes or no?"

Asked in a mockingly official tone of voice, the question caused Tania to wince but she had no choice but to answer.

"Yes, he did. Satisfied?"

Jaimie was merciful.

"OK, Miss Heywoode, we'll put you on probation for now. So, you want me to go and look at the car, right?"

"If you wouldn't mind, yes." Then she asked: "Why do you always call me 'Ms Heywoode'?"

Jaimie said:

"Well, this is a formal relationship, I got to address you formally."

She didn't know what to make of it. Jaimie said:

"Alright, let's go."

Tania walked to the other side, got in. As Jaimie started to drive, she asked:

"Why do you drive this? This is the kind of car we use for rough terrain, back home."

"I'm a rough man, it suits my style," he answered, half-serious.

They joined the traffic on the main road.

"I hope it's not inconvenient, I mean..." Tania began.

"As a matter of fact, I did have plans to go somewhere. You just caught me."

"Oh, I'm sorry."

"It's just this agency I'm with. I need to check if any work's come up."

"You're looking for another job?" Tania seemed interested.

"Not really, I'm just trying to get into movies."

"Movies? You mean, acting? You're an actor?"

"Yeah, I'm trying to get a break."

There was a smile on her face now.

"Why, you find that funny?" Jaimie asked.

"No, I just didn't know you were into that."

He was watching her.

"OK, say what you think. Come on..."

Tania shook her head.

"I'm not thinking anything."

"You wanna come along? Maybe you could get a break too."

"No, thank you."

"No, you don't want a break or no, you don't wanna come along?"

She shrugged.

"I'll come along if you want me to. I don't want to disrupt your career."

Jaimie could swear he heard a note of sarcasm in the remark. They drove down, leisurely chatting. Tania seemed a little less uptight today. Whether she was being genuinely friendly or it was only that she needed him to get her out of her predicament with the car, Jaimie couldn't tell but it was nice. The lyrics on the West Coast track were suddenly audible and seemed much ruder than Jaimie remembered them to be. He noticed Tania's reaction and smiled.

"A little too x-rated for you, uh?"

She simply glanced at him and asked:

"So, what type of roles are you looking for?"

Jaimie shrugged.

"Anything, really. If I can get a part, any part, I believe I'll get noticed and make it work from there."

"Have you done acting before?"

"Did a few plays back home, mostly community productions, you know. I got some work as an extra also, twice, but non-speaking parts. You done any drama?"

"Only at school, and I didn't enjoy it then."

"What was it?"

"Classics, that sort of thing."

"Where was that?" Jaimie asked.

"In Harrow."

"Private school?"

"Why do you ask?" Tania sounded suspicious.

Jaimie laughed. "Just to know."

"What was your school like?" she asked.

He said simply, with a little smile:

"Not private, that's for sure..."

She was about to say something, but Jaimie's pager started beeping. He unclipped it from his belt. ' CALL LORRAINE. URGENT.' read the message. Jaimie frowned. They were literally down the road from the agency, but he wasn't worried about that now. Lorraine wouldn't page him without a serious reason. His mind locked on the incident of the previous night.

"Something wrong?" Tania asked, noticing the change on his face.

"My sister-in-law called."

"I didn't know you were married."

"I'm not, my brother is, kinda..." he answered, picking a gap in the traffic to do a sharp u-turn. Then Jaimie put his foot down, expertly handling the jeep around side streets until he was back in his area. His mind was racing too, trying to figure out what could have happened. Beside him, Tania was quiet for a while.

"Maybe it's a bad time, maybe you should drop me off," she said tentatively.

Jaimie looked at her.

"Be cool, I gotta find out what's up first."

She didn't say anything else until the jeep screeched to a halt in front of Junior's block.

"You wanna wait for me?" Jaimie asked her as he switched off his engine.

Tania glanced briefly around the estate.

"I'd rather not."

"Come on then."

Jaimie was already jumping out of the car. Tania followed him as fast as she could, but was still only on the first landing by the time he rang the bell. Lorraine opened the door almost immediately, Keesha in her arms. She seemed upset.

"What's up?" Jaimie asked.

"Junior got arrested," Lorraine said.

66

Tania was just arriving.

"This is Ms..." Jaimie stopped short. "Tania. This is Lorraine."

Lorraine let them in. The place seemed upside down. She motioned at the chaos around her.

"They searched up the place."

Lorraine explained that the police had stopped Junior outside as he was coming home from work and brought him upstairs. Having found nothing they had still taken him in. Jaimie listened, his face closed up, his mind cold. Tania seemed totally bewildered. Something clicked in Jaimie's mind. He told Lorraine:

"Listen, I gotta go. Don't worry, he'll be out tonight. They ain't got nothing on him."

"What's going on, Jaimie? Is it to do with the problem with the white guy?"

Certainly seemed that way to Jaimie. He tried to reassure Lorraine.

"You stay here, let me go down to the station. I'll be back soon."

He started out. Tania said her "good bye" and followed him. Jaimie was already halfway down the stairs by then.

"What did your brother do?" she called out behind him.

"Nothing, it's a mistake."

"A mistake?"

"Yeah."

Jaimie was hurrying to his car, his mind working on overdrive. He figured the police were looking for a gun and as Junior was still officially registered at their address, that would be the very next place they were likely to go to. But should he go to the police station first or to the house? And even if he went home first, he didn't know where Junior had hidden the piece. Tania got to the jeep. Jaimie switched on his engine, still undecided. He didn't have time to make a choice however, for just as he was about to slip the Renegade into first, the sound of screeching tyres distracted him. Out of nowhere came a police car. It stopped right in front of the jeep, effectively blocking it in the parking bay. In a flash, Jaimie saw the doors open and heard:

"Nobody moves, stay where you are!"

Too shocked to move anyway, Jaimie watched the two policemen standing behind their car, guns pointed at him. A third officer was a little to the side at the back, giving the orders. Tania sat frozen in her seat, eyes wide open in surprise. Next came the commands, sharp, precise.

"Driver, very slowly, switch off the ignition. Hands above your head now, right. Slowly, step out of the vehicle. Now, down on your knees, lie down on the ground, hands behind your head."

Like in a trance, Jaimie obeyed, his jaws clenched in anger. It wasn't the first time, but that was back then...back home. Quickly, one of the armed officers approached him, patted him down quickly then cuffed him. The other one was by the side of the jeep now, checking Tania. Jaimie heard her protest, now recovered from the initial surprise.

"I demand to know what this is about. You have no right to search my bag, get your hands off me!"

But that didn't prevent the police from forcing her in the back of their car, next to Jaimie. At least they didn't handcuff her! A small group of curious residents had gathered, watching the incident. As one of the officers searched the jeep, Jaimie said to the one at the front:

"Could you ask him to get my keys?"

The policeman obliged. They weren't rude or anything, just very efficient. There was nothing to find in the jeep, so the officer climbed in the police car and they drove off under the interested gaze of the gawkers. The drive to Ladbroke Grove police station was short, silent. Jaimie was hoping they wouldn't go to his house. Tania sat beside, head straight, looking miserable. At the station they were led inside through the back entrance. The arresting policemen conferred with the desk sergeant then left, after removing Jaimie's handcuffs. From then, he and Tania were separated until an hour or so later when, after he'd been interviewed by two plain-clothes officers, he was brought back to the desk. Of course, Jaimie denied any knowledge of a gun and brushed off their suggestion that his brother had admitted to anything. He told them they had been misled in the first place. They wouldn't say where they got their information, but it was plain to Jaimie. So eventually, they all met back at the desk: Jaimie in a brooding mood, Junior looking even more upset and Tania who seemed about to explode. None of them could be charged with anything, nevertheless no apology was offered and Jaimie knew only too well that they were likely be under surveillance for some time. Outside in the mellowness of the descending evening, Junior asked:

"Lorraine OK?"

Jaimie nodded. Tania threw him an intense stare.

"I have never been so humiliated in all my life," she said coldly. Jaimie sighed.

"It's a misunderstanding, I'm really sorry about that."

"Sorry, you're sorry? They pointed a gun at me. I could have been shot!" She paused, looked away, visibly trying to keep calm. "Do you know what will happen if they contact my workplace?"

"They won't," Jaimie assured, "They don't want nothing with you, you just happened to be there, that's all."

She was still very upset, a deep line etched between her eyebrows.

"Hi, I'm Junior," Junior said to her, smiling.

Tania threw him a brief glance, but didn't even answer. Junior was not a man to let that phase him however.

"I feel responsible for all this," he told her nicely," Jaimie had nothing to do with it. In fact, it's all a big mistake. I was framed."

"Leave it, man," Jaimie said, "don't say nothing else. Let's go home." He turned to Tania. "Let's get a cab back to my car then I'll drop you off," he offered.

People often say that if looks could kill. Well, Tania's eyes were deadly. Facing Jaimie, she said very stiffly:

"I don't want anything to do with you, or even to see you ever again."

With that, she marched off down the road, into the setting sun. Jaimie called out:

"Hey! Come on, Miss Heywoode, don't take it like that!"

She didn't even turn, but kept on strutting forward angrily. Jaimie sighed, shook his head.

"Who was that?" Junior asked.

Jaimie didn't answer. He felt too dejected about the whole thing. To think that he had come all the way to England, started a new life and kept himself out of trouble only to find himself, once again, handled like a criminal! He took a deep breath and turned towards Junior.

"I thought they were gonna take me home, search the house."

"They did."

Jaimie stopped in his tracks.

"What?"

Junior nodded.

69

"They didn't find anything by Lorraine's, so they drove me home and searched the whole place."

Junior shrugged and kept on walking. Jaimie caught up with him.

"How come?"

With a wide grin on his face, Junior winked at his brother.

"I took a trip home during my lunch break."

Jaimie shook his head, relieved.

"So you're not totally crazy after all, thank God!"

They walked on, enjoying the freedom to be able to do so. A spell in a cell, even a brief one, makes you feel that way.

"What are we gonna do about the snitch?" Junior asked.

Jaimie took another bite from his cheese and tomato sandwich, put it back down on the paper and swallowed before answering Tony's question.

"Junior had gone to get it out a couple of hours before that."

He picked up his bottle of beer. Around them, at the wooden tables of the beer garden, the other lunchtime drinkers were chatting, enjoying a relaxed moment in the mild sun. Tony had been listening to Jaimie's story of the previous day and the look on his face was pure astonishment. He had called Jaimie at work that morning, offering to meet him for lunch. Caught up as they had been in their respective affairs, they had not seen each other for a few weeks, and from his tone Jaimie had guessed that Tony had problems. When he learned the latest from Jaimie however, Tony forgot his and wanted now to find out the extent of his friend's troubles.

"But what about the white guy? He's got a gun too, right?" Tony asked in a low voice.

Jaimie finished the sandwich in two hungry bites. He nodded gravely.

"Yeah, well, he probably works for the police, you know what I'm saying?"

"What?"

"That's the way I read it."

Tony couldn't believe it. He drank some of his beer but his sandwich remained untouched.

"So, what about the girl?"

"Oh, they released her too," Jaimie said, deadpan.

70

Then a broad smile broke on his face. Tony couldn't help laughing. He shook his head.

"You take this as joke! Jaimie, this is serious, man."

Jaimie leaned back in the plastic chair, exhaled.

"What can I do? This isn't my idea. The whole thing just fell on me, Tony." He added after a pause. "And I can't blame Junior either; he didn't start it."

Tony nodded, thoughtful. "So what you gonna do?"

Jaimie shrugged. "Wait."

Tony looked at him but asked nothing. He knew his friend enough to understand his way of thinking. All the same Tony felt disgusted by the injustice of the whole thing. He watched Jaimie leaning back in his large 'Knicks' tee shirt, downing the rest of his bottle of beer. Often he wished he could take life as easy, as coolly as Jaimie seemed to.

"Forget about that, Tony. How's life on your side?"

The question brought an instant pained look on Tony's face.

"Bad, man. My life's wrecked."

"Wrecked? What's up with you?"

It was Tony's turn to lean back in his chair. For a moment. Jaimie's story had made him forget the reality of his own predicament. Shaking his head sadly, Tony let out:

"My mother and Charlene had a row; everything is off."

Jaimie's eyes widened in surprise.

"Off? When did that happen?"

"Yesterday."

Tony's countenance darkened as he recalled it all.

"So what happened, man? Your mum dissed Charlene, uh?"

Jaimie knew of Tony's mother's frank speaking and meddlesome tendencies. He hadn't really seen Tony much since he had introduced the expectant Charlene to his mother, but apparently, the first meeting had been cordial enough.

"No man, it was the other way around. Charlene cracked up under pressure, opened up on Mum then walked out.

"What?! Charlene's bad like that?"

"Believe it, man. I told her to let Mum talk and not to get into no arguments with her. She agreed. But yesterday afternoon, things got ugly down there. I was at work when I get this call from my sister Cleo...you know Cleo?"

"I met her once."

"She said I had to get home right away. Mum was vexed, man, cursing... Took me the whole evening to calm her down. She wanted me to leave Charlene right there and then. I'm telling you, this is serious!"

Jaimie had to admit that it sounded really serious.

"So, what was the static about?"

Tony waited a few seconds, as if checking within himself for the right answer to that.

"The baby's christening."

Jaimie searched Tony's face for a hint of a joke that wasn't there.

"But..." Jaimie frowned, "...the baby ain't born yet!"

"I know." Tony sighed.

"So what's the kick up about?"

Tony took time to choose his words. The problem seemed both painful and unsolvable. Leaning forward over the table, he told Jaimie:

"Charlene came to the house to pick up Mum to go shopping for the wedding."

"The wedding?" Jaimie stopped him.

"Yeah, the wedding. Oh yeah, I haven't seen you since...anyway, we decided to get married just after the baby is born, then have the christening..."

Jaimie nodded, kind of shocked at the pace events had taken since they'd last seen each other. But Tony didn't have time to go into that now.

"So as she's getting ready, she's talking to Charlene about how the wedding should be and the people to invite, the food, you can imagine! Anyway Cleo was there with them, she was going along. So Mum starts talking about the christening now; that's when things turned bad. All the time, Charlene is sitting at the kitchen table with Cleo, while Mum walks up and down and tells them this and that while she's getting ready. So Mum tells Charlene that she's already talked to the minister of her church about the dates, and that they could choose one together. Like she's involving her, after all!"

Jaimie smiled and shook his head. Tony continued after a sip from his beer.

"Cleo said she saw Charlene get up slowly and turn to Mum. She told her quietly that her child would be christened in the same church as she was, and that her family were all Catholics and her child would be too."

Tony paused. Jaimie was frowning, taking it in.

"You can imagine the atmosphere in the kitchen! Cleo said Mum got cold on Charlene and told her that her grandchild would be christened in the Seventh Day Adventist church, and that was that."

"So what happened?" Jaimie pressed his friend. Though he could see Tony was upset because of the conflict, it sure sounded like an interesting story to him.

"Well, Cleo said she tried to cool things down but by then, Mum was getting hot and told Charlene outright that the Catholic church was wicked and...and that the Pope is Satan or something like that. Then she walked out, man."

Jaimie blew out some air through his lips.

"Hot stuff!"

"Jaimie man, this is not a movie, this is my life!"

"It is. What you gonna do?"

Tony seemed unsure, all he knew was that he wanted things back to where they were before.

"Your mother ain't gonna back down, right?"

Tony shook his head sadly.

"What about Charlene? Have you talked with her since?"

"Yeah, last night. She's another crazy one! She told her mother, man, and now it's like a family affair. They're into this church thing in a big way."

Jaimie didn't know quite what to say to make Tony feel better.

"What about you? I mean you're in the middle of it. It's your child too. How do you feel about it?" he asked finally.

"I don't know, I guess I didn't think about the details. One church or another is the same thing to me."

"Well, it looks like you're gonna have to take a position. It's your baby, man. You're the man!"

Tony winced. He looked totally bewildered by the whole dispute and felt powerless to solve it.

"What about the wedding?"

The query added to Tony's gloom.

"Same problem; both sides want their own way." Tony paused, then looked at Jaimie. "I have a feeling that Charlene's mother is stirring the whole thing up. She never really took to me. I'm not sure what's gonna happen, man."

Jaimie shook his head, sorry that his friend's life should have

73

taken such a disastrous turn. They sat in contemplative silence for a long moment until Tony asked:

"What time are you going back to work?"

Jaimie checked his watch and shrugged.

"No rush, I don't have much on anyway."

"Let's have another beer."

"I'll get it."

Tony was already up.

"No, it's OK. Let me get it."

He disregarded Jaimie's objection that it was his turn and walked to the bar inside. The two friends spent another hour sipping beer and talking in the hot sun. Most of the lunchtime drinkers had gone back to their jobs now but half a dozen people remained, mostly couples smiling at each other. Tony still hadn't touched his sandwich. Apparently his domestic problems spoiled his appetite. He asked:

"How is your acting career going, Jaimie?"

Jaimie made a face that said 'not so good'.

"No break yet, but I'm still working on it. It's gonna be hard, man."

Tony paused. "Remember I told you I talked to this friend of mine who works for an independent production company? He's coming back from holidays this week, I'll see him and find out if anything's happening."

"I appreciate that, Tony. It ain't easy but one way or another, I'm going to get on screen."

Tony smiled.

"You're determined, and that's the main thing in life. Hey, what happened to that story you were writing?"

"I'm still working on it, but it doesn't flow, if you know what I mean."

"Yeah, what was it called again?"

Jaimie recalled giving his friend a run down of what he thought at the time was a great idea for a film script. Eventually, his initial enthusiasm had gradually dried up as he strained to develop it on paper.

"I scrapped the title," he said, " 'cause I'm not sure where the plot is going. It's a kind of love story..."

Tony laughed.

"I can't see you writing a love story, no offence, Jaimie, but I see

74

you more in the gangster genre, you know I mean?"

Jaimie smiled, downed some beer.

"Yeah, you're probably right, but I've got to try it. I know it's in me, it's just hard to bring it out."

They kept quiet for a while. A light breeze was rustling through the neatly trimmed garden bushes behind them.

"So, what about that girl?"

Jaimie's mind was on thoughts of his own.

"What girl?"

"You know, the lawyer?"

"What about her?"

"You should check her out. She sounds interesting from what you told me."

Jaimie shook his head and laughed.

"Interesting? No man, try stuck-up, repressed and totally uncool. That girl's definitely not my type."

Tony threw his friend a sideways glance.

"You mean she didn't fall for your legendary charm."

"Tony man, I'm telling you this girl is on a different trip. I didn't even try to get through. Word!"

"Well, maybe you should. She can't be that bad, and besides, maybe she needs someone like you to straighten her out."

Jaimie laughed.

"That's a lifetime's work, and I ain't got that much to spare."

Tony finished his bottle.

"But you haven't got nobody right now, right?"

Shrugging, Jaimie had to admit he was kinda 'unemployed', as he put it.

"Alright, but how do you expect to write a love story; you're out of love!"

Tony's logic made Jaimie smile.

"Sure, I am. You know, I've noticed that you're always trying to push me into getting involved. Last year it was that friend of yours, what's her name again? The one with the big eyes. Nice of you but I'm fussy, you know what I mean?"

"I know. That's why you should try something different. So what about the lawyer; she's fit right?"

"Sure, but there's more to her and I can't handle the rest."

"I've got a great idea, why don't we go and see her. You can introduce me to her, I'll see what she's like..."

75

"Man, you got to be crazy," Jaimie laughed. "After yesterday, she don't want to see me, even in picture. She thinks I'm some kind of gangster! Check this out..."

Jaimie did a passable imitation of Tania's face and tone of voice outside the police station. "I have never been so humiliated in all my life!"

They both laughed hard.

"I've got to see her. Come on, man, I could do with a little entertainment," Tony said.

"You just love trouble, that's your problem. And who's gonna get the blame? Me again."

"Let's check her out, Jaim. Why, you got anything better to do this afternoon?"

Jaimie had to admit he didn't. All the same, he wasn't keen on the idea. Tania was not a social acquaintance and, the way things had been happening, was unlikely to be friendly. But Tony insisted, dared him, taunted him and before he knew it, Jaimie was driving out of Cricklewood with a grinning Tony by his side. He seemed in a better mood now, having pushed his family problems at the back of his mind for the time being. From his wallet, Jaimie pulled the gold-on-black business card, passed it to Tony who nodded appreciatively. The Friday afternoon traffic wasn't too bad, except on Kensington High Street, where the failure of a traffic signal at a junction was making things slow. Finding a safe parking space proved difficult, but eventually Jaimie was lucky enough to come upon a departing vehicle and squeezed the jeep in. He fed the costly parking meter, then he and Tony joined the flow of pedestrians. The area was busy, window-shoppers, idlers and tourists mingling on the pavements in a colourful, multi-lingual moving crowd. Jaimie found the solicitors' office on the first floor of a white stone building, above a shoe shop. He rang the intercom, waited. Tony looked at him.

"What are you going to say?" he grinned mischievously.

Jaimie didn't answer. A woman's voice came over, hardly audible.

"Hi. I'm here to see Ms Heywoode."

With a little click, the wooden door opened and the two entered, walked up the carpeted stairs to the first floor. At that point, Jaimie suddenly realised he was dressed a little too casually in his jeans and tee shirt compared to Tony's slacks and neat, short-sleeved

76

shirt. Why had he agreed to come here? Beyond a glass partition, a grey-haired, bespectacled woman was speaking on the phone. Jaimie and Tony approached the polished desk and waited for her to finish.

"We're here to see Miss Heywoode," Jaimie said in a polite tone of voice and with his most engaging smile, once she had replaced the receiver.

The woman smiled back, one of those condescending half-smiles that seem to come with certain positions.

"May I ask your name, sir?"

"Mr Charles, Tony Charles."

Jaimie gave Tony a little wink, then reverted to his 'diplomatic' smile as he watched the secretary press a button on the switchboard in front of her. Apparently, the name worked because she asked them to take a seat, which they did. As they sunk into the comfortable metal-framed leather chairs, Tony asked again in a low voice:

"What are you going to say?"

Jaimie shrugged, then said in an affected tone:

"My friend, Mr Charles, needs a good divorce lawyer." Jaimie held on to his own smile as he answered.

Then he added more seriously:

"You better pray she doesn't freak out on us!"

Before Tony could answer, a door opened at the far end of the corridor and a smartly-dressed woman stepped out. Tony watched as the attractive young woman with the sculpted brown features stopped in front of them. They both got up as one man, said "good afternoon." There was some fifteen seconds of silence as Tania stared at Jaimie. Something on his face must have touched her because, she said:

"If you would follow me, please."

They did. Tania's office was bright, sparsely decorated as any serious solicitor's office should be, with black metal cabinets and stacks of neatly arranged files on a table at the back, by the window. She sat behind her desk, dropped a cool gaze on both men seated in front of her. Jaimie thought he should start.

"Look, I know you might not be thrilled to see me right now, but I just wanted to apologise for getting you involved in this unfortunate incident yesterday. I hope you can understand..."

Tania switched from Jaimie to Tony whom she could feel staring at her. He smiled but she ignored him and turned back to Jaimie.

"So this is not a business visit?"

Jaimie glanced at his friend. He said:

"Well, my friend here, Mr Charles, may be in need of some legal advice on divorce matters, but..."

Tony prevented him from going any further down that lying road.

"But it might be a bit early for that." He cleared his throat and took up the defence.

"The truth is, Miss Heywoode, my friend Jaimie here told me how he unwittingly got you involved in some regrettable...misunderstanding, and although he didn't want to come here, I told him he should...to straighten things out and explain to you that he was just a victim of circumstances."

Tania listened to Tony, then looked at Jaimie who couldn't help admire his friend's eloquence. He nodded.

"It's absolutely true."

This time Tania looked up to the ceiling, sat back in her chair. Her face relaxed somewhat as she asked:

"I supposed it was a case of mistaken identity?"

Jaimie sighed and shrugged disarmingly.

"I was framed."

"It is not a very original defence, I guess you know that. Did they charge you?"

"No, I was innocent. I told you but you were kinda upset at the time."

Tania smiled a little and said:

"I don't know about you, but this is not the kind of thing that I'm used to. In fact this is the first time I have ever been treated like that."

"Yeah, I know and like I said, I'm sorry. I guess you probably got a totally wrong impression of me by now..."

Tania looked at him for a moment.

"And what is the right impression I should have of you, Jaimie?"

Surprised that she had addressed him by his name, Jaimie looked her deep in the eyes. She didn't flinch.

"Well, I'm basically a straight-up, hard-working, decent type of guy," he answered.

Tony had been watching the two of them. He told Tania:

"You know, Miss Heywoode, you're not at all like Jaimie said."

78

Jaimie threw him a warning look that said: 'What's up with you, man?'

But it was too late. Tania asked:

"And what did he say I was like, Mr...Charles?"

"Tony, call me Tony. From what he told me I imagined you to be more cold, you know, less accessible...I find you quite friendly."

'Tony, you snake you!' Jaimie thought to himself. He could see Tania's knowing look on him now, so he tried to limit the damage.

"All I said was that we always seem to meet in unfavourable circumstances."

"...And that I seemed a little...cold, right?" Tania added mercilessly.

Jaimie's ingenious smile was his best defence. He took the initiative and switched topics.

"What about the car? Do you still want me to do the job?"

Tania's face revealed that this was one of her more pressing concerns.

"I'd like to get that sorted out, yes."

"How bad is it?"

"It's only scratched on the paint, but it shows. It's got to be done before tomorrow."

Jaimie nodded confidently.

"No problem. If you want I could get what I need and pass by later." He couldn't help adding: "No need for you to drive down to the garage."

She saw the glint in his eyes but didn't take it as a jibe this time.

"OK, I'll be home by six-thirty."

"Right," Jaimie said, getting up. "I hope we didn't take too much of your time. I know you must be busy."

Tony got up too. Tania followed suit and came from behind the desk, to open the door. Jaimie ignored Tony's nudge and suggestive grin.

They walked back to the reception area where the grey-haired secretary was busy shuffling papers, the phone receiver trapped between her head and raised shoulder.

"Very nice to meet you, Miss Heywoode," Tony smiled.

"Likewise, thank you for coming." Tania said business-like.

She shook his hand lightly, then Jaimie's.

"Goodbye, and thank you," she told him.

He stood her stare for a moment and thought he could see

something new there, but maybe it was just him. He released her hand.

"Thanks for your time, Ms Heywoode. See you later."

Then he turned and followed Tony. Outside, the afternoon was unfolding lazily. The first thing Tony said hardly surprised Jaimie.

"This girl is wicked! What's the matter with you, Jaim?"

The ball bounced against the panel, dropped on the rim but bounced back out. Junior, who had been watching the outcome of his shot, jumped first to retrieve it but his brother jumped higher and knocked the ball away from him. Jaimie laughed as he ran back to collect it.

"I told you, you're out of shape, man!"

Hands on his knees, getting back his breath, Junior watched his brother coming towards him, bouncing the ball teasingly. It was almost eleven o'clock in the morning and although they had come out early enough to play before the sun got too warm, the temperature was starting to take its toll.

"Time out!" Junior called.

"You just had one. Come on, homie, push yourself, you're trailing by six points!"

Jaimie faced his tired brother, dribbling the ball from hand to hand and down between his legs, all the while keeping it just out of reach of his opponent. Arms apart, Junior made a valiant attempt at defending. He read Jaimie's light shuffle which was always the sign that he was about to make his move. Junior focused on the ball, ready. Jaimie came in closer with every cautious bounce of the ball. Just as Junior leapt forward, Jaimie made a lightning-fast dart to his right, bouncing the ball out of his brother's reach, then a skilful and daring pass which sent the ball bouncing between Junior's legs. The rest was rapid, merciless. Junior turned around in time to catch the end of the slam dunk and watched helplessly as the ball slipped inside the rim. He sighed heavily, shook his head.

"22 to 14!" Jaimie announced in a TV commentary style. "...six minutes on the clock, and the new jack visiting team is looking mighty tired...have they got enough juice left to catch up with the old school champions?"

"Forget it, man."

"You're giving up?" Jaimie smiled as Junior stood there, hands on his waist, visibly winded.

80

It was Junior who had dared to challenge him to a one-on-one and now looked like he regretted it. All Jaimie had said was that he seemed to be getting fat since living with Lorraine. Junior said he wasn't and eventually the challenge was issued. It did both of them good though; it had been a while since the two brothers had played together. With his girlfriend and daughter away for the weekend, Junior had decided to come and stay at the house where they had been having a ball. What better way to start Sunday than with a good basketball game?

"Let's get some drinks," Junior offered.

Jaimie threw the ball to him playfully.

"I'm still the champ, right?"

"Yeah, yeah, you're still the champ."

They walked out of the court, went around the block to the newsagent. Junior drank almost all of the water in his bottle right outside the shop, then splashed some over his head to cool himself. They got home and Junior won the age old toss of the coin to use the bathroom first, so Jaimie sank into a chair with his newspaper. Junior turned on the stereo so loud it threatened to blow the roof off.

"Yo, turn that shit down!" Jaimie shouted above the music. It was one of those jungle tracks that Junior relished so much and Jaimie still found hard to relate to. The level went down.

When his brother finished, Jaimie used the bathroom, then came back down to the kitchen where Junior was busy making himself a triple decker giant sandwich with smoked salmon, pepper, cucumber, mayonnaise, cheese, tomato, HP sauce and lettuce.

"Putting on more weight, uh..."

Junior ignored the remark. Jaimie picked up some juice from the fridge and sat at the kitchen table, barechest and in his shorts.

"So what's the programme, Todd..."

The reference to Jaimie's nickname was only as a counter for the 'weight' joke, he knew that.

"Well, amigo, I don't know what your programme is but personally, I have a four o'clock appointment, so..."

Pressing down on his sandwich so he could bite into it, Junior asked:

"What kind of appointment you have on a Sunday?"

"A private appointment."

Chewed, swallowing and nodding with satisfaction, Junior

smiled.

"Oh, you have a date. So who is it?"

"Like I said, it's private."

Another bite, another smile.

"I bet it's that girl, the rich girl. What's her name again?"

Jaimie took another sip of the juice.

"As a matter of fact it is, but don't get the wrong impression."

"Oh no, I won't." Junior sat at the table, looked at his brother with a kind of suggestive smile.

"What you got to say?" Jaimie asked.

"Nothing, man, I'm just glad you got a date. I think it's time you had a little fun, it's good for you."

Jaimie stopped him.

"Alright, first of all it's not a date. Tania and me are just talking. I think she's interesting to talk to, that's all."

"Yeah, sure, I'm with you. So where are you and...Tania going?"

"Why you wanna know?"

"Just asking."

"We're going to the movies, alright? She also happens to be interested in cinema."

"Can I come along?"

The question had its purpose, and Jaimie didn't even grant it a sniff of an answer.

Junior put down the remainder of his sandwich, stretched then sipped from his glass. He grinned at his brother.

"Right, so you're going to the movies on a Sunday afternoon like this with a wicked browning, to talk about cinema?"

"That's right, and before you go any further; she's not my type, OK?"

"So why are you being so defensive?"

Jaimie looked at him. He was usually the one with the keen psychological insight. It seemed as if Junior was using his style...

"I know what you're thinking, man, but I don't look at women that way no more. I need a little sophistication, a little...refinement. That woman is nice, she's educated and we're friends now, no thanks to you."

He had told Junior of the visit he and Tony had paid to Tania at her office and how he had managed to change the impression she had of him because of the police bust. Since then, he had fixed the small scratch on her father's car and talked to her on the phone a couple of times in the last few weeks. Junior was unconvinced that Jaimie's intentions were strictly honourable.

"I gotta get dressed," Jaimie said, getting up from the table.

"What's for lunch?" Junior asked, still munching his sandwich.

Jaimie was almost out of the kitchen. Without turning he said nonchalantly.

"I'm having lunch with Tania."

"Aaahhhh!"

He heard Junior's knowing roar behind him. Fifteen minutes later, Jaimie wandered through the living room sporting a neat, printed bowling shirt and a pair of white slacks. He picked up his sunglasses from the bookshelf.

"Have a nice day," he said.

Junior was into the Italian football match on the TV screen but not so much that he would pass on the chance for a last remark.

"Watch out for the lipstick traces, home!"

Jaimie shook his head and left.

She wore no lipstick anyway. The only sign of make-up on Tania's face was a faint black liner that accentuated the slant of her light-brown eyes. Her long wavy hair clipped back by a golden brioche lightly brushed over shoulders left bare by her summer green and white dress. She had hardly touched the ice-cream Jaimie had insisted she order, while he had distractingly picked at his while listening to her. After lunch at a Chinese restaurant, they had taken in a movie in Leicester Square and as they rejoined the busy Sunday afternoon crowds, Jaimie had proposed a dessert, which he realised was just a ploy to prolong their date. She knew that, apparently, but had simply smiled and agreed. The atmosphere between them was light, easy-going and much more friendly than their first few encounters. Jaimie, who had experienced her more icy side, was surprised how cool Tania was now. She was like another person altogether. He told her so. She shrugged and simply said that she took time to warm to people. As they sat face to face across the small table on the first floor of the cafe, with the hustle and bustle of the street below them, Jaimie realised he was enjoying the afternoon immensely. He was trying hard to keep his mind in control.

"So you don't like ice-cream?"

"I do, but I've had more than enough to eat today."

"Why, are you on a diet?" he asked.

She took the question for what it was and didn't answer. She wasn't exactly skinny but anyone who suggested the young woman had weight to lose had to be out of their mind.

"So, what d'you usually do at the weekend?"

Tania shrugged.

"It depends. Sometimes I go and visit some family outside London, but mostly I stay home. I don't really go out that much."

Jaimie nodded, pushed further.

"What about dates, you get taken out much?"

"Now and then." She caught an expression in Jaimie's eyes. "Why did you do that just now?"

"What?" he asked innocently.

"That face. You did the same thing earlier on."

"Oh, it must be a nervous thing, I can't help it," he lied.

Tania laughed, shaking her head. She was sharp enough to catch on.

Jaimie sighed.

"Can I be straight with you?"

"Please."

"OK, check this out," he started. "I'm in a difficult position right now. Because we started on the wrong foot, I got this perception of you which was...well, which was wrong. So over the last few weeks, talking to you even only these few times, I found out you're kinda nice, and...I'm surprised. I find myself wanting to ask more personal things, you know what I'm saying?"

She listened, looked away for a few seconds then asked:

"So, what do you want to know?"

"What's your position?"

Jaimie looked serious. Tania frowned slightly.

"My position?"

"Yeah, you know, who's the man?"

"Oh, I see."

"I already assumed there's a man but I just wanted confirmation, you know how it is."

Jaimie saw Tania looking at him straight, her eyes deep in his as if she was trying to read something there.

"Well, to satisfy your curiosity, there is a man," she accentuated the last word to sound like him.

"And...how is he?" Jaimie asked slightly deflated.

84

"He's fine, thank you." Tania answered, looking a little surprised.

Jaimie's laugh was genuine. It sounded funny to him.

"No, that's not what I'm asking." They both laughed at the joke. "I meant, what's he like?"

"What's he like?" she repeated.

"Yeah, I'd just like to know, what's his style, what has he got? He's a lucky man, he's gotta have style!"

Tania gave him another deep glance.

"Should I take that as a compliment?"

"Hmm yes, to you."

"Thank you. Well, he's sensitive, caring...and funny."

Jaimie nodded, reflecting on it. Then he ate a spoonful of ice-cream, before asking again:

"And where is he now?"

She shrugged.

"At home with his family, I imagine."

"He's married?!"

The way Jaimie punctuated the question with a raise of his eyebrows, made Tania laugh.

"He lives with his parents."

"With his parents? Damn, you dating a teenager! Alright, I ain't asking nothing more," he said. Then he remembered something. "I'd like to invite you somewhere," he said tentatively.

"Really, where?"

"I told you I have a radio programme. Next month, they're having this big celebration for the anniversary of the station. There'll be some live bands, PAs and all the DJs on the station. I'd like you to come."

Tania thought about the offer.

"I'm not sure..."

"You'll like it," Jaimie said. "There's gonna be all different styles of music. It would be a nice day out for you. I'll be playing too..."

She smiled.

"When is this happening?"

"August the twenty-fifth, it's a Saturday."

"I'm really not too sure I can make it."

"Why not?"

"My mother's birthday is the twenty-sixth. She has a garden party every year, I'll have to help her get everything ready the day before."

"Oh, well, I'm sorry I'm gonna miss that garden party," Jaimie shrugged. "Tell me, is it a big thing, I mean does your mother invite a lot of people?"

"Not that many, only family, friends, some of my father's associates. Maybe fifty people or so," Tania explained. Then she asked with a little smile, "Why, would you like to come?"

Jaimie hadn't really thought about it, but he nodded.

"Sure, if you invite me. I have to expand socially, meet people..."

"OK, I'll give you an invitation."

Jaimie considered the novelty of going to a garden party.

"What's the dress code like?" he asked Tania.

"Anything really, as long as it looks smart."

She was watching him, probably wondering if he would really come.

"I know what you're thinking," he laughed. "You don't believe I'll be there, right?"

"I'm trying to imagine you mingling with my mother's guests."

"Oh but I mingle very well, with all kinds of people. I'm a homeboy basically, but a very versatile homeboy!"

Tania laughed, that high, fluttering laugh she had. Then she said:

"Actually, I'm sure my brother would love to meet you."

"Really?"

"I think so. He's a homeboy too, at least that's what he wants to be. You being a hip hop DJ from the States, that would make his day."

"Alright!" Jaimie exclaimed. "An ally in the family, that's good."

"Except that he probably won't be home that day; he's not on good terms with my parents at the moment."

"Why's that?"

Tania explained that her seventeen-year-old brother had recently been suspended from the private school he attended, for discipline problems. Her parents had been called to see the principal and considering the offender had changed school twice in three years, they were understandably less than pleased with him. Jaimie said he understood the way Tania's brother felt.

"It's hard to be that age for a boy, you know. There's so much uncertainty inside, so many things you become aware of. School is the last thing you care about."

86

"You seem to know a lot about that," Tania said. "Were you like that too?"

Jaimie winced.

"Hmm...a little," he said vaguely. "My brother was really the one with the discipline problems at school."

"By the way, how is your brother?"

Jaimie laughed.

"He's OK. He wanted to come along when I told him I was out on a date with you."

"Really?"

"Yeah, I told him we were just friends, but he's convinced I have ulterior motives," Jaimie said, as if nothing was further from his mind.

Tania's squinted her eyes, searching his face.

"Do you?" she asked.

He left the question hanging in the air, knowing now that he couldn't truthfully answer negatively. Sighing, he shrugged.

"I think I'll take the fifth on this one," he said finally, knowing that, as a lawyer, she would appreciate the legal reference. She gave him a knowing look, then asked:

"Are you going to keep staring at that ice-cream or are you ready to go?"

Jaimie smiled, shook his head and got up.

In the three following weeks, Jaimie didn't see Tania, nor did he call her. Sure, he felt like it, but he had decided it was better that way. Since she already had a boyfriend, he reasoned that there was no point fuelling the attraction he had felt developing. To him, at this point in his life, women meant problems. Not right away maybe, but past experience had taught him that once the honeymoon was over and familiarity set in, invariably the whole atmosphere changed and so he stuck to his resolution to concentrate on his work. August was in full bloom, with blue skies and warm evenings, yet Jaimie spent most of his spare time in his room in front of the computer or leaning back in his big swivel chair, meditating on the story he was writing. After meeting Tony's producer friend, he decided to scrap the elusive love story he had been trying to finish. It wasn't so much that what the man told him changed his mind, rather their conversation triggered something in him which made him understand where the problem with his writing was. He couldn't feel the love he was writing about, not in the tone he wanted to write it in anyway. The intention was there, he wanted to describe softness, sentiments and warm embraces but he just could not get the right words out. An uneasy feeling hung over him all day at work after he returned from the meeting, he hardly ate and, although he did his job as conscientiously as always, his mind was not really there. By the time Jaimie got home in the evening, he knew what he really wanted to write but had repressed all along. One of the first things he learnt at the performing arts night school he had attended back in New York surfaced from his memory: 'you can only write well of what you know personally or what you have thoroughly researched.' That maxim spelt the reason why he had had so many problems writing his intended story. Of course he had felt the warmth and strength of love, experienced the light-headedness of passion and so should have been able to relate to it and put it down on paper. Yet what superseded these feelings in his mind, what stifled their memory and refused to remain buried in his subconscious was the sourness of repressed love-pain, the only too vivid reminiscences of an injured and still convalescent heart. So that evening, Jaimie opened a six pack of Budweiser and opened a new file on the computer. He didn't quite know what to call it and didn't care for the moment; what mattered right now was to channel the flow of images he could feel streaming up into a story, his story. At first he found himself unable to formulate in words the images in his memory. Finally he realised that, if he wanted to put it down at all, he would have to detach himself emotionally from what had happened. That night, Jaimie lost all sense of time, only switching off the screen when he realised his eyelids could no longer keep up with his racing mind. For three weeks, all his waking time was spent re-living the sometimes exhilarating but often hurtful episodes of his teenage years on the streets of his Brooklyn neighbourhood. Finally, early one Monday morning, he delivered two hundred and forty seven printed pages bound in a plastic cover to Julian Whitfield, Tony's independent producer friend. Then he tried to forget all about it and unwind...

CHAPTER SIX

"Distant lover...you should think about me...say a prayer for me..."

Jaimie was crooning at the top of his voice, doing a passable Marvin Gaye impression to the song from the car stereo. Or so he thought anyway. Not that he cared much how he sounded. His elbow resting on the edge of the open window, he was negotiating his way through the early morning traffic. His appointment wasn't until eleven, so he had more than enough time to make it to Islington but he had gotten up early anyway, spurred on by the bright sun. The summer was on, cool and light and Jaimie felt right. There was nothing like a Marvin selection on a morning like this! As far as Jaimie could remember, even at the height of his hardcore days, the man had always been his favourite singer, bringing relief to whatever ache his soul was feeling at any time. Only Marvin could turn a song into a prayer in that special way! And then, apart from the sweetness of the morning, Jaimie knew something else made him feel right, although he really didn't want to admit it to himself. He just couldn't accept that he, Jaimie, hardened and cynical as he had become could start to feel this good about a woman. To be fair, he had not seen Tania since that 'ice-cream' day and had made only one brief phone call to her office the previous week. Still, it was nice just like that; nothing going on but the mind.

Marvin stepped up the pace with 'How sweet it is...' as Jaimie cut through St John's Wood. As promised Tony had hooked him up with Julian, his producer friend. After they met, he had asked Jaimie to bring him what he had. What Jaimie had amounted to no more than a few dozen typed sheets and to be truthful, he wasn't too sure where it all started but Julian had said to bring it all anyway. So Jaimie spent two whole weeks typing feverishly until he got what seemed to him like a complete story, something that sounded coherent. Whether it was a good story he couldn't be sure because it was so close to him and, after putting down on paper such an important and painful part of his life, there was no way he could be objective about it, he knew that. The hurt was still there, buried, repressed, held in check, but simmering deep in his heart. To confront it, Jaimie had to relive the story again, consciously, scene by scene, ten years after. It was like an exorcism, kind of, and Jaimie did it. It all happened very quickly and in less than two weeks of intensive writing, he had his story. Whether it was technically good enough was another matter; script writing was something Jaimie had learned succinctly during his night classes back in New York but at least the story was readable. So he delivered the draft to Julian's office and waited. It took three weeks but the man got back to him, and now Jaimie was on his way to hear what he thought about the story.

Julian was cool enough for a white guy. He had this relaxed, amiable attitude that seems to go hand in hand with a middle-class background, the self-assurance of someone whose pre-occupation with artistic achievement stems more from the need for recognition by his peers than from financial concern.

By the time Jaimie reached Holloway Road, it was still only 10.20 am.

"Oooh, I want you...but I want you to...want me too," Jaimie's voice pleaded in tune with Marvin's. The big McDonald's sign probably triggered the thought that he had left home without eating anything, so he manoeuvred slickly ahead of a 279 bus to cut a right turn. Luckily, a removal van was good enough to pull out of its parking space so Jaimie eased the jeep in then walked back to the high street.

The queue wasn't that long. Asides from chicken, Jaimie was a sparse meat-eater, so the English breakfast was not for him. He ordered pancakes and syrup, two donuts and a large orange juice, which he received with a teasing smile from the pretty, petite, dark-skinned young woman behind the counter. As she dropped the change in his open palm, Jaimie gave her a 'I-know-what-you're-thinking' grin, took his tray and walked upstairs. The place wasn't too busy. Jaimie ate slowly, thinking of nothing special, peering out the window at the flow of people across the junction. After he had finished eating, he left the cafe and joined the crowds in the sunny street once again.

The offices of Triple Eye Films, Julian's production company, occupied the first floor of a building not far from the Business Design Centre. Jaimie climbed up the stairs and entered. The secretary wasn't the same one he had met on his previous visit. This one was older, fatter and the eyes behind the squarish tinted glasses said she was loath to interrupt her gossiping on the phone. She said "hang on" into the receiver.

"Good morning," Jaimie smiled at her.

"Good morning, can I help you?" she said, eyeing him wearily.

He dismissed a mischievous 'I don't think so' thought from his mind and answered:

"I have an appointment with Mr Whitfield."

The receiver still hanging in her left hand, the plump secretary ran a finger down the ledger in front of her.

"Your name is...?"

"Hannen, Jaimie Hannen."

She found it.

"I'm afraid Mr Whitfield is running a little late this morning."

"That's OK, I'll wait," Jaimie shrugged. He went to sit on the leather couch and grabbed a magazine. The woman went back to her phone call, keeping a low voice to keep Jaimie from hearing any of her no-doubt highly confidential chatter. Twenty minutes later, an apologetic Julian pushed through the glass door.

"Jaimie, hi. I'm really sorry about this. I got delayed. Have you been here long?"

"That's OK. How you doing?"

"Fine, I'm just rushed off my feet. We have this film at post-production stage and it's taking longer than it should. Let's go in my office. Marjorie, hold my calls, will you?"

The sweetly-named Marjorie smiled officiously and said she would. Jaimie followed Julian inside the oversize office with the obligatory black and white photos of the producer with some TV personalities on the walls. Julian dropped his attache case by the desk.

"Can I offer you something: beer, whisky, soda?"

"Just water, thanks," Jaimie answered as he sat down.

"Very wise, I wish I could give it up," Julian smiled, taking drinks from the small fridge by the window. He handed Jaimie his water, mixed his before leaning back into the swivelling armchair.

"OK, well, I read your script. In fact I read it three times, that's the reason why I took a little longer before I got back to you."

Jaimie took a sip and nodded quietly. Julian downed some whisky soda then declared:

"It's a great story. I hope you won't mind, but I gave it to my associate to read. Is that alright? And he said the same thing: a very powerful story."

"But..." Jaimie started.

"But? Why d'you say that?" Julian smiled.

"I'm sure you're about to qualify the compliment. You're a producer right?" Jaimie grinned.

Julian nodded, amused.

"Well, yes, I'm going to qualify. It's a great story and I would like to shoot it..." he paused, "but I wanted to talk to you about it. Not about the content, like I said the story is very strong. I'm thinking about the...feel of it."

"Yeah?"

Julian was choosing his words carefully. He wet his lips again before continuing.

"I like the plot, it's gripping, very raw but what I would like to talk to you about is the emotional colour of the story."

Jaimie waited.

"What I mean is that there is an intensity of feelings that comes across, it is almost sentimental...tell me, is it a true story?"

"Yeah, it's a true story."

"Were you involved?"

Jaimie nodded soberly.

"Yeah, I was...involved," he said.

"I thought so. I guess it wasn't easy to write."

"Does it show that much?"

Julian smiled.

"Not in the style. It's just that it sounds very personal." He added: "But that's good, very powerful."

Jaimie was thinking: 'what is he getting at?'

"So what are you thinking, Julian; you really want to make it?"

"Oh absolutely," he straightened up behind his desk. "But I would like to tighten the script a bit, I mean make it more action-packed, dispense with some of the sentimental aspects."

"So you think it's too soft, right?"

"Hmm...I wouldn't say soft, but I think we need to make it leaner, more simple."

Jaimie thought about that for a few seconds, then he said:

"You know, things like those that happen in the story are painful, they reach deep. You need to show the effects, how it changes the characters."

"You're absolutely right," Julian nodded, "but the focus has to remain on the cinematic mode. I mean in a book, you have the scope

92

to explore feelings more, to go deeper into the psychological aspects of things, but here, we have just ninety minutes and the audience needs to be kept on edge. You see what I'm trying to say?"

Jaimie could see. He asked:

"Don't you think we run the risk of falling into the same trap as other so called 'rap movies', where the characters always seem to act impulsively, without thinking and all the audience remember is the violence?"

Julian swivelled a little in his chair. He said, smiling:

"Not if the script is clever."

"Right...so you're serious about this?"

"Quite serious, yes. In fact we've been looking for a story with a kind of...street feel and this is definitely it. Now, I don't know if you want to work on the second draft alone or will you need some help?"

"I'm gonna get you a second draft to look at, then we'll talk."

"Excellent!"

Jaimie allowed himself a grin; at least things sounded promising.

"It's on!" he said.

"It's on!" Julian repeated, laughing, imitating Jaimie's Brooklyn accent.

When he got to work that afternoon, Jaimie found a carburettor problem on a Pontiac waiting for him. It was one of those 'priority' jobs Paul entrusted to him from time to time, as he knew they would be done promptly and to the satisfaction of the owners who didn't mind what the job cost as long as their prestigious vehicles were back on the road after the briefest delay. Since Jaimie got a bonus in it too, everyone was happy. Today's problem required real understanding of that type of engine but Jaimie eventually had the monster sorted out and the timing reset. He stretched satisfyingly and went to sit on the wall outside, cold beer in hand. He felt light, the sun overhead bathing his face and chest. It felt like one of those days when you feel you could accomplish anything. The morning meeting with Julian had lifted him up, given him a positive sensation about what he really wanted to do. To think that he was working on a script that was going to be filmed sounded, well, unreal. But Julian sounded serious and the arrangements they had discussed included money to be paid to him for 'script development', so it couldn't be bad! As he sipped some of the chilled Bud, Jaimie reflected that he had just about got a foothold in

93

the film industry he had so longed to penetrate. To think he was getting a break not as an actor, as he was trained, but as a writer, that was even more kicking.

Driving back from the meeting, Jaimie had reflected back on what Julian had said. Of course he was right in the sense that even now, Jaimie could not be completely detached from events that had so decisively shaped his consciousness as a teenager. Here he was, ten years older and still he had felt the claw in his stomach when he had spent those nights in front of the computer, tripping back through his short time with Anita, his old girlfriend. The only difference time had made was that he had learned to switch mode, escape the memory track and focus, like it was never there. The stretch he'd since done in prison plus the time spent in that army camp had been enough for Jaimie to steel up inside against any hurtful memories. He took another swig of beer...

Brownsville, summer '84. The intense heat had him and the crew guzzling forties all day. He was heading for his eighteenth birthday, school was out and all over the projects, the basketball courts were busy. The groups of pretty girls in fly, short clothing had the boys in the 'hood outplaying each other in skills and stamina on the burning asphalt. The heat was everywhere, in the stainless blue sky, behind the smiles of the honeys and in the bugging out of the restless homies. Whenever things boiled over in one of these games, the displays of dribbling and the acrobatic slams ended in a wild scramble. Sometimes these basketball contests degenerated into fierce disputes and, since many youths were already strapped by then, ended up costing the life of one of these young athletes. Jaimie could only remember one incident when shooting actually took place on the court and a player died. In the Black and Latino neighbourhoods of New York, the gangs were getting edgy, more crazy. The sweltering heat, the easy access to guns and the flood of crack which had taken over the streets each contributed to rising levels of violence. Whereas previously excessive bravado and a little tough-talk posturing had sufficed to sort out inter-gang rivalries, there now seemed to be a systematic recourse to gunplay, a willingness to fire shots. The Black Tomahawks, the gang Jaimie was affiliated to, now went out strapped at all times. Although he was still in high school, most of his spare time was spent hanging out with the homies. All through the summer vacation, he was out

94

there, to the consternation of his father who had little illusions about the youngsters who were blowing their car horns in front of the house for his son. Pop knew Jaimie was not himself inclined to do wrong and was only following his friends, but he was worried all the same. What could he say to an eighteen-year-old kid who acted like he knew the world, just like they all do? Jaimie was never disrespectful to his father; he would listen patiently to his warnings and advice before disappearing out the door to do exactly what he wanted. Pop could only pray that the taste for easy money and fast living didn't get the better of the boy. Jaimie himself wasn't worried. He felt grown up, fearless and yearned for the challenges every new day brought his way.

But even the excitement of his new life faded right off when Jaimie met Anita. He now knew she alone could have made a difference, kept him in school, away from the wild ways he was falling into. Yet maybe if he hadn't met her and been through the pain he wouldn't have become so hard inside and reckless, maybe... For all the 'ifs' and 'maybes', Anita was an episode of Jaimie's life he probably wouldn't have run from, even if forewarned. That August evening when they first met, Jaimie's mixing had been, by all accounts, magical. So good in fact that the crew they were competing against got angry, knowing from the reaction of the audience that they had lost the contest. They were bad losers. On neutral ground, things would have just settled down but this was the Bronx, their home turf and so when Jaimie saw the commotion starting in the opposite corner, he warned his boys to be ready for an emergency exit. The first gunshot hit the ceiling, exploding loudly over the tumult of the restless crowd and provoked a huge stampede. In the confusion, Jaimie reached outside and, having been separated from his crew, decided that it was best to make it to the nearest subway. Sure enough once he got there he found Twist, his closest homeboy, about to board a train with three girls from their neighbourhood. Two of them Jaimie recognised as the sisters of one of his friends on the block, but the other one, a petite Puerto Rican with long curly hair, he couldn't recall seeing before. She had come along to party with her friends. Somehow girl crews were less rigidly divided along racial lines and it wasn't uncommon for Latinos and Blacks to mix. So the five of them travelled back south to Brooklyn. Just what Jaimie first said to Anita he never really remembered but they got talking, and kept on talking so much so

95

that by the time they got to the neighbourhood, he found himself walking her to her block. She was just seventeen, with brown skin and dark eyes. Jaimie learned that night that she lived with her mother and aunt, since coming from Puerto Rico five years earlier. Her speech had that Spanish flavour Jaimie subsequently got to love, as she talked to him of life back home and what she intended to do after completing school. It soon became clear to both that they were having trouble leaving each other. When Jaimie eventually went to bed that night, he had all but forgotten about the party, the crew, the fight and everything else about the evening. The very next day, he called Anita and they went to the movies. After that, the spell was on. His friends teased him about it at first, thinking it was just going to be another one of those short-lived, sex-based relationships that were the norm for all of them. But, deep inside, Jaimie knew from the start that it wasn't anything like that. Whereas he didn't take the girls he was dating seriously, and there were a few just then, Anita had him thinking about her all the time. Twist asked Jaimie about her and quickly realised that his friend had got the bug for the pretty Latino girl. Jaimie wasn't even listening to his words of caution about the problems a love like theirs could bring. By the time summer ended and school started again, everyone in the area knew about them, but that was cool, especially because Jaimie was one of the most popular boys around. A skilled basketball player and good track athlete, he was also generous and generally nice to everyone. Yet he was also known to be no pushover and his reputation as a tough fighter had earned him props.

Anita was the first girl Jaimie really introduced to Pop. One evening he walked in, pulling the shy girl behind him and told his father, "That's my girl!" Pop had been nice to her. The next day he told Jaimie: "Your girl's real pretty, where she from?" Just like Twist before, Pop had asked his son if he was serious about her and what did her parents think about it. Truthfully Jaimie answered that he had not yet met her mother but that wouldn't be a problem. In fact, that was just where the problems started. Anita's young aunt was cool when her niece told her about Jaimie. She knew situations like that could prove difficult, but Anita seemed so happy, so in love that she took to Jaimie immediately when she met him. When the mother realised what was happening, her instant reaction was to put a stop to it. Jaimie tried to do the right thing and went to see her but, although she was polite enough to him, the scene she caused after he left drew tears from her daughter. Anita cried because she couldn't understand what it was her mother, whom she was close to, was so mad about. To her Puerto Rican or Black was no different. After all, her own father had been as dark as Jaimie! In defiance of her mother, she kept seeing Jaimie and eventually, when the pressure got too much to bear, ran away to live with a friend. Things being the way they were, and the two youngsters clinging to each other through the adversity, love overtook caution: Anita got pregnant. Jaimie decided then that he would face the challenge of life and assume his responsibilities. He quit school and started looking for a job. He told Pop too, but what could his father say? His mind was made up and there was no turning back.

For a while, Jaimie and Anita were happy. They managed to survive and the little they had satisfied them, so engrossed were they with each other and the baby growing inside of her. The tragedy that was to shatter their dream happened in the form of Anita's older brother, Miguel. A hoodlum of some notoriety, Miguel was released in late winter from the pen where he had just served three years for robbery. When he learned from his mother about the situation, he got worked up and set out to find his sister. Grown up with the street values of the Latino gangs as he was, the news was nothing short of an insult. Naturally violent and driven by a warped sense of family honour, Miguel hunted his sister down and when he finally found her, the beating he unleashed on the unfortunate girl sent her to hospital. Jaimie never forgot the rage in his guts when he saw his girlfriend inert on that bed. By then, Anita was six months pregnant and although the doctors did all they could, the little girl they delivered survived only eighteen hours. All that time, Jaimie and Anita prayed and watched the tiny baby fight for life. But she died, and for both parents the horror was just too much too bear. Anita recovered physically but her mind never healed. She refused to even see her mother and went to live with an older relative of her late father. Inside Jaimie something had snapped. He tracked down Miguel, determined to kill him viciously. Of the violence of that night, Jaimie recalled little except for the enduring image of the barrel of his gun already inside the mouth of the bleeding, broken-up Miguel and Anita's aunt holding onto him, begging for the man's life. How she got there when she did, and what she said that released his finger from the trigger,

Jaimie had no idea but somehow he let Miguel go. For the young couple, things could never be the same again. Anita wasn't insane, strictly speaking, but he just couldn't get through to her anymore. The drama had been too much for her young mind and she seemed to have retreated into a world of her own. Eventually, she left town one day and Jaimie never saw her again. He drowned the screaming pain inside with an orgy of recklessness that should logically have resulted in his death. Fate didn't grant him that release, so he learned to live with the memory but the scar never really healed.

The beeping, regular and insistent, was spoiling the sweetness of the dream, one of those you know you are going to want to remember when you wake up. But Jaimie could feel himself slipping out fast. He stirred and one conscious thought flashed in. 'Today is Saturday!' Beep-beep-beep. Jaimie stirred. A filtered flash of light caught his half-closed eye. With a heavy sigh and stretch, he reached out to the bedside table for the pager. He pressed on the green button, the number wasn't familiar. That was enough not to disturb his Saturday morning rest. This was a 'day-off' Saturday, which only came every two weeks! Jaimie tensed his aching leg muscles and sat up slowly. He winced. The two hours work-out at the gym the previous afternoon was claiming its revenge. The three Budweisers in the evening was adding to his physical troubles. Massaging the back of his neck, Jaimie picked up the phone from the floor, wondering who in the world this 'Lyn' could be. He dialled and waited through a couple of rings. "Yes hello, I'm Jaimie. Someone called Lyn left a call on my pager...is..."

"Oh hello, it's me, Lyn," the voice cut in, hurriedly.

Jaimie still had no idea who he was talking to.

"I'm Martin's sister. D'you remember me?' she said.

"Martin?" Jaimie was scanning his memory in rapid mode.

"You know, Martin...Tino...from the team..."

There it clicked; Lyn, Tino, the team. Martin, or 'Tino' as he was more popularly known to his friends, one of the star players of the junior basketball team.

"Tino! Right, yeah, what's happening, Lyn?"

Jaimie recalled Lyn being introduced to him after one of the games.

"I'm sorry to disturb you but...I thought..."

"Sure, no, don't worry. What's up?"

98

The voice was weaker now:

"Tino's in hospital. He was arrested last night..."

"What? In hospital!? Where?"

Frowning, Jaimie was absorbing the shock of the news. He asked her a little more before putting down the receiver. It took him no more than twenty minutes to shower and dress, then he left for the hospital. On the way, Jaimie kept turning over in his head the scraps of information Lyn had given him. Tino was a tall fifteen-year-old kid with a mischievous smile and easy going ways. He attended college seriously, played ball the rest of the time. What the hell could have happened? His sister was close to tears on the phone.

Jaimie always felt there was something haunting about hospitals. They held too many bad memories. This one was huge, modern, pretty almost, yet as he stepped out of the elevator and pushed open the door to the ward, he still didn't like being there. A middle-aged couple was standing over a woman in bed, on the left. Jaimie spotted Tino's sister on a chair at the foot of the last bed, near the window. He walked down, she watched him, her eyes locked into his from behind her glasses as he stopped beside her. She said something which Jaimie barely heard; his gaze was on the respirator covering the face of the young man on the bed. Jaimie took a few steps, stood over Tino, lifeless under the white sheet. The little he could see of the youngster's face showed dark bruises staining the brown flesh around the eyes. He looked like a car crash victim.

"The doctor said he will be alright," he heard Lyn's toneless voice.

"Alright?!" Jaimie repeated almost despite himself.

She sobbed, started crying quietly. Jaimie came to her, patted her shoulder.

"Take it easy, he'll be OK," he tried to sound reassuring.

"What happened?" he asked after she had composed herself.

"We got a call from the hospital this morning. We came with my father, and found him like that. Daddy went to the police station. They said they found drugs on him and that he resisted arrest."

"Drugs?! What drugs?"

"I don't know..." Lyn sniffed.

"Where's your dad now?"

"He's gone back to work, he'll be here soon."

Jaimie recalled Tino telling him how his father had raised him

99

and his sister on his own after their mother walked out years before.

"You spoke to the doctor?"

Lyn nodded.

"Yes, he said Tino's got a fractured skull, two broken ribs, sprained wrist and bruising."

She had listed the injuries calmly, almost as a doctor would, but as she stopped, tears started rolling down her cheeks again.

"It'll be OK...be strong," Jaimie told her.

He felt angry inside. He stayed for a little while, talking to Lyn, reassuring her as best he could, as if he could. She said she was waiting for her father to return, so Jaimie told her he'd be back in the afternoon, to call him if she needed to, then he left.

Tino didn't regain consciousness until the Sunday night. Though he couldn't speak yet, his eyes moved around the room, taking in the circle of familiar faces anxiously looking down at him from above. His father, who had kept vigil on a chair for most of the past two days smiled nervously as he watched his son move his head slightly. Around the bed Lyn, their aunt Barbara, Jaimie, Junior, Richie and Erwin, Tino's two best friends, all wanted to say something to him, something meaningful but somehow everyone found it hard. The doctor, who had come with some nurses as soon as he was notified of the improvement, had told the youth's father that he was "doing fine" but he would have to remain in intensive care before he was moved to a ward. Tino was breathing normally, his eyes were swollen under the white bandage around his head. It was after eleven when Jaimie took his leave with Junior, Richie and Erwin. Though they were all relieved by Tino's improving condition, there wasn't much conversation in the jeep as they drove across west London under a fine drizzle. Junior turned to Richie on the back seat.

"So they charged you too?"

"Yeah," the youth nodded.

Jaimie had by now gotten the whole story from Richie: A group of them had gathered near the Grove station, ready to go to a jungle dance in the Queen's Park area. As they waited for a few more friends, talking and taking in the sound from their 'beatbox', a cruising police van on its Friday evening patrol pulled them over outside the tube station. From demanding that the music be turned off to insisting on an on-the-spot body search, the officers behaved so rudely that eventually, an angry exchange developed. The overtly racist tone of the incident escalated right there and then, as a small group of commuters stopped to find out what was happening. When one of the youths being searched suddenly made a break for it across the road and disappeared into a side street, the police got the excuse they needed to start manhandling the others. Another police vehicle arrived and, under the howls of protest of the gathered crowd, Tino, Richie and another boy were bungled inside the van and and taken away. It was sometime later that Tino was beaten in his cell. Since they had been separated on arriving at the station, Richie couldn't tell Jaimie anymore. The police wanted to know the identity of the runaway but he'd told them he didn't know him. Before Jaimie could ask the question, Junior turned again to Richie:

"How come you had that shit on you, man; I didn't know you was into that!"

Richie sighed dejectedly.

"I'm not...I got it from somebody..." He added, "I never took it before."

From behind the wheel, Jaimie frowned.

"You should know better than that, Rich, man."

Richie could say nothing. The whole thing made him feel really bad, it was like a curse to him. He knew from the start he never should have accepted to take the stuff.

"Tino take E's?" Junior asked.

"No, no. He got it same time as me."

"So why did you buy it?"

Richie looked uneasy but Junior wouldn't let him off until he knew the whole story.

"We didn't pay for it. We was gonna take it at the dance. Cooler said it wasn't dangerous or anything..."

There was silence in the car for a while. Erwin was keeping quiet. As Tino's other 'key' spar, he would have been involved in the incident had it not been for his girlfriend who had delayed him that Friday evening. Jaimie asked.

"Tell me, that guy, Cooler, he's the one who ran, right?"

"Yeah," Richie said quietly.

Jaimie sighed.

"That shit is ill, Rich, it can't help you."

He paused.

"Cooler's not your friend, man."

101

Erwin spoke.

"That's how he makes his money. He's always juggling."

"Yeah, he's juggling with your life," Junior sneered.

Jaimie dropped off Erwin by his flats, then Junior at the estate. The rain was still coming down, thin and insistent. As they were going over the bump to the entrance of the blocks, the beams of a car taking the corner at speed flashed full into Jaimie's windscreen. He braked hard. The car's engine roared as it geared up and sped past the jeep.

"What the f..k's up with him?" Jaimie growled.

He pulled into the estate. Junior looked at him.

"Did you see the car?"

"Not much of it, the guy had his beams on..."

Junior said:

"That's the same car...when we got busted."

"What? What you saying?"

But Junior was certain.

"The police car, Ford Orion. I saw the reg at the back...M972 MRX."

"You remember that!"

"You bet, it's useful."

"You saw the cop?"

Junior shook his head. "No, I couldn't make out who was driving, but there was a woman in the passenger seat."

Jaimie stopped in front of Junior's flat.

"Call me tomorrow," he told his brother.

Junior said he would, took his leave and climbed up the stairs. Jaimie drove off, said little to Richie until he got to his parents' house. He stopped his engine, Richie hadn't moved.

"What did your mother say?" Jaimie asked.

Richie hesitated.

"She's upset. She said she trusted me and she's scared of this court business."

"You'll get off with a fine, that's all. But that's not the problem. Let me ask you again; you do drugs before?"

"No, Jaimie man, we was just gonna try it. Cooler takes it, he said it was safe."

Jaimie sighed, he looked Richie straight in the eyes.

"Oh, so your friend Cooler sells the stuff, gives you one, telling you it's safe and you believe him!"

102

Richie bowed down his head.

"I'm sorry. I didn't think."

"Right," Jaimie paused, then he told the youth, "OK, now you got to go and explain that to your mother, and try to convince her that from now on you will think, so she can trust you again, alright?"

"Yeah."

"Tell me, that Cooler, where does he get his stuff from?"

"He's dealing for some white guy," Richie said.

"What white guy? You know him?"

"Some guy, I seen him talking to. He drives a Jag."

Jaimie thought of something. Richie added:

"I couldn't say nothing to the police..."

"Yeah, I can dig that." He placed his hand on Richie's shoulder.

"OK, you go home now and you think about all this. It's bad but it could have been worse. I'll probably see you at the hospital tomorrow."

Richie climbed out of the car and walked slowly up to his front door. Jaimie watched him until he got inside, then left. Back home, he felt the bitter taste the whole affair had left him with. Like he had told Richie, 'it could have been worse'. Youths like him were straight, good at school and good athletes but how long could they stay that way? All it took was one little slip, one mistake and they'd find themselves on the slope. It was hard enough to have to face the police and their hateful practices every day, but the drugs... Drugs were everywhere and it seemed that no amount of advice or warnings could deter many youngsters from dabbling in them. That night, as he sat working on his script, Jaimie's mind kept drifting to the grey car he knew was parked under Junior's window.

CHAPTER SEVEN

Presumably, the neighbours had been informed, yet, from behind the curtains of several of the pretty houses, busy eyes were peering at the array of expensive cars parked all along the street. In fact, the line of vehicles stretched right up to the main road, giving the usually quiet residential neighbourhood a festive appearance. Jaimie had to reverse and drive around the next two adjoining streets before he found space. He walked slowly back towards the cul-de-sac, slipped on his jacket and fixed his tie. Although suits weren't his thing, the formal occasion warranted a formal dress code and he wasn't about to be the odd one out. "I'll be looking out for you," Tania had said on the phone. She'd even sent an official invitation to his house, so there was no missing it. Now here he was, all dressed up and ready to mingle. 'I'm moving up!' he reflected, amused, walking down towards the gates of the residence.

The previous evening Jaimie had managed to coax Tania down to the radio station anniversary jam. By then she had completed arrangements for the garden party and decided to reward Jaimie's persistence by checking it out. The Saturday night event had attracted thousands of ravers and the big tent set up in the park for the occasion hardly contained the crowd. In fact there seemed to be more people outside than under the huge canvas. Most people moved from one stage to the next to sample the diversity of music pumping through, only the die-hard regulars of certain sets remained loyal to their favourites. At first, Tania had looked a little bewildered by the size of it all. On the other hand, her brother Carl whom she had brought along at Jaimie's invitation had felt at home right away. A fifteen-year-old gangly youth with the outward street-smartness of his age group, Carl got into the rhythm of things so fast that it wasn't hard to guess that this was his world. Tania had explained to Jaimie with a kind of embarrassed smile that her brother was giving their parents the world of trouble, the most recent offence being getting kicked out of an expensive private school for smoking cannabis. Carl apparently resented all forms of authority and was the despair of his father who had set so much hope on him. Since he had himself been a military man and thus inclined to discipline, the gap between father and son had grown to become unbridgeable it seemed. All this caused some friction in the household, Tania told Jaimie. Carl, to all intents and purposes, was a 'homeboy', he could see that. They got on right away. In fact, Carl explained, his sister needed to date a guy like Jaimie, a hip hop DJ and from New York at that. To him it was just like a miracle. For the whole of Jaimie's set, the youth had remained right behind him, intently watching his every move on the turntables, taking in the expert mixing with visible envy. When he hit the dancefloor, it wasn't hard to guess what he spent most of his time doing. Carl sure could dance. Tania too warmed up to the party atmosphere and even got involved in a little dancing albeit of a more discreet style than her brother. Not all the sounds there were to her taste though and she certainly wasn't down with the hardcore jungle beats, but all in all, she enjoyed herself. When they left, Carl made Jaimie promise he would show up at the garden party the next day so they could talk some more about music.

'Talk about a change of scene!' Jaimie mused to himself as he stepped up to the big gates of the mansion. 'No ravers, no homeboys and definitely no G's!' The two couples now handing their invitations to the white jacketed attendants were black alright but from the other side of the social fence, so to speak. The men, late thirties, neatly groomed and sporting well-cut suits, the women in evening frocks with just enough jewellry to feed an inner city family for a couple of months. Jaimie came forward, invitation in hand, and smiled to the largest of the two men in black bow-ties. After a glance at the card, the man asked, looking at him almost suspiciously:

"Are you alone, sir?"

With a feigned look of surprise, Jaimie quickly checked behind him, then raising his eyebrows, he said to the unsmiling doorman:

"Damn, she must have given me the slip!"

The two attendants looked at each other. At that point, Jaimie noticed a feminine silhouette coming through the sizeable crowd entering the house. Tania had seen him and was making her way to the gate. Though he knew it was her, the woman in the long, off-the-shoulder black dress with her wavy hair cascading stylishly down from a gold clip atop her head, could have been someone else to Jaimie. She reached, smiling.

"It's alright," she said simply, "he's with me."

105

Jaimie couldn't resist giving the two attendants a cheeky little wink as he stepped past them. He could smell Tania's perfume as she slid one arm under his and walked him in. He felt nice, but acted natural, adopting the blasé expression of a man accustomed to such social occasions as they joined the other guests. To the left, Jaimie could see a line of dressed-up tables laden with an impressive range of food, with uniformed waiters attending to them. Further down, under a round thatched roof, was the bar. More waiters circulated through the crowd with trays of drinks.

Huge garden lamps diffused soft lighting throughout the courtyard. Out of strategically hung small speakers, the light jazzy sounds blended in with the chatter of the distinguished guests.

"I guess you had a hard time parking," Tania was saying.

"Oh, I found somewhere."

Jaimie kept looking around the grounds as they were making their way towards a sitting area to the right.

"This is nice, real nice," he said appreciatively.

"I didn't think it was your kind of scene," Tania smiled.

"I could get used to this, I'm quite versatile, you know."

She laughed, let go of his arm. They sat at one of the small garden tables where a young woman was busy sipping from a champagne glass. She looked up at Jaimie and smiled.

"This is my cousin, Millie," Tania said.

Jaimie smiled back, shook the outstretched hand.

"How you doing?"

"Fine," Millie answered.

The two young women had an obvious resemblance; same elongated eyes and high cheekbones. Otherwise Millie was darker in complexion and had dimples. She told Jaimie:

"You're the man from the club. I heard about you."

"Good things, I hope."

Millie smiled, nodded.

It seemed all nationalities were represented amongst the guests in the courtyard. Jaimie remarked to Tania:

"Your father sure knows a lot of people!"

She shrugged.

"They're business acquaintances and long time friends."

A waiter arrived, Jaimie couldn't tell on whose orders, with a bottle of champagne on ice and three tall glasses. He set the glasses down on the table, then deftly popped the cork and proceeded to

106

pour out the sparkly liquid before disappearing as neatly as he had arrived. Champagne wasn't Jaimie's usual fare. To be truthful he could only remember trying it on two occasions. But tonight was no ordinary occasion. Confidently, he picked up his glass.

"What shall we drink to?"

"To friendship," Tania proposed.

"Yes, to friendship," Millie seconded.

They knocked glasses and sipped. A quick glance at the label confirmed Jaimie's suspicion that he was drinking an expensive nectar, he tried to define the taste but it was just...smoothly drinkable. They chatted for a while, of all and nothing. Millie asked Jaimie about New York. She'd been there several times but never to Brooklyn. In fact, she seemed interested to know more about Jaimie. He skilfully answered her questions then shifted the focus onto her and learned that her father and Tania's were cousins. When he died during the 'troubles' in Liberia, she was taken to England and raised by Tania's parents.

Jaimie could feel a kind of pleasant lightness, which he put down to the atmosphere and the company. When Tania excused herself to go and greet some people, Millie poured out some more of the champagne.

"I'm not sure how much of that I should drink, you know. I'm kinda new to it," Jaimie said to her.

"You have nothing to worry about, this can't hurt you...Tania said you're really good with cars..."

"That's my line of work." He asked in turn: "What do you do?"

"Oh, I work in a laboratory." She sipped some champagne. He could see her eyes on him over the edge of the glass.

"Really! Doing what?"

"I did a biology degree, so for the last few years I've been working for a pharmaceutical company."

Jaimie laughed.

"You say it like it's really dreary. Don't you like your work?"

"Yes, I do, but it's just a job." She added: "My real interest is painting."

"So you paint?"

"A little, I'm not very good yet but I'm working on it."

For a while, Jaimie listened to Millie's discourse on the different schools of painters, throwing names which, apart from maybe two or three obvious ones, he had never heard. She seemed to know

107

what she was talking about, her passion shining through as she tried to impart to him some of her knowledge of the art form. He was impressed. Under pressure to reveal more about his interests in life, Jaimie let out that he was something of a writer, a budding one really, just starting out, he said modestly. Whether out of genuine interest or because of her third glass of champagne, Millie seemed to find that fascinating. Tania came back and proposed that they should check out the 'buffet', letting Jaimie off the hook.

The diversity of dishes on offer was truly impressive. Jaimie couldn't remember ever seeing that much food at any one time in his life. He reflected that some 'cordon bleu', high-price catering firm had been hired. Some of the dishes were so intricately decorated that it was hard to even tell what food it was. He surveyed the options quickly then asked one of the waiters for smoked salmon, bean salad and a few of the light brown delicacies the waiter said were called 'pommes souflees'. Tania and Millie went for an artistic lobster dish, to which they added touches from a few other trays. Tania then led the way to a little corner to the left side of the house where some logs had been carved into seats and from where they could survey all the festive activity. While eating and keeping track of the jazz selection, Jaimie noted with amusement how the distinguished guests had started warming up under the influence of the plentiful supply of liquors. Most of the women seemed partial to champagne, it seemed.

"I bet there must be quite a few lawyers in here tonight!" Jaimie said.

Tania smiled.

"Big ones too."

"So you know a lot of these people, right?"

She finished chewing before motioning towards a little group near the victuals tables.

"You see that man over there, with the two ladies in white...he's a lawyer, from Houston, Texas. One of the biggest, handles large oil companies' contracts mainly."

Jaimie nodded knowingly.

"A fat cat!"

Millie laughed.

"Fat enough! Wouldn't you like to be that rich?" she asked him with a glint in her eye:

He scooped the last of his bean salad, then admitted:

"I could do with half his bank account, you know what I'm saying?!"

A Japanese couple, soberly dressed, was walking away from the tables, apparently discussing the merits of the cuisine on their plates. Tania pointed them out.

"That gentleman there is one of the biggest bankers in Japan. He knows personally most heads of states in Africa, has residences in the States, England and France."

Jaimie put down his plate, sighed contentedly.

"Big timers. And they all find time to come to your daddy's garden party. He's got to be real big!"

Tania shrugged as if it was no big deal.

"He's made a lot of business contacts over the years."

She smiled as she looked over towards the centre of the courtyard.

"He must have heard his name being called."

'Daddy' was walking through the crowd from the far side towards the buffet, pausing here and there to answer greetings from his guests.

"Come, I told him I invited you." Tania got up, taking Jaimie by the hand and the three of them crossed the lawn towards Mr Heywoode. They caught up with him by the buffet.

"Dad, you remember Jaimie?"

Mr Heywoode turned and looked at him.

"Certainly," he said smiling. "Nice of you to come. How are you?"

Jaimie shook the offered hand.

"Fine, I'm enjoying all this."

"Did you sample the buffet?"

"Yes, thank you. Your daughter has been looking after me well."

Mr Heywoode nodded and said: "She's a good hostess."

Then he gave his order to one of the waiters.

"How's business?" he asked.

Jaimie shrugged.

"Not bad, keeping me busy..."

Tania said she was going to see how her mother was doing. Millie followed her after a little sly smile to Jaimie. Mr Heywoode got his plate and invited Jaimie to join him.

"What are you drinking?" he asked, stopping a passing waiter as they made their way to some tables to the right corner near the front wall.

"I'll have a beer, I think I'd better keep away from the champagne."

They sat. Two bottles of chilled German beer arrived promptly. Jaimie sipped his while his host dealt with his food. Though he was around fifty, with his tall frame, neatly-trimmed moustache and piercing eyes, Mr Heywoode could have passed for less. He was visibly a man who took care of himself, the dark blue suit fitted him perfectly. Jaimie noticed a single gold ring with an intricate symbol on his well-manicured hand.

"I really like the way you set up the whole party," he said. "Your guests are having a good time."

Mr Heywoode stopped munching to taste his beer.

"Most of them are old friends. A little relaxation is good for business too."

"The music's just right. Did you take care of that yourself?"

"Oh sure, I just dug inside my collection. Do you like jazz?"

Jaimie nodded.

"I grew up with it. My dad was a musician at the time, used to blow the sax."

"Really?"

They talked some more about music. Jaimie discovered that Tania's father knew his jazz. Mr Heywoode was pleasantly surprised that Jaimie was also a connoisseur.

"You seem to know a lot. Usually young people of your generation are into more modern sounds, like rap."

"Oh, I'm into that too, but I'm versatile. You like rap?"

Mr Heywoode made a comical frown.

"I can't say I enjoy it, but my son plays it so loud in the house that I have no choice at times. Have you met him?"

"Carl? Yes, I met him yesterday."

Mr Heywoode finished his plate, wiped his mouth with the serviette.

"Tell me, what d'you think of him?"

Jaimie paused.

"Well, he's like most teenagers, a little wild but I think he's basically a good kid."

Mr Heywoode seemed to ponder Jaimie's answer, then he said:

"I guess his sister told you I'm having some problems with him."

110

"She mentioned Carl's got problems with authority."

The matter seemed to make Mr Heywoode thoughtful. After a sip, he said:

"He's my only son, you know, but I'm not sure what to do with him anymore."

"He's got to be interested in something," Jaimie offered reassuringly. "I'm sure he'll find his way at some point."

"Let's hope, at some point..." Mr Heywoode dismissed the problem from his mind. "What about you?" he asked. "Have you got any plans for the future? You're good at what you do..."

"Yeah, but I'd like to see if I can try something a little different at the same time. I started to do some writing lately."

"Really? Are you writing a book?"

"I got this script, you see, and I might be able to get a film deal."

That seemed to catch Mr Heywoode's interest.

"Have you approached any production companies?"

Jaimie nodded.

"Yeah, I'm negotiating something with an independent at the moment. Triple Eye films, have you heard of them?"

Whether Mr Heywoode had or not, Jaimie wasn't to know for now, for suddenly, the man he had previously met under stressful circumstances, appeared from behind him. Eddie, minus gun, wearing a black tie and sharp black suit, didn't even glance twice at Jaimie. Mr Heywoode listened passively as the man whispered in his ear.

"Would you excuse me," he said to Jaimie.

He got up and followed Eddie towards the entrance gates through the idling guests. Jaimie watched the two men disappear from sight. Loosening his tie once again, he thought of something, dismissed the idea, then he looked around. No Tania or Millie in sight. The last beer had straightened him out, so to speak. Count Basie was on the wire. At least he was having a great time, so far. He grabbed his half-bottle of beer, got up and headed in the direction of the gates through the chattering crowd. When he got to where he could see the entrance without being noticed, he eased up innocently behind two middle-aged oriental-looking women and watched discreetly. Of the three new guests by the gates, Jaimie could only see the front man clearly; a squarely built, unsmiling giant of a man in a light grey suit, with a felt hat he wore a little inclined like they used to do back in the old days. He was a big man

111

with a baby face. The two men behind him, darker than him in complexion, were the proverbial 'little and large' but each as cold-looking as the other, despite their evening suits. The three men were squared up to the two bow-tied attendants, the large bald man Jaimie remembered as 'dog-man', Mr Heywoode and Eddie, standing just behind his boss, loose.

Without even thinking about it, Jaimie slid on the other side of a group of drinkers and ended up behind one of the trees that lined the front wall. He eased back against the trunk, wet his lips with some beer and watched. He could see Mr Heywoode seemed less pleased than his unexpected guest. They spoke for a short while but it was hardly a brotherly reunion. Then Mr Heywoode and the man in the hat started off towards the house, leaving the bodyguards to face each other rather stiffly. At that point, Jaimie felt a squeeze on his arm.

"It's not very polite to spy on people, you know..." Tania reproached him mockingly.

"You're right."

She pulled him away. "Come, let's sit."

He followed her back to their seats.

The guests were becoming acquainted and the good humoured banter filled the garden. From where he was now, Jaimie could just about catch a glimpse of the mysterious guest's minders, standing by the gate, tense. Jaimie asked Tania:

"Do you know them?"

A waiter appeared but neither of them was thirsty. Tania knew what he was asking.

"They're with Colonel Liston. He's an old friend of Daddy's."

"Old friend?" Jaimie remarked ironically. "Seeing your father's face, I'd say he wasn't invited tonight!"

Tania looked at him, shrugged.

"I haven't seen him for a long time. Colonel Liston and Daddy go back a long way. They were in the army together back home. I think they had a fall-out some years ago."

Jaimie took a little time to take it all in. He was naturally inquisitive and the situation seemed worthy of interest, but Tania didn't seem inclined to talk about it. He was considering whether he should probe further when Tania explained:

"We used to go on holiday with Colonel Liston's children. To us, he was like an uncle. He took his family to the States before the

112

coup. I thought they were still there."

Jaimie was listening.

"So your father was an officer too?"

"Yes, he was. He was Director of Customs at the time," Tania said.

"What about that man, Colonel Liston?"

Tania answered the greeting of an older lady passing their table, smiled to her before getting back to Jaimie, serious once again.

"He was Commissioner of Police," she said.

Jaimie leaned back in his chair, shook his head. An intrigue from faraway places against a background of gourmet food and high-flyers...Dinah Washington's intonations floated through from the speakers into his brain, loosening his concentration.

"Your father really knows good music," he told Tania.

She didn't answer, so he followed her gaze to the two 'old friends' walking back across the grounds towards the gate, side by side, Mr Heywoode politely answering a few words from some of his happy guests. Colonel Liston's face still harboured that semi-grin which didn't reveal much about his real state of mind. By the gate, the stand-off was unchanged. There was a brief exchange between the two men, before Colonel Liston elegantly turned and walked away, his minder close on his heels. Mr Heywoode said a few words to Eddie then walked back towards the house.

"A short visit..." Jaimie mused.

Tania seemed to be thinking.

"Here they are! Where did you two disappear to?"

Millie's voice reached Jaimie and as he turned he saw her approaching their table. With her was a woman which he guessed to be Tania's mother. Her cream suit and pearl necklace against the black of the silk blouse spelt taste, designer prices, subtle 'chic'. Tania got up, Jaimie did too.

"Mother, this is my friend Jaimie."

Smiling, Mrs Heywoode studied Jaimie for a moment.

"How are you? Are you enjoying yourself?" she asked.

"Fine, yes, very much, thank you," he answered with his most honest smile.

"Tania, could you come a minute, I'd like you to meet someone."

Tania followed her mother leaving Millie with Jaimie.

"I was wondering where you'd got to," Millie said.

"Oh, just mingling."

113

A waiter stopped by the table and promptly poured her a glass of champagne. Jaimie declined the offer to have one too.

"I'm driving home," he said.

But Millie insisted; it was a party and he was a strong man. She said a little drink couldn't move him so he got another beer, to please her. They made small talk, at least it sounded like it, then she asked:

"You're not married, are you?"

"Why, don't I look like a married man?"

"Oh, you are?"

She seemed surprised. Jaimie laughed:

"I no longer am."

Then of course, she didn't allow him to stop just there. He had to go through the whole story for Millie who refused to be put off by vague answers. He was spared further inroads into his life by the arrival at their table of two well-dressed young men whom Millie introduced as school friends. They sat and the four conversed pleasantly for a while. Jaimie learned that they were also sons of exiled Liberian diplomats and had studied in America. Howard, 'Howie ' to his friends, the slightly older of the two knew a couple of spots in East New York so he and Jaimie hit it off and from him Jaimie learned a little more about their country.

Some of the guests had started to leave, but a sizeable crowd was still moving around the place. Tania reappeared and proposed a second trip to the buffet. Despite the relatively advanced hour, there was still a nice choice of desserts. Another iced champagne bottle appeared at their table and Jaimie found himself accepting another glass. After a while, Howie and his friend opted to go to some club in the West End but Jaimie declined their offer to come along. He was working in the morning and besides, didn't really feel like leaving. Tania, of course, couldn't leave but Millie, who was by that time rather merry, after failing to sway Jaimie, followed the two men. Tania and Jaimie sat quietly, while around them people shuffled to and fro to Ella Fitzgerald's silky tones. Tania's eyes rested on her father, taking leave of a white-haired gentleman by the gate.

"Is everything OK?" Jaimie asked.

"Yes," she turned to face him, saw his insistent, expectant look and sighed. "Well, I don't really know. Daddy seems a little concerned about...the visit. He wants me...all of us, to adopt security

114

measures for a while."

"Security measures?" Jaimie repeated, intrigued.

"Yeah, you know," she laughed a little to ease the tension. "It's not that bad. You just learn to be aware. We grew up with that kind of thing."

Jaimie shook his head.

"This is England. You don't have much to worry about here."

"You never know. Last week, twice, I was sure someone was following me."

"Really? Where?"

"After work, I'm almost certain."

It all sounded very mysterious, unless Tania was mistaken. Jaimie asked:

"How serious is this thing with the Colonel?"

Tania seemed preoccupied by precisely that. She grimaced.

"I'm not sure. Daddy never discusses his problems. I'm sure he'll work it out."

Jaimie couldn't see himself drinking much more champagne. Most of the guests had by now gone or were going. Garden parties were early dos after all. A few scattered groups around the courtyard continued their discussions under the cool night breeze. All in all Jaimie had enjoyed his first garden party. He said:

"I guess I'm gonna have to leave you soon. It was real nice of you to invite me."

"I'm glad you came," Tania said simply.

"I could get used to this kinda thing, you know. Maybe I need a little sophistication in my life."

She watched him adjust his tie and laughed.

"Well, I'll make sure to invite you to the next one."

"Alright. And I hope you'll get me a special pass?"

She searched his face.

"Pass...what pass?"

"Well, I wouldn't like to get caught in a curfew when I come to pick you up next week..."

He got up, she did too and they walked slowly towards the gate.

"Did we make a date?"

"Oh yeah," Jaimie dropped casually, "I forgot to tell you. Next week Friday, I'm taking you to a real hot place on the north side."

She smiled, "Oh, I see."

But that didn't mean 'no'. Maybe Tony was right, it was time to take control of this, Jaimie thought to himself.

"And furthermore, Miss Heywoode," he stopped and faced her, "I think I should warn you that from now on, from tonight, I'm gonna be looking for you. I don't care if you don't take my calls, I'm gonna be shooting at you, it's on!"

Tania looked into his eyes to see if he was joking.

"Is it the champagne?" she asked facetiously.

"Uh-uh, not even that!" he threw her a meaningful gaze, his eyes deep into hers for a few seconds, until she moved her head slightly. He told her straight: "You're in a world of trouble."

Tania knew now he was serious. She asked quietly:

"So what brought that on?"

Jaimie changed his stance, looked at the pretty woman in front of him silently for a moment.

"You're staring," she said.

"Damn right."

"Now you're swearing too."

Jaimie could hear Louis Armstrong's trumpet kicking waves in the background. He said:

"Are you ready for this?" She waited. "OK; the way it is...so far, I've been keeping a real low profile with you 'cause you were playing hard with me, and that was cool, that was cool...but now, I'm gonna be checking you out. I've got to see you very regularly."

"Yes? I didn't know that." She seemed amused.

His eyes were searching hers, on and off.

"I didn't tell you before because I thought maybe you'd be too much of a society girl..."

She frowned a little but he didn't let her stop him.

"...But I was wrong. I think you're really...nice."

She stood his look just long enough then took his arm and marched him gently on down. At the gate a few couples were taking leave of each other with much niceties.

"By the way; what happened to Carl? I thought he wanted to see me tonight," Jaimie remembered.

"Oh, he was here earlier then he got a call from his friends and disappeared. That's how he is."

They stopped on the other side of the gate, in the semi-darkness of the street. The sounds of departing cars fading in the distance as the street reverted back to its peacefulness. Jaimie noticed Eddie looking their way from the entrance.

116

"So, we're on for Friday?"

Tania didn't seem sure. Then she asked:

"You remember a conversation we had over some ice-cream?"

"Hmm, yeah..."

"Well the situation is still the same, I'm not really free, you know." She added: "But we can still be friends."

Jaimie cringed.

"You know it sounds really ugly. Why do women always say things like that? You know it's the last thing a guy wants to hear!" He mimicked a woman's voice: "Why can't we be friends?"

Tania couldn't help laughing. He got just that little bit closer.

"No, seriously, I can't take that 'friend' thing, not with you."

Tania didn't say anything, neither did she pull back the hand he was holding.

"Look, I'm cool. I can dig your situation but how serious is it?" he asked. "First of all, where is he?"

"Where?"

"Yeah, I mean, if he's the man, he's supposed to be here."

"He's abroad," she said.

"Abroad," he repeated.

"Hmh hm."

"OK, let him stay abroad, because on Friday I'll be picking you up to wine you and dine you, so be prepared."

"Have I got a choice?"

She could feel how close he was, but didn't move. That was as close as Jaimie had ever got to her and he realised right there and then that he liked the feeling. In fact he was in no hurry to leave.

"No," he said softly, "you're trapped."

"OK," he heard her say in such a sweet tone of voice, Jaimie felt a tingle in the back of his neck. Then she eased up a little from him, he released her hand and the fleeting magic dissipated. He could still feel her eyes watching him.

"Are you OK to drive?" Her voice was back to normal.

"Sure. Are you OK?"

"Yes," she said, "call me."

That request, again, was a first.

"You can count on that! See ya!"

Jaimie was slowly backing up, she waved.

"Good night."

Tania watched his silhouette melt away in the darkness.

117

CHAPTER EIGHT

With the start of the academic year, the streets were filled with noisy and unruly students. It was part of the cycle of seasons. The little group of schoolgirls darting recklessly across the road, seemed to have no care for their lives and forced Jaimie to brake sharply. One by one they stepped onto the platform of a moving bus and climbed up. Jaimie sighed. Sometimes he reflected that he'd love to be that age again. But then again, he wouldn't like to do the whole teenage trip over... He eased off the clutch pedal, moved on slowly behind the line of vehicles. The day had been greyish, with showers threatening but never quite falling. In the passenger seat a brooding Tony seemed lost in meditation. It wasn't like him, but considering the crazy scene they had just been through at the hospital, it was understandable. His face reflected how little sleep he had had in the last twenty four hours.

Charlene's labour had started prematurely just before midnight. Tony had driven her down to the hospital and stuck by her, like a dutiful husband. He was a little tense but after a while, he got used to the wails of pain and simply did his best to talk to her, although there wasn't much he could say to help her. He waited, all kinds of thoughts going through his mind; moments like this, the birth of your child, do that to you he found out. He sat for almost an hour on a plastic chair in the hall, his head in his lap, not sleeping, just letting images of his past jump about in his head. And he waited. The nurse monitoring Charlene said that she was 'doing fine' (by the end of the night, Tony had grown to hate that expression...). It takes a long time, sometimes, she said. So Tony waited, making regular trips inside the room, asking dumb questions like 'are you alright?' to the semi-conscious woman. Finally it happened. He'd just been in the room and was absent-mindedly watching the coming of the dawn through the waiting room window when he heard the shuffling of hurried feet and the jingling of a trolley being rolled down the corridor. Tony remembered later arriving at the door of the room and hearing Charlene bawling out in pain. The nurse who was closing the door of the delivery room stopped and looked at him, waiting for him to enter but he shook his head and remained standing on the spot. He didn't move until he heard another, high-pitched wail ring out from behind the closed door.

Jaimie got his friend's call on the pager and drove to Tony's house at lunchtime to meet him. They stopped to eat in a pizzeria on the way to the hospital. When they got there, Charlene was sitting in bed, her tiny baby in a white gown asleep in her arms. She was pretty, with a full head of shiny black hair and her mother's copper skin and high cheekbones. On the window side of the bed sat Charlene's mother, sister and aunt with a similar kind of studied expression on their faces. Across from them were Tony's mother and two older sisters. Tony kissed his wife and smiled at his sleeping daughter. After saying 'hello' to everyone and admiring the baby, Jaimie pulled himself a chair and sat back. Nothing much was being said around the bed, at least not by the women. In fact the atmosphere was almost hostile. Everyone present was extremely pleased about the birth, of course, except that both families resented Tony for not calling them when Charlene's labour had started. Tony decided that it would be best that way and, judging by the present turn of things, congratulated himself on his decision. And as he found out quickly enough, the debate which divided them throughout Charlene's pregnancy had finally turned into an irreconcilable difference.

"What are you gonna call the baby?" Jaimie asked innocently. He felt both grandmothers' stares reach him.

"I'm not sure yet," Charlene said with a diplomatic smile. She looked happy cradling her baby, in fact it suited her. The matter of the baby's name hadn't been worked out yet since it was directly connected to the problem at hand. Jaimie's question poured oil on the fire, as they say. Up to the moment Tony and Jaimie arrived, Charlene had managed to keep things under control, skilfully deflecting any acid remarks from her mother. Here was the bone of contention: should the new baby be christened or baptised? Now, the issue might have sounded trivial to some people but to Charlene's mother, for one, nothing was more essential than that her grand-daughter should be properly baptised at the Sacred Heart of Mary Catholic church she had frequented every Sunday since arriving in England in the fifties. Tony's mother, on the other hand, had no intention of letting her only son's child, the flesh of her flesh, be handled by anyone else but her local Seventh Day Adventist minister.

There had been no room for agreement in the past weeks and

119

there wasn't any now. The two sets of women on either side of the bed were on a minimum level of verbal exchange now. Charlene pretended not to notice the cold vibrations; she was happy and wanted everyone else to be also. Jaimie was oblivious to any hostilities. He was being nice to everyone, complimenting Charlene, trying to make pleasant conversation. He'd come along to see Tony's baby. He had no idea this was the first time in a long while the two families had met. The day of reckoning was at hand, but Jaimie was unaware of it until Charlene's mother told her daughter in a tight voice:

"Back home, we have the baptism certificates of all the women in the family, all the way back to six generations. You were raised a good Catholic, Charlene, and so should your daughter."

So far, Tony had ignored her snide remarks on the topic, as he had done for the past months. But Jaimie noticed the sudden frown on his friend's face. He watched him turn to the slender, brown-skin woman, her handbag clutched tightly on her lap. His mother could see him getting hot, but didn't say a word to hold him back.

"Yeah?" Tony said, with a side grin that spelled no good. "Well this is not back home, wherever your home is, and let me tell you something..."

"Tony!" his sister called out feebly.

"You see this child? She's my child, in case somebody don't know. And I am no Catholic. As a matter of fact, I don't go to no church so don't think anybody is going to put their hand on my child to talk any foolishness over her!"

Under the effect of his anger, Tony's accent was drifting rapidly to his Jamaican roots, making the speech all the more stinging. For a second, Tony's mother looked as if she wanted to say something but Tony didn't pause long enough for any interruption.

"I will name my child like how I feel fe do it, without no church business, and anybody don't like it can stay ah dem yard. I don't care, y'understand!?!"

With that he got up. No one spoke and Tony didn't expect an answer neither. Jaimie was finding it hard to repress a smile at the offended 'Catholic' faces. He said light-heartedly:

"OK Tony, what d'you say we pass back later."

For a moment, Tony looked as if he was about to unload some more arrows into Charlene's mother but, after a glance at his newborn daughter, he simply walked away and out of the ward.

120

Jaimie sighed and smiled apologetically to the women.

"It's a very emotional time for him. You all have a nice day," he said before following his friend.

"Should I drop you home to get some sleep, or you wanna come along to Junior's?" Jaimie asked.

Tony shrugged.

"Ah, I'll sleep later. Let's go."

Jaimie had called his brother from the hospital in response to the message on his pager earlier on. Junior was sick apparently, a cold he said. By the tone of his voice, Jaimie could tell his health wasn't the real problem.

The Grove was alive with throngs of children on their way home from schools, besieging sweetshops, the older boys busy taunting groups of girls. The long-awaited rainfall fell lightly from the skies, Jaimie switched on the wipers.

"So I guess the one-on-one we talked about for this weekend is out, uh?"

Tony smiled.

"No way! I'm gonna need to be fit, the pressure is on now."

"You're right, homes; and it's here to stay," Jaimie laughed.

By the time they parked in Junior's estate, the rain was pouring down. Upstairs, Lorraine let them in. The way she answered his greeting confirmed Jaimie's suspicion that Junior had, once again, messed up somehow. He and Tony went to the living room, sat down.

"Wilfred, where are you?!" Jaimie called mockingly.

"Is that his name, Wilfred?" Tony laughed.

"You didn't know? Yeah, he was named after my father."

"Wilfred!"

"Hey man, what's funny about my daddy's name?" Jaimie clowned, as if he didn't know?

Lorraine had disappeared in the adjoining kitchen. A little voice was calling:

"Uncle Jaimie. Uncle Jaimie! "

He entered the kitchen and the little girl giggled in her chair. Her mother had been trying to convince her to finish her meal but it wasn't going too well. The rice and fish fingers had all but disappeared while the spinach remained untouched. When it came to greens Keesha could be real stubborn. Jaimie opened his eyes

121

wide.

"Ooooh Keesha! Keeshaaaah, you know you need to eat that spinach. Otherwise you'll be weak, then those big girls at school gonna beat you up. You got to eat it, you know that."

Jaimie's reasoning didn't work too good. The little girl giggled but refused the offering nevertheless. After a few more attempts, he managed to trick her into eating a spoonful of spinach stuffed in the remaining quarter of a fish finger, but that was it. Jaimie smiled and smoothing her hair back serenaded his little niece:

"*What can make me feel this way...My girl, talkin' 'bout my girl...*"

Keesha giggled some more.

Lorraine marched into the kitchen just then, a sour look on her face. Jaimie guessed that it had something to do with his brother.

"What's Junior done now?" he asked her.

"You ask him."

Jaimie decided to do just that and he made his way to the living room.

Junior was sitting across from Tony, in his dressing gown and looking rough.

"Boy, you look like you sounded on the phone, what's up with you?"

Junior looked stressed.

"That woman, man. She's pressuring me, I can't take it," Junior said, in a low voice.

"OK, what's the story?"

Tony's smile suggested that he had been privy to a 'sneak-preview' of the said story. It seemed to have lightened his mood.

"Your bro's been busted," he told Jaimie.

"Busted?!" Jaimie sat up in his chair.

"Shhhhh! Take it easy, man," Junior urged him.

"Busted?!" Jaimie repeated, lower. "Again?"

"Look, I ain't been busted," Junior corrected. "I ain't done nothing."

It sounded feeble. Jaimie shook his head and laughed.

"Come on, I'm like your lawyer, you know that; you tell me the truth, I'll tell the lies."

It didn't cheer Junior up but he knew he couldn't hold back from his brother. He coughed like a real sick person a few times, convincingly it must be said, then said:

"I came home late, so she's getting all upset over that."

Jaimie threw him his 'lawyer's look'.

"Uh-uh, so...what time did you get home?"

"Around three..."

Jaimie blew out a little air, shook his head slowly. He said:

"So, you get home at four in the morning, then you're too wrecked to make it to work in the morning and you don't know why your wife gets all upset just for that?"

"First of all, we ain't married, right..."

It was weak, sad...and Junior knew it. In fact, it sounded very much like an admission of guilt. Jaimie fixed his brother like a judge.

"You, went on a shakedown. Don't even try..."

Junior's face was pitiful.

"Alright, I was with some friends."

Jaimie shook his head again, even Tony shook his head this time. "Homeboy, I know you and you look as guilty as a nigga with a ton of shit in his trunk," Jaimie told his brother. "You were knocking boots and the play took you over. You looking washed out, man."

Junior shrugged. He didn't like being told that but it had to be said.

"It wasn't my fault," he said, dismally.

"So what exactly happened?" Tony asked him, keeping close. He was back in good spirits now, having found someone with greater problems than his own. He and Jaimie leaned forward conspiratorially to hear the story. Junior cast an apprehensive glance towards the living room door and started, really low:

"It's this girl from work. She's been onto me for a while. We're on a vibe, you know." He added, a little urgently: "But I told her straight, she knows my situation and everything."

Jaimie and Tony nodded knowingly.

"Anyway, yesterday after work she asked me out for a drink, so I said alright. I was just going to have one beer and get home, you know what I mean?"

Nods again from the two listeners.

"So, uh, we had this drink, but then some people showed up that she knew from before so we all had a drink together... What?!"

The tired Junior in his dressing gown stopped in mid-flow, puzzled by his listeners' condescending smiles.

"Go on, homie, we're with you!" Jaimie reassured him.

Junior was trying to retrace in his memory the exact sequence of

123

events of the previous night. It seemed difficult.

"So after a while, they all decided we should all go to this guy's house for another drink. One of them had just come back from Greece. Paulo, that was his name...I tried to get away but they wouldn't let me, man, you know how these people are, man. So I followed them...and that was my mistake."

Junior paused, leaving the climax hanging. They waited.

"Come on, man! Tell us the story!" Jaimie growled.

"Come on, Junior!" Tony seconded in urgent, hushed tones.

Junior went on:

"So we ended up at this guy Danny's house, nice guy..."

"The one from Greece?" Tony asked.

"No, Paulo was the one from Greece."

"Go on, man," Jaimie urged him.

"You shoulda seen this house, man. Three bathrooms, jacuzzi, poolroom, a wicked place, somewhere near Croydon. They poured out this liquor the guy, Paulo, had brought back from Greece...ozi, uzi or something..."

"Ouzo," Tony corrected.

"Yeah, that's it, ouzo, man. That stuff is deadly! Whatever you do, don't ever drink that shit, I'm telling you Jaimie..."

"Right, but you did so just tell me the whole story," Jaimie wanted details.

"So they put on some music and everybody started dancing and all that, it was nice, we drank some more of this ouzo stuff and then..."

"Then what?" Tony couldn't wait.

"I can't remember what happened exactly...but the next thing I know I was upstairs with Karen," Junior said with a puzzled look on his face.

"Karen; that's the girl from your workplace?" Jaimie asked.

"When you say 'upstairs', you mean, in the bedroom?" Tony offered.

"She's the one, yeah...in the bedroom, right."

Junior paused again.

"So you realised you were in the bedroom with...Karen, right? So what happened?" Jaimie sounded like someone listening to the blow-by-blow account of a boxing match.

"Well, I was...you know, working..."

"What?" Tony interrupted again, in a lower but more urgent

tone. "You just found yourself doing it, just like that?"

Junior eyes darted towards the half-closed door, fearful that Lorraine might overhear. He whispered:

"Like I told you, I don't remember what happened. I must have fallen asleep after that. I woke up around two o'clock, I felt dizzy."

"What about Karen, what did she say?" Tony was curious.

"Karen? Oh she was gone, man. Everybody had left when I woke up."

Jaimie was shaking his head from side to side. He heard Junior say:

"I tried to get up for work this morning but I felt sick."

"What a night!" Tony mused.

"It's not funny, man. Lorraine freaked out on me!"

Jaimie wasn't surprised. The story he'd just heard summed up well enough Junior's life and its many misadventures; he never meant things to go that way but somehow they usually did. What could he say to his younger brother? He smiled:

"Whatever you do, don't go to Greece, alright?!"

Tony laughed, but Junior couldn't. His 'butt' was 'in the sling' as they say, and it was no joking matter. He frowned.

"Thanks, you're a great help."

"What can I do? Lorraine's angry right now. You gonna have to work it out. Ain't nobody can help you."

"I was thinking of coming home for a few days, give her time to cool off."

Jaimie held out his two hands in front of him.

"Don't even consider that! That would only make her angrier. Besides, she'd only follow you and I don't want no fight at my crib."

He and Tony enjoyed the joke, doing their best to keep from laughing too loud.

"No, seriously, you got to talk your way back in, slowly," Jaimie advised his brother. "Be nice, take her out, do some housework."

"Act like you're sorry, apologise," Tony agreed.

"I ain't telling her the truth..." Junior stopped them.

"Not if you're sane and you love life!" Jaimie warned.

He got up.

"Where you going?" Junior asked.

"Home. Now I seen you safe, I'm gone. I have a life too!"

Tony got up also. Junior seemed sad to see them go.

125

"I know you; you'll find a way to get through to her," Jaimie assured him.

"Take it easy!" Tony said.

They started out.

"Later Lorraine!" Jaimie called out.

They left and got back on the street where the rain had stopped and left the roads shiny in the early evening illumination. Already, the days were getting shorter.

On the way to Tony's house, Jaimie stopped to buy two beers at a local off-licence.

"Have a drink to celebrate the birth of your pretty daughter, daddy!"

He grinned, handing one to Tony. 'Daddy' seemed content enough at the end of the day. He asked as they entered his street:

"By the way, what's the news on your girl?"

"My girl?" Jaimie repeated.

"You know who I'm talking about!"

"Oh that girl. Nothing man, she ain't my girl."

He parked the jeep.

"It's that cold, uh?"

"Yep. Why you always trying to push me onto her anyway?"

Tony smiled mysteriously. "I think she suits you."

"Serious?" Jaimie asked. Then he shook his head. "I ain't heard or seen her in two weeks."

"But, the garden party and all that? You seemed well in, man."

"Yeah, well, she's busy apparently."

Tony looked at his friend, pulled a face.

"Busy? Busy?! You, the great Jaimie are interested in a girl and she's busy?"

"Oh I ain't that interested," he shrugged before Tony's scrutinising gaze. "Alright, I'm interested, but she has somebody."

Tony told him: "I seen that girl, she looks good, and she likes you too."

Jaimie sighed.

"You got to play harder than that, Jaimie."

"She's a rich girl, man. Rich girls are different. You can't shake them too hard, you got to have style, be nice."

Tony laughed. "Rich girls are no different from your average inner city girl, believe me. They just want someone to rock their world, someone who tells them things they've never heard."

Jaimie reflected that it was probably true. Tony continued:

"As a matter of fact, that's why that girl likes you. You're a homeboy; she's not used to that. You got to forget that nicely-nicely approach and give her some homeboy style. Be firm."

What Tony said made sense. Jaimie smiled.

"Sort of like you today?"

"That's right, like that."

They laughed.

"You going back to the hospital tonight?" Jaimie asked.

"No, I'm too tired, I'll go in the morning." Tony stretched. "I think I'll drink that beer and get some sleep."

"Alright, call me tomorrow, I'll pass down there."

Tony stepped out of the car.

"OK, drive safely."

"Yeah. Sleep good, Daddy!"

Tony closed the door. Jaimie left him and drove back down. He got home, had a shower, a light dinner then settled down to watch a movie. Before the end of the video, he could feel his eyes closing so he switched it off. Upstairs in the bedroom he succumbed to sleep easily with the sound of raindrops tapping out a rhythm on the roof above.

By morning, everything was dry. A beautiful early sun had risen over London town. Like most Thursdays, Jaimie got up early and jogged to the sports centre for a light workout. It was a routine he tried to stick to, with the Tuesday night jogging and the Saturday afternoon game with the junior team at the community centre. Sometimes Junior came along on Tuesday nights but these days it wasn't that often. As for Tony, he showed up once in a while to take part in the Saturday game but with his new responsibilities, he was going to be out for a while.

Back home there was time for a shower and rapid breakfast and Jaimie still made it to work on time. He felt energised, fit and happy and ready to start a new day. Paul seemed to have had one of those nights again. Jaimie avoided any early conversation with him, knowing he 'd be back on course after his first drink of the day.

At lunchtime Jaimie hit the high street for a sandwich. Lots of people, lots of noise.He noticed three pairs of female eyes following him, but Jaimie simply smiled and walked on, real laid back, even though the last woman, dressed elegantly with sensual features stirred him a little. She reminded him of someone. He dismissed the thought. Back at the garage, the thought was still with him, hanging at the edge of his mind. 'Should I call?' he asked himself as he slipped his overalls back on. He was still toying with the idea as he got underneath the pick-up truck. The proposed date with Tania after the garden party hadn't materialised. When he had called, she had sounded a little restrained, saying she was busy, couldn't make it that week. Jaimie had called once more after that and although she was nice on the phone, made another excuse so he said he'd call back and didn't. True, he was busy too, but he knew he caught himself thinking of Tania often enough. He even saw her in a dream once but was unable to recall anything about it when he woke up. He could have gone out with several other girls by now, but he didn't really feel like it. Even Brenda still called from time to time, making barely veiled suggestions and he'd been close to giving in on a few occasions. It made him smile to think that he, Jaimie, could have become like that, refusing girls.

With Cypress Hills' *A to the K* blaring through his headphone, Jaimie got busy with the truck. He soon finished fixing it and called Tony at work, just in case, but they said he had been in and out. He wasn't at home either. "Be firm!" his friend had told him. The advice was sound and, as Jaimie scrubbed his hands, a different outlook was shaping in his mind. By the time he changed, checked out and stepped outside, he was thinking, 'she likes me, really'. He got to the jeep, grinning. His mind was made up.

An army of traffic wardens had invaded Kensington, ambushing the unsuspecting and the absent-minded. Jaimie watched the owner of a gleaming Saab plead, in vain, as a diminutive, stout warden was writing him his ticket. This was rush hour, the best time for 'hunting' and the warden mercilessly hooked her plastic-wrapped ticket under the Saab's wiper and walked away. It was still a little early, so Jaimie neatly eased the jeep behind a company van across from the lawyer's office and waited, sipping on his Ribena.

Just before six, a gleaming white Mercedes with tinted windows double-parked in front of the office. Jaimie watched the passenger door open and was only mildly surprised to recognise the ubiquitous Eddie, yet again dressed in a suit, his face unsmiling as ever behind dark glasses. Eddie scanned the street, taking in the continuous flow of pedestrians on both pavements. He didn't seem to pay any special attention to the red jeep across the road.

Then he simply leaned against the car, arms crossed on his chest, ignoring the intense gaze of a male traffic warden booking an unfortunate van driver a little further up the road. Jaimie smiled to himself, swaying rhythmically to Tupac's *Me Against The World*; the security measures were in force. 'Eddie might not be happy to see me again', he reflected, amused.

A couple of minutes after six, they emerged from behind the door. Tania, her usual elegant self in a beige suit, paused on the pavement and turned to say something to the man. He was tall enough, medium-built and light in complexion, with glasses. They say first impressions are everlasting, well, apart from the fact that he had a good guess who the guy was, Jaimie could never have liked a man wearing that jacket! A checkered, black and white tweed with burgundy pants! 'The guy's either a jerk or he's been brought up in the woods,' Jaimie said to himself. The 'clown', as Jaimie decided he must be, was saying something to Tania who listened then turned away before answering. He held his arms open in an apologetic gesture, then she said a few final words before walking off towards the Mercedes where Eddie was holding open the rear door for her. The man with the jacket adjusted his horn-rimmed glasses and walked on up the street. 'It's my time', Jaimie thought, dropping the empty Ribena carton. He got out of his car, dodged a couple of cars to cross over and reached the Mercedes. Tania must have sensed his closeness for she turned just as she was about to climb in. She didn't seem surprised to see him.

"Hi, I was in the neighbourhood," Jaimie said.

She looked at him and smiled.

"Really?"

Eddie remained holding the car door open, frozen, unsmiling. Jaimie raised a friendly hand.

"Hi, it's me again."

Eddie barely acknowledged him, a little twitch at the corner of his mouth maybe, but no more. Jaimie looked deep into Tania's eyes; they were hard and focused. She waited, silent.

"I know you probably didn't expect me but...I really felt like seeing you, and I thought maybe you were feeling that way too but you didn't know if I was upset about you cancelling our date, so...I came to pick you up. I'm not upset."

He stood there grinning at her. She said:

"I'm sorry, I couldn't call you."

"I accept your apology," he told her, generously. "So, what are

129

you doing now?"

"I'm about to be driven home..."

"You don't like it, uh?" he smiled.

"One of those things..."

Jaimie felt like he could stay right here, in the setting sun, just talking. It was a strange sensation, intriguing. She waited, said:

"You're staring."

He sighed.

"Yeah, it's compulsive, I got to see a doctor, you know..."

"Be firm!" Tony had said. Eddie was still watching him. Jaimie rubbed the back of his almost shaven skull.

"Alright, it's like this, I want to see you. I'm determined and I ain't gonna give up. You can set my man Eddie here on me, or even your two dobermans but this ain't gonna change nothing. We have to talk."

He was sure he could see a hint of a smile on her inexpressive face.

"Talk about what?" she asked.

"Oh there's so much I could talk to you about, you know...but if you want to choose the topic, it's cool with me. Just let me drive you home. I need about half an hour alone with you."

Tania seemed to be giving it some thought. She turned to Eddie and said something Jaimie couldn't hear. The man answered her but she shook her head and said: "It's alright, you can follow." Then she told Jaimie, "OK, let's go."

'Alright, it's on!' he was thinking as he walked her across the road, feeling confident, and helped her aboard the jeep. They drove out, the white Mercedes in tow. Jaimie lowered the volume on the stereo, too late to spare Tania a spice of heavy-worded lyrics from Tupac.

"You'll get to appreciate it, eventually..." he joked. She pulled a frown which spelled 'I don't think so', but said nothing.

"You're surprised?" he asked.

"Not really, I knew you would come here this week."

He looked to her, in profile, serious.

"You knew I was coming here?"

"Yes, I dreamt it."

This time he turned from the road, imprudently.

"What? You dreamt I was coming to pick you up from work?"

"I did," Tania insisted quietly, as if it was nothing extraordinary.

Jaimie smiled, shook his head.

"You're kidding, right?"

No, she wasn't.

"This is a good sign," Jaimie smiled.

"Is it?" Tania asked in a non-committal kind of voice.

"It sure is! In fact I'd go as far as saying you're thinking about me, subconsciously. That's what Freud said, you know!"

"Oh, you're a psychoanalyst too?" Tania teased.

"Well, in my spare time."

They shared the joke, she relaxed a little now.

In the rearview mirror, the white Mercedes still trailed.

"This security thing is still on, uh?"

She nodded. "Yes, for a while."

He watched her, then remarked in a detached voice.

"Before I forget, tell your friend he should really ask somebody about dress style. He looks positively uncool. What's up with him?"

"That's is a typical macho response," she said.

She seemed amused by it.

"Here we go," Jaimie sighed. "You gonna get into that male-macho complex thing, right? "

"So...you came to surprise me, you thought, and you saw me coming out with a man whom you assume to be my boyfriend. So, because of your alleged interest in me, you make a point of attacking his dress sense to belittle him in my sight probably, and further your cause."

She stopped and it was just as well because Jaimie had so much to say, now that things were going smooth.

"Now we're talking!"

He diverted his attention for just long enough to let a bus back into the flow of traffic. Their escort was still in sight, one vehicle behind. Jaimie asked Tania:

"Could you push this mirror a little way out?"

She put her arm outside to move the large side mirror.

"Yeah...a little more...that's it, no; too much..."

Then he heard Tania say:

"That's the same car. It's them!"

Jaimie frowned, looked at her.

"What's up? Who?"

"It's them, in the car behind, the brown Ford..."

"Who's that?"

Tania seemed serious, her brow creased as she stole another look into the side mirror. There was a brown Ford right behind them, with two men inside but Jaimie could only see the silhouettes through the half-tint of the windscreen. The driver wearing a cap and his passenger. They didn't seem to present any immediate danger. Yet Tania insisted:

"They're the men who followed my car twice in the past month."

"You sure it's the same car?"

"Of course I'm sure; it's the same licence plate."

Jaimie was thinking. Eddie in the Mercedes was following the brown Granada. Apparently, he didn't recognise the car.

"What d'you think; anything to do with the Colonel's problem?"

"I don't know."

It all sounded a little crazy to him. But then again, he was at the garden party and the Colonel was real enough. Mr Heywoode took things seriously enough to have his daughter escorted to and from work. Beside him, Tania seemed concerned, her eyes checking the car behind them. It wasn't fear though; she seemed intrigued rather than shaken. She said:

"Let's find out who they are."

Jaimie looked at her seriously. A voice in his head was still saying 'Don't do nothing crazy'. Nowadays he listened to that voice.

"Whatcha thinking about? What about your bodyguard?"

"By the time we tell Eddie, they'll be gone."

Jaimie still couldn't figure out how Eddie, vigilant as he was, could not have noticed what was happening. There was only one way to let him know. Jaimie looked at Tania.

"OK, we're gonna find out."

"They can drive, be careful," she remarked.

Inside himself, Jaimie wasn't worried about the driving part; that was his forte. He was wondering if the two men tailing them were strapped. They were approaching Kilburn station, at medium speed, trailing behind a line of cars all manoeuvring to overtake two buses. Jaimie saw what he was looking for, indicated left to turn into the gas station. Ideally, the 'tail' would follow and the Mercs as well. Could the trap work so easily?

"What are you doing?" Tania asked.

Jaimie didn't answer. He drove slowly inside the forecourt of the station, sighed as he watched plan number one fail. The guys, whoever they were, weren't that green and to make it worse, Eddie drove in too. Jaimie shook his head; if the tail didn't know about Tania's bodyguard, they would now! He slowed down by the pumps, watched the Granada stop under the bridge, waiting for them no doubt. The Mercedes pulled to a halt behind the jeep. Slowly releasing his clutch pedal, Jaimie asked:

"How's Eddie at speed driving?"

Tania gave him a puzzled look, but Jaimie wasn't expecting an answer. If Eddie picked up fast, it would help but one way or another, he would find out what was going on. The little voice was still whispering 'Don't go crazy...' but Jaimie nodded and gassed down, shooting out on a sharp right turn and back onto the main road. The oncoming traffic was lighter, as the cars could now overtake the stationary buses. The Granada jumped forward as the jeep appeared behind it, the hunter was now the hunted. Jaimie's unexpected manoeuvre had taken Eddie by surprise and the Mercedes was only just leaving the gas station.

The Granada pushed up to overtake two vehicles before finding a break in the flow to avoid the van ahead. Jaimie had to wait until it passed to go after the fleeing car. He geared up, zoomed past three cars but the Granada had plenty of power and was keeping its distance. Jaimie glimpsed the Mercedes behind, ignoring the Highway Code in its attempt to catch up with the runaway jeep. Eddie was probably having a brain haemorrhage trying to figure out what the hell was happening. Losing Mr Heywoode's daughter surely was the last thing he wanted to happen to him. Jaimie was well over the speed limit by now, the 4.2 engine roaring loudly as he followed the Granada. It was still speeding away in the descending evening. So far all lights were on green, but the one ahead was already changing to red. The Granada had no choice but to slow to a halt beside another vehicle. Jaimie closed down the gap. Eddie was sure to arrive any moment now. Tania had not said a word for the last ten minutes. She was watching the car. Jaimie pulled his handbrake and opened his door. He was going to find out what all this was about and who was following them. He had only just stepped down from the jeep when to his surprise, the Granada was moving! With its wheels locked full on right and with a screech of tyres, it shot back up the other way, forcing a small car coming in the opposite direction to brake sharply. Jaimie swore, jumped back in the jeep, turned his steering wheel furiously and hooked a vicious 'wheelburn' in first gear. Eddie in the Mercs was only just arriving at full speed. The Granada was a good four hundred yards in front but Jaimie was cold now; he didn't like the way he'd been hoodwinked. Whatever was on Eddie's mind that exact minute, no one could tell but suddenly the Mercedes cut across the road heading straight for the jeep.

"Watch out!" Tania cried out.

Jaimie swore.

"What the fuck is he doing?!"

He couldn't believe that Eddie was about to crash into him but the big car was coming ominously closer. Tania tensed herself in her bucket seat. Arching his body, Jaimie dropped back in second gear and turned his wheel. He hit the pavement, just as the Mercedes' tyres skidded to within two inches of his door. Jaimie caught a final glimpse of the brown Granada shrinking in the distance. Eddie jumped out of the Mercedes with a furious look on his face, but Tania had unbuckled her belt and climbed down to ease things off. Jaimie couldn't tell in what language they were speaking but he could see from Eddie's face that he wasn't enjoying it. The man answered something but she wasn't of the same opinion. Jaimie said:

"What's wrong with you, man? You made them get way."

Eddie looked at him, cold behind his shades. With his suit and tie, neatly polished shoes, he looked like an FBI character from an old gangster movie.

"My job is to get Miss Heywoode home safely, not to chase cars."

As cold as that, and he didn't even sound angry. Tania looked at him with a mix of frustration and resignation.

Jaimie flapped his arms open, shrugged. It smarted him a little inside that the Granada outplayed him like that.

"Let's go home," Tania said calmly. Her composure had returned.

"Don't lose us this time," she chastised Eddie as she climbed back in the jeep.

Mr Heywoode listened carefully as Tania recounted the incident to him. They were seated in the grand living room, with the chandeliers hanging from the ceiling bathing them in a warm glow. Eddie had disappeared somewhere in the house. Mr Heywoode

134

asked his daughter only one question:

"Did you see the faces of the men inside the car?"

She shook her head negatively. Jaimie had been offered a beer. From where he was sitting, he could see the lit-up garden through the large french windows, right down to the shrubs and trees at the back. The evening news on the large-screen television in the far left corner talked of natural disasters and man-made catastrophes. After Tania excused herself, Mr Heywoode asked:

"You didn't damage your car, I hope?"

"No, I managed to avoid the crash."

"Eddie is a very conscientious person. All he is concerned with is my daughter's security. It was nothing personal."

"I understand that," Jaimie said.

In fact there was a lot he didn't understand, but he refrained from asking too many questions. Mr Heywoode was his usual dapper self: grey suit and tie. He got up to pick up some ice from the drinks trolley near the mantlepiece.

"Actually, I was going to give you a call this week. I have something I want you to take a look at for me."

Jaimie took his eyes off the framed picture of Martin Luther King on the back wall.

"Really?"

Mr Heywoode sat back down. He handed Jaimie a polaroid picture.

"Have a look a this."

Jaimie looked at the print, nodded. With a hint of admiration in his voice, he said: "Plymouth Belvedere, classic."

"1957, original chromes..." Mr Heywoode smiled. He seemed happy that Jaimie had immediately identified the shiny black car on the photo.

"Ever worked on one of them?"

Jaimie nodded, "Once, in the army. This officer had one. He was a classic car fanatic. Great ride. This one must be expensive."

Mr Heywoode sipped a little of his whisky, grinned a little.

"It's worth it to me. You see I have been collecting classic cars for years. I had six original models back in Liberia. Beautiful cars!"

"You left them down there?" Jaimie asked.

The man had a fatalistic shrug.

"The Oldsmobile is the only one I managed to save... So you were in the army. How long did you serve?"

135

'Serve is the right word', Jaimie mused to himself.

"Oh, only two years. I'm not exactly a veteran," he said.

"How did you like it?"

Remembering that Tania had mentioned her father being a military man, Jaimie sidestepped.

"They let me out of jail once in a while to work in the motor pool," he laughed.

Mr Heywoode laughed too, and then Mrs Heywoode made a timely entrance in the room.

"Well, good evening."

As she walked across to Jaimie he had time to notice again how much Tania had taken her eyes and high cheekbones. He got up.

"Good evening," he smiled, shaking her offered hand.

"How are you?"

"Fine, thank you."

The neatly pulled back black hair and sober dark blue suit gave Mrs Heywoode an almost scholarly look, belied by her smile.

"You are just in time for dinner," she said, turning to her husband who took his cue and finished his glass before getting up.

"I don't think I should..." Jaimie started. He suddenly became aware that a jeans and multicolour summer shirt might not be the proper dress code here, but Mrs Heywoode was polite enough to ignore his attire.

"Oh but you must stay, I have already made the arrangement."

In that case there was no turning away the offer.

"Well, it's very kind of you, thank you," Jaimie said.

Mrs Heywoode escorted him towards the open door at the end of the room.

"Is my husband trying to get you to work on one of his toys again?" she asked pleasantly, but loud enough for Mr Heywoode to hear. "Please say you can't do it, otherwise he is going to buy more."

"I know how he feels," Jaimie sympathised, "they really are beautiful cars."

They entered the dining room where the table was set on a light blue cloth with double plates, forks and spoons. The maid was placing two bottles of wine on the table.

"Have a seat here," Mrs Heywoode told Jaimie. He sat at one side of the long table. The hosts took their places at either end of the table which, since it was a fair size one, put them at some distance

136

from each other. It all looked a little more formal than Jaimie was used to, but he wasn't phased by it. He decided to play it by ear. Tania walked in and smiled on seeing Jaimie seated at the table between her parents.

"There you are!" she said.

She had changed into a loose fitting white and brown robe. Her face was relaxed, rid of the tension that was there before. TV voices drifted in, low. Mrs Heywoode directed the proceedings, they made casual conversation and the atmosphere was light. As for the food well, the food was just fine, spicy, succulent to a point. Mrs Heywoode, who led the discussions, seemed to be a woman of some education and wide-ranging interests, while her husband contented himself with expressing the politically correct point of view on whatever the item of discussion. Tania wasn't saying much. Jaimie reflected that she must have inherited her father's sobriety with words. Her mother, by contrast was vivacious, and gracious at the same time, with a affectionate laugh that rang high and youthful.

By dessert time, Mrs Heywoode had guided them through a medley of topics on the rainy tendency of the summer, the frequency of train accidents and suicides on the underground (she worked in a hospital), today's young people's lack of dress sense (with references to Carl, her absent son), and the iniquitous greed of taxi drivers (Mrs Heywoode didn't drive and had no desire to either). Tania listened to her mother with amused indulgence.

"Tell me, Jaimie," Mrs Heywoode said, smiling, where in New York did you say you were from? We have relatives there, you know."

Jaimie was trying to make up his mind about the dessert; should he take any, and if he did which one of the three varieties on the maid's tray would he opt for. He turned to his hostess.

"Brooklyn."

"Brooklyn, really?" Mrs Heywoode's relatives didn't live in Brooklyn. "We are more New Rochelle."

"New Rochelle, yeah, I've been there a coupla times," he said casually, unwilling to elaborate.

"What was it like growing up back there?"

He couldn't swear for it but Jaimie felt she was probing. He sighed with concentration.

"Well, it's hard to say really, looking back now..." he started.

To his left, Mr Heywoode was carefully peeling an apple, apparently unconcerned. Tania was watching him in her casual way, with eyelids so low you thought she was sleeping.

"...As a kid, you always find ways to have fun I guess, no matter how little you got, but let's say that a lot of people from my side never really manage to raise themselves up."

Jaimie busied himself buttering one of the small cuts of french bread he'd picked from the basket.

Maybe Mrs Heywoode loved dialogue, or maybe she just hadn't met someone like Jaimie before.

"Surely some of your friends too have managed to succeed in life," she said.

Jaimie wasn't about to discuss the fate of most of his friends. He smiled as the thought crossed his mind. He caught Tania's deep glance, but he didn't know what she was thinking, so he said:

"I didn't know him that well so I can't call him a friend of mine, but Mike Tyson made it, and he's from Brownsville."

That brought a spontaneous smile from the placid Mr Heywoode.

"Mike Tyson comes from your neighbourhood?"

He sounded genuinely and happily surprised.

"Yes, sir," Jaimie nodded. To be truthful, he had always felt a sort of 'territorial kinship', in a manner of speaking, with the boxing champion and son of the Brownsville projects.

"Mike is my homeboy."

"Homeboy!" Mrs Heywoode cut in. "That's all Carl is ever talking about: homeboys. Oh my God, Jaimie, don't tell me you used to be in that kind of life..."

Jaimie's first reaction was to burst out laughing, but he held back. Mrs Heywoode's face and tone of voice just then would have cut nicely in a rap video. In any case, Mr Heywoode prevented him from allaying Mrs Heywoode's fears.

"I watched everyone of his fights, and whatever anyone says, that young man is gifted."

Jaimie felt good to hear that.

"Yeah, he whooped them all. Mike is the man!"

"I thought they should have kept him in prison a little longer; it was dreadful what he did to that poor girl!"

Jaimie tried not to stop munching. Mrs Heywoode was finishing her fruit, not specially concerned what reaction her remark had

138

caused with the two boxing aficionados. Jaimie saw a slight puzzled frown on her husband's face then it was gone. Tania said:

"Yeah, he became very conscious in prison."

Jaimie confirmed: "But, you know, he shouldn't have been jailed in the first place because he was not guilty of anything."

Tania held her breath, waiting for the answer she expected from her mother across the table.

"He was found guilty, I'm sure."

"Sure, and it was a set up 'cause most people know that girl was frontin'," he said as diplomatically as he could.

He had to straighten Mrs Heywoode out on that. He added:

"Because he came from the streets, Mike's life has become a symbol to all the young kids. He made it and he's remained true to himself, he didn't sell out. It's a story that's really powerful with the young kids back in the projects."

"Personally, I think boxing should be banned anyway; it is much too violent, but never mind. Should we pass in the living room for coffee?" Mrs Heywoode got up from the table, her husband did likewise. Jaimie wasn't going to be left behind. As he stood up his eyes caught Tania's discreet smile towards him. It was a good sign, he thought.

Jaimie was impressed by the size and the beauty of the living room. He didn't know much about antiques but he guessed there were some pricey ones there. The maid was waiting with an ornamental pot of coffee. Tania took milk with hers, her mother drank it black without sugar. Jaimie, seated comfortably across from the two women, declined. He never drank coffee, as even the smallest cupful could keep him awake all night.

"Jaimie, I have something much better than that coffee. What do you know about cognac?" Mr Heywoode said, getting up and going to the brown wooden drinks cabinet.

"Apart from Hennessy, not much I'm afraid, sir."

And downing ounces of a liquor does not a connoisseur make.

Just then, Eddie stepped in, quiet and sharp as ever, minus his shades. He stood to attention waiting patiently to catch his boss' eye. Mr Heywoode turned to him.

"Should I bring the car in sir?" Eddie asked.

He had not even glanced at Jaimie since entering the room.

"Not yet; I need to send you out later."

Eddie nodded before disappearing. Mr Heywoode returned to

his guest.

"This is something I brought back from France last year. I bought a couple of bottles from an old peasant in the countryside."

Jaimie looked at the dark glass ringed-top beer bottle. It looked like bootleg stuff if there ever was! Then Mr Heywoode filled the two small 'shot' glasses on the coffee table. Mrs Heywoode was sipping her black coffee, taking in the TV, not really sharing the experience. Tania also, but she seemed mildly amused at her father's enthusiasm for his foreign brew. Somehow Jaimie was sure the two women were watching him.

"Taste it!" Mr Heywoode told Jaimie, sipping from his drink. He swallowed, then coughed appreciatively. The smell of the liquor hit Jaimie as he brought the glass to his mouth. He sipped a little of the colourless liquid. For a second, as it ran down his throat, he recognised a fruity aroma, maybe pear, then very quickly a line of fire travelled down his digestive tube, into his stomach. He coughed, tried to contain it, coughed again, saw the two women's identical expression, something in their slanted eyes that spelled, 'You been caught, sucker!' He smiled bravely when Mr Heywoode asked:

"What d'you think?"

"Pretty good," he nodded, his chest on fire.

This was no Hennessy or malt liquor! Mr Heywoode sat back and warmed up the remaining half of his glass in his hand, Jaimie replaced his on the table, thinking of the best way to avoid finishing it.

Fortunately the phone rang. Tania started to get up.

"Finish your coffee, I'll get it," Mrs Heywoode told her. She got up and walked to the shelf near the grandfather clock. *'Siege this morning in a south London street...'* the woman on the TV was saying.

"Hello...hello..."

Mrs Heywoode replaced the receiver. She shrugged, came back to sit down, then it started ringing again. Mr Heywoode took his eyes off the screen, looked at the telephone. He got up. His wife's eyes followed him, so did Jaimie's.

"Hello...yes..."

Mr Heywoode replaced the phone after a few moments, having said nothing more. He sat back down, picked up his glass, took a sip. He was acting perfectly normal and Jaimie couldn't read much on a face as impenetrable as his, but he could feel something, a

140

subtle change of atmosphere in the room. He didn't catch Mrs Heywoode's swift eye contact with her husband. She said:

"Tania, why don't you show Jaimie around. I'm sure he would love to see the whole house."

"Yes, OK." Tania stood up.

Jaimie too.

"It's a listed historical mansion, you know," Mrs Heywoode pointed out to him.

"You have a beautiful place here," Jaimie said and followed Tania. He was happy to escape the liquor and for a little time out with Tania. She led the way up the staircase.

"There are five bedrooms upstairs, two bathrooms, one at each end of the landing," she said.

Through the window at the top of the stairs, Jaimie could see his car parked in the courtyard and the shaven-headed guard with the dogs on his way towards the back of the house. He turned back to Tania.

"Does your mother know about the situation? She seems so cool..."

"You know, my mother went through really difficult times. She does not scare easy, but...no, she doesn't know much and she doesn't ask."

"I bet she's asking your father about that phone call though," Jaimie said.

"Come and see the guest rooms."

She took him right to the end of the landing, opened the door to a lovely large bathroom with an oval bath tub and gold taps and trimmings.

"I really have to come and spend the weekend here some time. What d'you think?" Jaimie asked Tania as she closed the door again.

He was leaning against the wall, quite close, close enough to smell the fragrance of her perfume. She gave him a knowing smile.

"You think that because you had dinner with my parents, you've got it made. How sly of you!"

He laughed.

"I wouldn't say I have it made, but things are looking better than yesterday! You didn't call me so I had to change strategy. How many guys have made it to the dinner table?"

She shook her head, moved away.

141

"This is the main guest room." She opened the next door.

Jaimie was impressed. The windows looked out on the garden, the carpet was thick and the four-poster bed with its drapes stood high and majestic.

"This is really nice, very big, lots of room..."

He'd moved close to her again, and she didn't seem to mind.

"Which one is your room?" Jaimie asked.

"Why?"

"I'm just curious."

"Yes, you are... This is my parents' room." She pointed to the door opposite. "I don't sleep on this floor." They walked back towards the stairs.

"Are you gonna show me your room?"

"Certainly not!"

"Why not?" he pressed on.

"Because a woman's bedroom is a very private place."

"And a man's bedroom too, but I'd let you see my room if you asked."

"Yes, I bet you would..." Tania said, with a suspicious glance. He stopped her by the window.

"You haven't told me about the man with the jacket."

She smiled.

"There's nothing to tell. He's a friend."

They stood in the semi-darkness, on either side of the window frame. Outside, the garden lights threw shadows across the grave drive. Jaimie was struck by a feeling of intimacy.

"I'm asking if that's the man. You could at least tell me..."

Tania laughed lightly.

"Why do you want to know? And why do you think I have a man anyway? Can't I be single?"

"Single?!" Jaimie exclaimed. "A woman like you can't be single, shouldn't be single. That's a crime! So...is he?"

She sighed.

"I've known Bernard for a long time, since secondary school. He's a very bright person and he's always ready to help."

"Bernard! Man, that's some name."

"You would like him, he's very nice."

"Sure, Donald Duck is nice, but I can't quite picture you with him."

"You know, you shouldn't be like that," she said admonishingly.

142

"I have to be like that." He crossed the divide and stepped closer to her side of the window. "I spent two weeks trying to get your picture out of my mind, but it didn't work, so I decided to follow my inclination. You see..."

"Your...inclination..." she repeated.

Jaimie stood over her now, close, but his arms by his side, not touching her. He expected her to move away but she didn't.

"That's right; I've got this really strong attraction that keeps drawing me to you."

"Really? Since when?"

"Since...since the day I crashed...sorry, you crashed into my car. I can say that you crashed into my life!"

She laughed.

"You didn't like me that day."

He edged a little bit closer, her eyes didn't shift away as he looked into them.

"You were obnoxious that day."

"Oh really?" she said, ready to step back but he took hold of one of her hands, gently.

"Listen, I couldn't see the real you, because the first few times you were really difficult to talk to, but I can sincerely say I have always liked you." He added: "In fact, you're the nicest woman I have met since I arrived in this country."

This time, she grinned dismissively.

"Go away, flattery won't get you anywhere."

"Maybe not, but I mean it."

"Well, I think you are a nice person too."

"So how come you didn't even call me once?"

"I couldn't."

"Because of him?"

She laughed quietly. "Don't be silly?"

"You burned my number?"

"No, I didn't." She could see he was waiting for an answer. "I was sick," she said seriously.

"Seriously? Sorry, I didn't know. What was it?"

She hesitated before answering.

"It's just something I suffer from, it comes and goes...I'm alright now."

Jaimie felt her pull out the hand he was still holding. He let it go.

"Are you afraid of me?" he asked.

"I've never been afraid of anyone. I'm keeping my distance with you, which is not the same thing."

"Why's that?"

She took a little time to answer, glanced away then said:

"It sounds bad, maybe I shouldn't say it like this...there's a lot of things you don't know about me."

"OK, but there's a lot you don't know about me too," he pointed out. "That's why we should get closer..."

"Jaimie..." He liked the way she called his name, but her face was serious. "I think you're a nice person, and I'm glad to have you as a friend..."

He waited for the 'but'. Tania sighed.

"...But I don't think you should see me as anything else. It's not to be."

Jaimie raised his eyebrows.

"What 'is not to be'?" he repeated. "Why couldn't you see yourself with a man like me?"

Suddenly she was almost apologetic.

"Please, don't take it personally, I only meant we're not really compatible..."

"How do you know?" he asked. "I feel good when I'm with you. What about you?"

Tania sighed and gazed out of the window towards the gates of the mansion where two men in suits were casually leaning on the Mercedes, chatting and smoking. Then she turned to Jaimie. He sensed she was holding something back. Searching into her eyes, he said:

"I feel there is something between us. I just need to know if I'm mistaken or if you feel it too."

They held each other's gaze for a few seconds. Then she said in a low voice: "It's nothing to do with us as people, it's just..."

"Tania!" a voice called from downstairs.

Jaimie sighed: "Your father's checking up on you!"

"No he isn't, he trusts me."

Jaimie rolled his eyes like a schizo. "Yes, but does he trust me?"

Tania laughed.

"Come on, let's go back down."

Jaimie followed her. At the bottom of the stairs, Mr Heywoode was holding the telephone.

"Millie's on the line for you."

Tania took the phone. Mr Heywoode turned to Jaimie with a proud smile.

"What do you think?" he asked.

"Very stylish, I like it." Jaimie looked about the house impressively.

"Come with me."

They left Tania with her call and Jaimie followed his host out, around the back to the garage area, past the neat rows of tomato plants and peas.

"You do the gardening yourself?"

Mr Heywoode laughed as he lifted one of the garage shutters.

"Oh I'm much too busy for that. That's Tania's corner."

"Really?" Jaimie couldn't believe it. This was yet another side of her personality.

"Voila!"

Mr Heywoode stood by the open shutter. Jaimie recognised the classic shape right away, the same as in the picture. At first sight the black of the original paintwork had lost its lustre and the chrome needed polishing but the car looked impressive under the garage neons all the same.

"Let's roll it out."

Mr Heywoode opened the car door, Jaimie helped him to push from the front and they eased the monster out. Jaimie admired the Plymouth's lean, powerful curves, like an animal poised to pounce. He watched Mr Heywoode lift up the bonnet on the massive engine. Dark, dried oil smudges tainted the pipes.

"It was parked for some time; someone who emigrated owned it. I traced it to the man's brother in Yorkshire. He had it in a barn..."

Mr Heywoode was shaking his head slowly in incredulous wonder. How could anyone with any feelings left in their heart keep a jewel like this car in a barn?

"It needs to be stripped down and cleaned up, then we'll see if it kicks."

"Are you very busy?" Mr Heywoode asked.

"Not that I can't get to it by next week..."

"Good, good!" Mr Heywoode seemed pleased. They pushed the Plymouth back into the garage.

"How about another beer?" Mr Heywoode offered.

"No thanks, I should be getting home, I've got work to finish."

"Oh, you're doing some overtime?"

145

Jaimie smiled. "No, I'm doing some scriptwriting."

"Oh yeah, I remember you mentioned something about that the last time. You're serious about it?"

"Yes sir; I'm definitely gonna make a movie."

Like an old reflex from his army days, he addressed Mr Heywoode as 'sir' for even with his jacket off and tie loosened, there certainly seemed to be something of the officer about him.

"How much money do you think you're going to need?"

The question almost surprised Jaimie. He shrugged:

"This producer guy I'm talking to says it can be made for a million pounds."

"A million pounds..."

Jaimie nodded.

"How much would it recoup?"

"Maybe five in this country...I'm guessing. Why, you thinking of getting into movies?"

Mr Heywoode smiled.

"I know a few people in Hollywood...I can't say I have really thought about it seriously, but then again, all it takes is one film, right?"

"Right."

Tania appeared from inside wearing a little grin on her face.

"Is he going to save the car?"

"It's all up to him now, he's the car doctor."

Jaimie laughed at the joke.

"Yes, I'm on the case. I was just telling your father I should be on my way."

Mr Heywoode rubbed the back of his neck, inhaled the cool night air. He seemed in deep thought for a few seconds. Then:

"I'll see you next week then?"

"You most definitely will. Have a nice evening, sir."

'There I go again!' he thought as he turned to follow Tania. They walked together alongside the rows of tomatoes.

"I didn't know you could grow vegetables..."

She smiled modestly.

"My father thinks it's hard work, but they grow easily." Tania looked up at him. "Why are you grinning like that?"

He was about to answer but she shook her head with a knowing smile.

"So, how many guys have come here to dinner before me?"

She shook her head again without answering.

"OK, you see my point," he laughed, then remembered something. "Oh, before I forget, I want you to come somewhere with me next Saturday. This is official."

"Where? Another jungle rave?"

Jaimie caught her snide remark.

"Come on, you love it! No, this is serious. My friend Tony, you remember Tony? Yeah, well, he's having a naming ceremony for his young daughter."

"Really?"

He smiled.

"Yeah, really. So I want you to come with me so everybody can see what a nice couple we make."

"You'd better stop that," she told him, half-serious.

"How about it? Come along. It's gonna be fun."

"Yo, Jaimie!"

Out of the darkness of the garden, Carl bounced into view, waving. From under his baseball cap, a bright smile shone through.

"Hey, you can bring Carl along too."

"Bring him?" Tania dismissed the idea, laughing. "Not if it's a formal occasion like you said! And anywhere rap doesn't play, Carl doesn't go."

"Lighten up, I think you're too hard on him. That kid's got a lot of potential."

The 'kid' reached them and offered a ghetto greeting to Jaimie, said, "What's up, Tan?" to his sister, stood there, tall for his fifteen years, grinning.

"I was just leaving," Jaimie said. "I've been here a while!"

"Really? Oh man, I wanted to talk to you about some tracks I'm working on... Yeah, I'm kicking rhymes..."

"Oh my God!" Tania winced.

But Carl wasn't joking; he had already pulled a cassette out of his jeans pocket.

"Maybe you could help me."

You could tell it meant a lot to Carl. Jaimie was about to reassure the young hopeful artist when a glance at Tania's face stopped him. She was staring towards the gate where one of the guards was shouting something. The other rushed to the Mercedes where Luke, the dog-man, was pulling on the leashes of his growling beasts. The man who had shouted left Luke and the dogs and ran to Tania. He

147

must have been in his late twenties, with strong open features which right now expressed nothing but fear. Short of breath the man said one word to Tania. Jaimie had never seen her face like that before, eyes frozen. Tania asked something in their language, and the man repeated his one word. Then Tania started towards the gate.

"Hey, what's up?" Jaimie called out. But Tania was already gone, the guard close behind. Whatever it was, it was scaring the hell out of the guards. Jaimie looked at Carl and started after Tania just as Mr Heywoode appeared at the front porch.

"What's going on?!" he called out heading hastily towards the gate with surprising swiftness.

With a terrified look on his face, the guard was pointing to something on the bonnet of the Mercedes. Tania stood staring at the object, motionless. Eddie who had sprinted after his boss, alerted by the shouting, froze by the car and drew a breath, for once losing his cool. Mr Heywoode's face was expressionless, focused on the small green lizard like he'd never seen one before. Behind Tania, the voice of the guard repeated his word again, this time in a low groan. Luke had to flex his muscles to keep hold of the canine monsters, barking wildly. Six men, a teenager, one woman and two nervous dogs all staring at a small, motionless creature. For a while, no one said anything. Jaimie looked at Tania, then at her father but they were both perfectly still. It was Carl who asked the right question.

"Is it dead?"

"No," Tania said almost normally. "Give me your handkerchief."

Carl frowned, puzzled. Tania was stretching out to him, so he dug in the back pocket of his wide jeans, pulled out a white and black bandanna and was about to replace it on second thoughts, when Tania grabbed it and turned towards the bonnet.

"Hey, that's not a handkerchief, that's my bandanna!" he protested, but it was too late. Tania folded the square of cloth and walked around the bonnet. She was now behind the immobile lizard, her eyes studiously watching it. She bent forward over it. In the background the guard said that word again. Very naturally, very gently, Tania picked up the reptile in the fold of the bandanna, lifted it up, then turned it around to face her. Her face was grave but her voice didn't betray her thoughts when she said:

"Carl, take it and put it in something in the garden. Don't let it

148

die."

"What?"

Carl saw something on her sister's face that cut his protests short. Ignoring the muffled warnings of the guard he took the animal from Tania and walked off into the semi-darkness of the garden. Tania walked back around the car. Mr Heywoode fired a few rapid questions at the two guards in their language. Both shook their heads. Eddie spoke to them in a harsh tone of voice, but they answered him plaintively, the braver of the two trying to get an answer out of their boss. Mr Heywoode glanced at him then finally nodded. The two guards moved as one man, half-walking, half-jogging towards the back of the house. Jaimie turned to Tania. She seemed deep in thought. He waited a little, unsure as to what his first question should be. He was still a little phased by the whole incident and didn't quite know what to make of it.

"Uh, what's up with the guards?" he asked.

Tania turned to him and said quite naturally:

"They are so superstitious!"

CHAPTER NINE

One soca, two socas, three socas. A section of the little groups of guests 'chilling out' in the garden, politely voiced their disapproval. Someone from inside the lounge called out, "Jungle!" Another, gruffer voice shouted, "Shabba!" Laughter all around. Tony's young cousin who was taking care of the music had so far managed to satisfy his public. Night wasn't upon them yet, nevertheless the occasion had turned out really nice and relaxed. The warm September weather continued, a mellow evening breeze had followed a splendid afternoon sun. A good time was being had by all. Tony's mother had been hovering around throughout, ensuring that everyone was taken care of. Tony had been heard to call out, "Rest yourself, Mom!" several times during the afternoon but the excitement of her grand-daughter's naming ceremony had charged up her energy. Jaimie watched her fussing over everyone, insisting that everyone take another piece of the cake she'd baked.

"Jaimie, what you doin' hiding? You want some more chicken...some left, you know!"

Tony's mother was as grey as she was vivacious, small in size but with inner strength and a great sense of humour. She had immediately taken to Jaimie when Tony brought him home one day and now, a year later, he was like a member of the family and as she did with her son, she thought nothing of delivering a sermon to Jaimie on any topic. He always listened respectfully and they usually agreed on most things. Tony had great fun watching his mother trying to arrange Jaimie's life and head like she'd done with him.

Tony's mother had won the battle of the naming ceremony party. After careful consideration, Charlene was forced to acknowledge that as so few of their friends and relations would travel all the way to Wolverhampton where her mother lived, the best alternative was Tony's mother's house. Charlene's mother stuck to her guns (figuratively speaking) for two whole days. After that Tony's mother took control of the whole thing. It was all happening very nicely. Jaimie even saw Charlene's mother smile once or twice. Not at him though, mind you. The good part had really been the actual ceremony.

150

Although the invitations said '3pm', things didn't really start until an hour later. All the parties essential to the naming ceremony were present, so everyone took their position on the rows of chairs arranged in the lounge. Jaimie sat in the third row alongside his party. Besides Junior, Carl and Tania, Millie was there also, Tania having told Jaimie how much her cousin wanted to attend and he said she was welcome. Feeling neat in his two-piece white linen suit, Jaimie sat between the two women, with Carl to the right of his sister and Junior on the other side of Millie. Carl the 'homeboy', forewarned by his sister that he would only come if formally dressed, was wearing a very proper Click suit in two tones of blue that she couldn't object to. Tania herself, fashion conscious as always, looked very nice in a white suit with green geometrical patterns. Hardly by coincidence, Millie had on a light green dress with white trimmings. Jaimie felt proud of being with them. Facing the guests, Tony and Charlene sat on two armchairs, the tiny little baby asleep in her mother's arms. Tony's dark suit and tie contrasted happily with his wife's red and black dress. In the first row, from left to right were Charlene's mother, her two sisters, then Tony's sister, his mother and, at the end of the row, his father. Though separated from his wife for several years, he was always close to the family for the separation had never been that real. Tony's parents were like many first generation immigrant couples who, though they experienced storms in their union over the years, nevertheless knew there was always enough of the original love which had brought them over left to make it work. Charlene's own father had passed away a few years earlier.

In the second, third and fourth rows sat an assortment of cousins, aunts and uncles, nephews and nieces and close family friends. All together, around forty persons witnessed the event.

After greeting his guests, Tony said a few words to explain the significance of the occasion, briefly summing up the African custom of naming a new born child and stressing its importance for his/her future. He diplomatically avoided the contention which had divided both families, only mentioning that he believed God's presence was guaranteed by the goodwill and prayers of all those assembled. The baby, pretty in her frilly white dress had fallen asleep. Tony's mother was heard to say that it was a good sign. First, both parents read a chapter from the Bible: a psalm for Tony and a passage from the Book of Judges for Charlene. After this,

Tony announced he would first tell his daughter the names he and Charlene had chosen for her, then declare them to the audience. Since not even the two grandmothers had been privy to the choice, there was some anticipation on both parts. So the little girl was gently awakened by her mother. Tony took her up and whispered a few words in her ear, kissed her before holding her up to the audience as he said:

"She will be named Amani Maryam Ella."

Comments arose from the seated guests and it was Charlene who then explained the reasons for their choices.

"Amani, her first name, means wishes or aspirations, because this is our first child and she represents our aspirations. We named her Maryam after the mother of Jesus, because she was blessed in having a special child. Finally her third name will be Ella, like the great jazz singer Ella Fitzgerald, a great artist and a strong black woman." Charlene paused, then with a little grin, declared:

"Ella also happens to be my mother's name..."

Everyone applauded. The honoured grandmother tried to repress a proud smile but both parents saw it and knew they had made the right decision, as it was essential that all should feel pleased with the names given. The little girl herself was by now smiling, which was taken as a sure sign that she liked her names. Then the parents invited the guests to pronounce a blessing over the child, starting with the grandmothers and grandfather. So, one by one, every person present in the room approached the baby and spoke a few words over the child. Jaimie caught Tania's apprehensive look when Carl took his turn but the 'homeboy' spoke well and intelligently. Once it was over, Tony's mother invited the guests to partake of the buffet. A few more people had arrived meanwhile and had quietly taken seats at the back. Now everyone made their way to the dining room next door and honoured the food and drinks provided, while in the background soft music played.

Jaimie smiled:

"No, thank you Ma, I'm really full."

She squinted at him.

"Full? You a big man; you can't full so easy! Have a piece of cake..."

Rather than protest again, Jaimie took another piece of cake. She said:

"Your girlfriend looks nice. I hope you're going to do like Tony and settle down."

Jaimie smiled broadly at the diminutive woman with the piercing eyes. He placed one hand on her shoulder and instead of pointing out that the nice girl wasn't exactly his girl, he said:

"You know, I'm really proud of Tony, and I guess you too, especially you, can be proud of him. I hope to be able to follow in his footsteps, some day, soon maybe."

Tony's mother was glad. She knew it was sincere.

"Good, good. You want another drink?"

"No, thanks. This one's still new."

She smiled and left him there, walked on through into the lounge. Jaimie took a deep breath, looked around the garden at the well-dressed men and women, enjoying themselves and celebrating life, as much as the specific occasion of the naming ceremony. It was all part of the cycle of human life anywhere, this gathering of family, clan or nation. Events like this gave meaning to one's life. "Life gives life," Jaimie repeated to himself several times, the words taking on a deeper meaning each time. He was discovering, or rather experiencing, right there and then that he still felt very much alive inside and, maybe for the first time in many years, he was feeling good about himself. At moments like these, life could be so sweet. Through the open sliding door, Carl appeared, bottle of beer in one hand, a piece of cake in the other. He stepped down, looking sharp in his blue suit. Jaimie laughed:

"I can't understand how you're so skinny and you eat like a bear, man!"

Carl laughed also.

"Did you taste this curry goat thing? It's wicked!"

Apparently, the youth had already eaten two plates of the dish.

"Tania OK?" Jaimie asked.

Carl nodded, swallowing a bite of his cake. "Yeah, she's gone upstairs with Tony's wife to change the baby...I checked out the guy playing the music; he's got some jungle tracks but he doesn't want to play them until later."

Jaimie nodded, taking a swig of his beer. He knew Tony's mother had given strict orders as to what music shouldn't be played in her house, well aware of the content of some of the popular records of the day. The one playing just now was safe enough: 'R.E.S.P.E.C.T' was what Aretha Franklin was talking about.

153

"What about my tracks, Jaimie. When you gonna check me?"

Jaimie studied the youngster for a moment.

"So you wanna be a rapper?"

"I have lyrics, my friends say I'm good..."

Jaimie downed some beer. "Maybe you are, but it's not that easy. There are thousands of kids out there who want to be rappers too. Most of them don't really know why, it just seems to be the way to make some fast money. You gotta know what you getting into."

"How did you start?"

The youngster seemed eager to learn, but what could Jaimie tell him?

"I never was a rapper, I'm a DJ. DJs started hip hop music. The first man who started scratching was a Jamaican called Kool Herc. There were other guys before him, like Grandmaster Flowers and Pete Jones who used to mix Philly R&B choruses with party tracks in the early seventies, DJ Hollywood and a few other. But Herc was the one who invented 'break beats' at block parties in the Bronx. That's the foundation of hip hop music. After him you had Afrika Bambaataa, ex-gang leader in the Black Spades, who founded the Universal Zulu Nation in the South Bronx. He did that to stop the wars that were killing a lot of kids. A lot of gang members followed him and got into hip hop at that time. When Bambaataa played at the Roxy in downtown Manhattan, you had celebrities, rappers, break-dancers, graffiti artists, hustlers; everybody wanted to be down with hip hop. Hip hop was a free-form expression then. Everything was progressive. At the Roxy, you'd get all styles of music, but it wasn't just music; it was art, fashion, dance. It was a unique time, man."

Carl was listening avidly.

"That was the old school, right?" he asked.

"The old school, yeah. Back in the day, the first hip hop MCs were Melle Mel, Kurtis Blow, Busy Bee, Afrika Bambaataa, The Furious Five, The Treacherous Three, Cold Crush Brothers... You ever heard of Grandmaster Flash's *The Message*? That was the beginning of what they now call 'reality rap'. Those were the days..."

Jaimie caught himself feeling almost old as he said it. Remembering was making him feel warm inside. Those days were his beginnings, when he used to roam the city following the music, getting involved with older DJs, MCs, hustlers and players. He

154

could still recall the rush he felt walking inside those packed block parties.

"That's what I wanna do: reality-rap," Carl said.

"Reality rap, yeah. At first everything was reality rap because hip hop was born in a period when life was getting harder in the States. The kids started talking about it, talking about their lives in the projects, poverty, racism, police brutality. That's what hip hop is meant to 'represent', the rappers are supposed to be speaking for those who don't get heard."

"What about gangster rap?"

Jaimie sipped a little beer, observing the would-be rapper. He paused a little, choosing his words carefully.

"Gangster rap is something that the media created, that was what people like Afrika Bambaataa were trying to fight against. Check this out: back in those days, people did what they did to get attention but nowadays people are just in it for the dollar. When the record companies realised rap was big business, they started to market personalities. It wasn't about promoting the music anymore. They encouraged those young rappers who had talent to live up to the gang member image. That's what's been happening. They don't really care if kids end up dead or in jail, they're selling records and making themselves a lot of money. The kids who listened to hip hop at first weren't gangsters, but after a while they started to act out what the records were talking about. When I started out, an MC was supposed to move the crowd but not towards violence. Originally, hip hop stood for peace, you know what I'm saying?"

Carl seemed impressed by it all. He nodded. He would have questioned Jaimie further if his sister hadn't stepped into the garden and spotted them. Jaimie caught himself thinking how sweet she looked.

"How's the diaper changing going?" he asked.

She smiled.

"Fine, thank you. Carl, how many beers have you had?"

Carl had drunk enough to make him feel he was a big man. He said dismissively:

"This is nothing to me, it's light."

Jaimie laughed.

"Yeah, until it catches you by surprise."

"He came home drunk one night last month, you know!" Tania told Jaimie with a disdainful glance at her brother.

"I wasn't drunk," Carl protested.

"You were singing in the kitchen at two in the morning!" she pointed out mercilessly.

"I was just happy."

Jaimie and Tania exchanged a knowing smile.

One record ended, the first bars of Percy Sledge's *When A Man Loves A Woman* rang out. Carl shook his head and sighed dejectedly.

"I'm gonna check the DJ," he said, and walked back inside.

Jaimie looked at Tania admiringly.

"You wanna dance?"

She raised her eyebrows.

"I don't do that kind of thing."

He laughed.

"Are you enjoying the party?"

"Yes, thank you for inviting me."

"I'm glad you came."

Jaimie could feel Tania was relaxed.

"Would you like some wine?"

"No thank you, I had two glasses of champagne and that's my limit."

Millie, Junior and Tony came out in the garden.

"Don't they make a beautiful couple?" Tony asked Junior.

"Yeah, that's what I was telling him," Junior grinned.

Tania didn't comment on it, so neither did Jaimie.

"Everything worked out well," he remarked to Tony.

"Yeah, I didn't know so many people would turn up but everybody's having a good time."

Millie was sipping something which looked like whisky and explained her detached smile. She and Junior looked like they had become good friends. Two young women came up and called out to Tony, asking him if the DJ was going to play any jungle. Tony said he would make sure he did. One of them, slim with a bob hair style, threw Jaimie a clearly seductive look.

Dusk was slowly descending on the garden. The music had gone uptempo and funky, attracting the younger guests into the lounge for a 'shakedown'. Millie giggled as Junior whispered something in her ear. When Junior disappeared inside and while Tania was talking to Tony, Jaimie sidled up to her.

"Having a good time?"

She smiled.

156

"Oh yes. What about you?"

Jaimie nodded.

"I'm OK."

She looked across to her cousin. "How is it going?" she asked Jaimie, nodding in Tania's direction.

Jaimie noticed the amused glint in her eyes.

"It's hard to tell. I was hoping you could help me out maybe..."

"Help you out?"

He kept his voice low, just in case.

"I can't get much out of her. She's being nice to me but at the same time she's keeping her distance."

Millie shrugged.

"Tania is not easy to understand. I'm probably the closest person to her but even I can't always figure out the way she thinks."

Jaimie emptied his beer.

"Check out the situation: I'm trying to get through to her but it's not easy for me because I don't want to get too heavy, you know what I'm saying? I mean she's probably not used to guys like me, in fact I don't know what she's used to."

Millie laughed, tried to contain herself but laughed heartily under Jaimie's perplexed look.

"What's funny?" he asked.

"I'm sorry, I'm not laughing at you," she paused and observed him.

"You really like her?"

"Yeah, she's got something..."

He glanced towards Tania, now involved in a three way conversation with Tony and one of his woman friends.

"...Maybe you can straighten me up on something," Jaimie continued. "There's a guy I saw with her once outside her office, Geràrd or something like that, kind of a colourful dresser with glasses. Is he her fiancé or something?"

Millie started laughing again.

"Take it easy, what did I say?"

"It's just the way you said it. I know who you're talking about: Bernard is his name."

"Bernard...right."

"Bernard is the son of the ex-ambassador to the USA. They've known each other since school."

"Sure, but what's his position?"

157

Millie stole a glance at her cousin. She said: "You're going to get me in trouble."

"Why?"

"Because Tania trusts me and she wouldn't like me to divulge details of her private life."

Jaimie looked at the young woman with a penetrating look.

"Come on, Millie. You know I like her and I'm trying, but for all I know I could be wasting my time. I mean, she's a society girl and maybe she's not taking me seriously, but I'm gonna play my cards all the same. I just need you to gimme a little insight."

Millie shook her head.

"You're a dangerous man, Jaimie," she smiled. "OK, there's a lot you're going to have to find out for yourself but all I can tell you is that Bernard is the man her parents would like her to marry. He comes from a very good family."

Jaimie thought about that for a moment. He recalled something Tania had said.

"Am I right in thinking that this 'class' thing is working against me?"

Millie thought about the best way to put it.

"You know, I guess every nation has its race and class prejudices. For us, because of our particular background, we grew up with a certain mentality. That's why our parents would look at a man like Bernard as the ideal husband for their daughters. Do you understand?"

"Sure, I understand. But does she love him?"

Millie pulled an enigmatic face.

"You'll have to ask her yourself."

Jaimie sighed:

"Thanks, I know that you know but you're holding back on me. I thought we were friends."

"We are, but Tania trusts me, so it wouldn't be right for me to reveal her secrets."

Jaimie looked a little dejected, or he feigned to be, and what she added couldn't make him feel any better.

"You know, Jaimie, I don't mean to discourage you, but you're going to have a real hard time to get through to Tania. She's a special woman."

"She's a wall of silence," he answered.

Junior reappeared with drinks. A glass of wine for Tania, one to

158

Millie and a beer to Jaimie. Tania tried to refuse but Junior, with his most amicable smile, insisted, telling her that she had nothing to worry about as his big brother would see her home safely. Then he and Millie disappeared inside the room as the long-awaited jungle rhythm started to play. Jaimie and Tania peeped through the sliding garden door and watched the dancing inside. Sure enough, Carl was in the middle, deftly executing his moves. Loosened by the liquor and encouraged by Junior, Millie was trying also, and getting the hang of it. Tania declined Jaimie's offer to show what she could do but dared him to join in, so he went inside and did his stuff. She laughed at his antics as he and Carl worked up a sweat but, she told him after, she thought he was quite good at it. It was now dark outside. Several of the older guests had already left but the party crowd was asking for more. The DJ responded to persistent requests and let off some reggae tunes. Jaimie finally convinced Tania to show her dancing skills on a crossover Shabba record and then on a ragga rhythm too. Jaimie was pleased to discover that she could hold her own on the dancefloor. After, as they sat in the dining area, he remarked:

"I know what it is with you; you're not shy but you're a very private person. You like to keep everything about you private, right?"

"I see you're still trying to analyse me."

"I've got to. I'm being kept in the dark here."

Tania smiled and shook her head. Carl came and said something to her. She answered but he insisted. Then he turned to Jaimie and said to him above the noise of the music:

"I want to go and meet my friends at a youth club. They have a session down there, but Tania says I've got to go home with her. Can you talk to her for me?"

Carl assumed that Jaimie had a certain influence on his sister. Not wanting to let the youngster down, he plead on his behalf, but Tania said that their mother wouldn't approve, not to mention their father who had become so preoccupied with security that he had insisted on Eddie and two other guards accompanying them to Tony's house. Eddie was to return for them when they were ready to go home.

Right now Jaimie felt an impulse to drive Tania off somewhere where they could be alone. He couldn't remember ever having had this strong a vibe about a woman since he'd arrived in England a

159

year or so earlier. Apparently, he was no longer as cynical about women as he previously thought. There was something in this one, or was he tripping? He leaned towards Tania.

"Why don't you give him a break; let him go."

"I can't, I have to keep an eye on him."

"He can take care of himself. Let him check out that jungle dance."

"Listen, Carl might look harmless to you but he's crazy. Things always happen to him." Tania added as an after thought, "And my father expects us back together."

Jaimie thought for a moment, then came up with a compromise:

"I have a great idea; why don't we take him there?"

Tania was thinking. "So are you ready to leave?"

He smiled.

"Leave here, yes. But I'm not ready to leave you."

Tania's face had that blank expression he'd learned to recognise, which masked how she really felt about things. A heavy hand on his shoulder spoiled the vibe of the moment.

"How's things, Jaimie?"

Junior stood in front of him, grinning confidently. He had come to ask a favour. Jaimie had always been able to 'read' his brother's intentions on his face.

"Not too bad. I see you're having fun..."

"Yeah man, this party's kicking."

Jaimie watched him, waiting. Junior had something on his mind.

"Yo, Jaimie man, what's your plan?"

"Why?" was Jaimie's cautious reply, because whatever plan he might have would definitely not include Junior and secondly because he asked, he had to be scheming something himself. And Jaimie had an idea what it was.

"Can you lend me your car keys?"

"Lend you my car keys? Do I usually lend my car keys to someone who drives like you do?"

"I wanna go home and get some records," Junior pleaded.

Jaimie looked at him.

"Junior, why d'you always try to lie to me? It ain't got nothing to do with music."

Junior shook his head, smiled.

"Jaimie man, don't be like that."

"I seen you, man, hanging out with Tania's cousin, real smooth.

160

I know what you're thinking, Junior, but forget it."

Junior smiled almost unconsciously as Millie came over and went to Tania.

"What are you talking about, Jaimie, we're just having a nice time. She doesn't go out much, she's enjoying herself."

"Hm-hm, so what's up with my car keys?"

"I was just gonna pick up some music with her and come back."

Jaimie sighed and shook his head with a sad look.

"Junior..."

"What?"

"You are a slimy snake."

"Come on Jaimie..."

Jaimie interrupted at him.

"You better say good night to that girl and go home to Lorraine."

"Lorraine's by her mother in Chester until Thursday."

"Right, you..."

Junior stopped him.

"Anyway, I don't know why you're talking about me; I know what's going down on your side."

Jaimie fixed him, growled quietly.

"Oh yeah, what's going down?"

Junior pulled a face then said:

"Not much, from what I hear..."

Then he burst out laughing, laughing like it was a great joke to him. Jaimie quickly reflected that Junior had been picking Millie's brain. His next thought was that Junior might in fact have learned the things which he needed to know or might at least be able to find things out."

"Junior, Junior, talk to me..." Jaimie patted his brother's back, affectionately all of a sudden. "My main man!" Junior watched him, wary of this friendly tone.

Jaimie checked behind him discreetly to make sure he wasn't being overheard.

"What's the story?"

"I don't know."

"What did the cousin say about me?"

"She said you're a nice man, and I said 'yeah, that's my big brother'."

Jaimie winced at Junior's laughter.

161

"So you ain't gonna lend me the keys?"

"I'm about to bust a move."

"Oh, so you have a plan?"

Junior smirked with a suggestive grin. "But you're gonna need me."

"Need you?" Jaimie laughed. "If you're ready I'll give you a lift home, but that is it."

Junior shook his head.

"You wanna run away with that girl, I know, but she ain't gonna move without her family."

"How d'you know that?" Jaimie asked.

"Because the other one is the same, they have to stay together. So how about a deal?"

Jaimie thought quickly, Junior was right. It had to be a collective play then.

"Alright, check. Let me do this."

"Go ahead, you're the man!" Junior was happy with that.

Millie drew Junior's attention, smiling.

"You two have a strong resemblance!"

Jaimie turned away towards Tania, leaving Junior to answer her. Carl was standing by the staircase, not really down with the soul sounds.

"I have an even better idea," Jaimie told Tania. "This is the play: we all leave here and drive Carl to the jam, then we can go and chill out somewhere."

Tania hardly seemed surprised.

"Daddy is waiting for my call to send the car."

Jaimie shrugged.

"Tell Daddy, everybody's going to a restaurant and that you're safe." "Lying comes easily to you," Tania observed.

'Damn', Jaimie thought. He said: "I'm a desperate man!"

"And now you want me to lie to my father?"

Jaimie said: "It's not really lying, it's more like...adapting the truth, you know."

He saw her fix him for a short second and heard her say as she got up:

"I suppose it makes sense."

He got up too, barely looked at Junior engrossed in a conversation of his own and went through to search for Tony.

The idea worked well and Jaimie had his time alone with Tania.

Carl was dropped off at the jungle session, together with Junior and Millie who were in a dancing mood anyway. That way Carl was under supervision and Jaimie was free. Free to convince Tania that it was time she should know where he lived. He was so good at it that before she realised, she was shown in and seated inside Jaimie's lounge. He played it cool, flicking on the cable TV, then getting her some juice, programmed the CD player, dimmed the lights and was back by her side in no time. Tania turned from the screen:

"This is a classic set up, just like in the movies, don't you think?"

Jaimie smiled broadly and nodded firmly.

"Yes, it is."

She laughed. "Millie didn't tell you what you wanted to know."

He studied her profile a moment then said confidently:

"You'll be telling me all I need to know soon."

"Oh yeah?"

"Yeah."

He was close now, and she had noticed him sliding over but had not moved. Eyes set on the dancing figures on the screen, she asked:

"You sound really sure of yourself. Should I be afraid of you? After all, I am in your house."

"Yes, you are and no, you need not be afraid. You've got nothing to worry about, because we're gonna agree, me and you."

"Me and you?" she asked, as his left arm slid sneakily along the top of the couch around her shoulders.

That was as close as he'd ever gotten to her, and unsure what she was thinking, Jaimie was playing it light. He said:

"That's right, you and I, Miss Heywoode."

"You prefer to call me that?"

He grinned:

"No, I like your first name, but you see, it's all a matter of stages."

"Stages?" she repeated.

Jaimie's right hand was caressing her hand. She kept watching the screen. He spoke in a mellow tone of voice, keeping the atmosphere easy between them, prolonging it for as long as he could.

"Hm-hm, stages. At the beginning I had to be formal, firstly because you were not very warm, and also out of respect for conventions."

He paused ever so slightly, tracing his fingertip down her arm.

She still didn't move.

"But now that we're on a different level, now that we're acquainted..." Words were coming easy to him, he found. "Now that we are about to get closer..."

He saw the beginning of a smile at the corner of her mouth.

"Closer?"

"Much closer..." he whispered in her ear and felt her tense a little. "Now, I'm gonna be calling you by your first name. You're not against getting closer, are you?"

She turned to look at him.

"I shouldn't be here, you know that?"

Jaimie searched her eyes in the semi-darkness.

"I know one thing: I feel nice when I'm with you."

It was intense that deep, probing eye to eye contact, and he found it amazing when she remarked, almost matter-of-factly:

"I know that song."

Amazing because Otis Redding's *Try A Little Tenderness*, purring away through the speakers, had always been one of his all-time favourite songs, and he wanted to believe in good omens tonight.

"Otis is right, I think I'll try tenderness..." he said softly.

Keeping real close to her, he talked to her about music and she told him her tastes. Time passed. Tania reminded him that they really should pick up the others now. Under the spell of this beautiful woman he'd longed to get close to, Jaimie had completely forgotten about the others. She agreed to give it another half an hour, so that they kept talking. They got up to leave, as Aaron Neville's *Tell It Like It Is* floated around the room:

"You believe in fate?" Jaimie asked.

She looked at him curiously.

"What made you ask that?"

He shrugged.

"I don't know. It's just that I feel comfortable with you, and I find I can talk to you like I've known you all my life. Maybe it was my fate to meet you."

She didn't answer directly.

"You know, I'm starting to think you crashed into my car on purpose..."

All Sunday, Jaimie hung around the house, doing nothing more than watch TV, eat and smile a lot. He'd woken up smiling and hardly noticed the rain outside. Funny what a woman can do... He sat down to do a little polishing to the script he'd been working on but realised that it didn't need any more. He kept going back in his mind to the previous day and especially the moment when Tania kissed him on the cheek as they were leaving. One little light peck, that was it and there he was, already thinking ahead, making plans. 'Get a hold on yourself, homes!' Jaimie told himself. But he felt nice, so he programmed the CD player and went about the house, grooving to the swingbeat sounds. In the afternoon, Junior called to say he would pass by later. He didn't.

Monday morning was dry, not very warm but still bright. At the garage, things were a little slow. The day went fast and by five, Jaimie checked out and drove home to change. There was to be a cocktail party at Tania's office the following Friday and to his delight she'd asked him if he would like to come along. Now that had to be a good sign. He accepted, of course. Since it was to be a formal occasion, Jaimie wanted to look the part. Then Tania said that she also had some shopping to do and the next thing, they decided to do it together. It was just too nice, the way things were running smoothly between them recently. There he was, dancing to the hardcore beat in his bedroom, like a little kid out on his first block party, and picking out some white slacks and a blue shirt from the wardrobe. One last look in the mirror. As he admired himself, he thought about Tania's remark that he should let his hair grow. He'd kept his head near-shaven ever since going inside. Now, on one little remark from a pretty woman he was about to change something as fundamental to his style as that! How fickle a man could be, he reflected, how easily led by a smile. The next thing she'd be asking him to grow an Afro! He laughed to himself at the thought of it, laughing all the way down the stairs.

Parking in town was an expensive business. Jaimie dropped in another pound coin; two hours should be more than enough. He adjusted his dark glasses, checked his watch; he was only a few minutes late. As he stepped around the corner onto Kensington High Street, it was as busy as any weekday, with people returning home from work or window-shopping.

He looked up and saw the white Mercedes, double-parked as usual. Jaimie scanned through the crowd and spotted Tania walking to the car, a burly man in a white short-sleeved shirt whose face Jaimie couldn't see, beside her. They were about twenty yards away. Jaimie saw Eddie, standing motionless by the open front door of the car. Standing in front of him was another black man of medium height and wearing a blue suit. Jaimie was closer now and saw the burly black man open the rear door of the car and usher Tania in. He'd never seen the man before. Tania's father seemed to have increased his staff lately. Another man, tall and dark with a little beard, leaned casually against the passenger door on the other side of the car.

Jaimie was near enough now, but suddenly he stopped. The glint of silver pointing at Eddie's stomach caught his eye. His mind clicked in overdrive as the memories of a life long past, flashed before him. In a few powerful strides he covered the few yards between him and the man in the suit, and hurled himself crashing into his back. Eddie had time to see the move but instead of sidestepping it, stood rooted to the spot where he received the full impact of the man with the gun hurtling towards him. The big guy with the bushy hair was about to climb in the car behind Tania. Seeing what was happening, he turned and went for Jaimie. Tania appeared at the door and climbed quickly out of the car. Somebody swore. Jaimie guessed that Eddie was grappling with the gunman. Meanwhile he had to deal with this one. Expecting a punch, he put up his fists in defence, but the man, taller than him with a protruding stomach, suddenly threw himself forward and held Jaimie in a powerful bear hug. Jaimie felt his strength seeping, in a few moments it would be all over. All in one, he arched himself for tension, kneed the man in the groin and headbutted him for good measure. The headbutt hurt him too but the big man let out a cry, before releasing him and dropping on one knee. Jaimie thought about kicking him but something told him to turn around. Tania's voice calling his name was the last thing he registered as the back of his skull exploded in pain and he tumbled at speed into a black hole.

His first conscious thought was 'I'm blind!' but then he realised he had a blindfold on and he was handcuffed. He didn't know and couldn't tell how long he'd been out or where he was now, but Jaimie's head felt shattered. He was aware of being pulled out of the car, helped up some stairs and finally he was sat on a hard chair in a room with the door shut on him. He forced his breathing to still his body and clear his head. Slowly, he regained control but his head ached bad. His hands were handcuffed behind his back so that he

166

couldn't remove the tight piece of cloth covering his eyes. 'What the hell is happening?' he thought. He knew Tania had travelled with him as he could now recall hearing her calling him just before he was dragged out of the car. He was worried about her now, more than about himself. Everything had happened so suddenly... Soon enough, he heard the door open. By the sound of the footsteps he guessed two or three men had come inside the room. There was a short silence. Somewhere inside another room nearby, the sound of a radio. Jaimie could literally feel eyes on him. He heard a noise like a lighter flicking open. Another few seconds of silence. Then a man's voice said, almost kindly:

"Untie him."

Right away someone stepped up to his chair and Jaimie felt hands push him forward and the handcuffs loosened up. He brought his hands in front of him slowly, massaged his bruised wrists. The back of his skull was hurting bad now and he winced as the blindfold was untied. The bright beam of the desk lamp in his face forced him to shield his eyes at first. The rest of the office-type room wasn't lit. 'It's just like in the movies', he caught himself thinking.

At the desk facing him, Jaimie could make out a large silhouette, the shape of a man sitting back with smoke drifting above his head. To the left of the desk, another man, whom Jaimie guessed as the man with the gun. The lanky frame to the right, in shadow, could have belonged to the man who had stood on the other side of the car. The man Jaimie had fought with had backed off to the wall after freeing him but kept himself in view. He was the only one Jaimie could actually see properly. The man behind the desk sighed heavily.

"Your boss will be proud of you. You did your best."

The voice was deep but at the same time smooth and without animosity. The accent could have been yankee, or something close and Jaimie had by now formed a pretty good idea of who he was presently facing. He cleared his dry throat.

"I think you got the wrong man..."

The red tip of a cigar glowed behind the desk. The man blew out smoke slowly before asking, conversationally:

"Are you saying I made a mistake?"

Jaimie cautiously explored with one hand the damage to his skull. The bump was too painful to touch.

167

"You sure did, and your boy who hit me from the back made a bad one too!" he said dryly.

The man got up from the desk and walked slowly, almost majestically, to where Jaimie sat. He was tall, of considerable girth although his well-cut beige suit didn't show it that much. Jaimie couldn't see his face clearly, but his head was bald and standing close as he was, Jaimie could smell drifts of perfume mingled with strong tobacco. He knew this was the man from the garden party. Colonel Liston Tania had called him. He was looking down on Jaimie, the cigar in his right hand level with Jaimie's face. The man sighed again.

"You're not one of Heywoode's boys, uh?"

"That's right. I'm just a friend of his daughter."

The Colonel paused then walked back to the desk. Jaimie heard him click his tongue, then he asked:

"And what is your name, young man?"

Jaimie could see what looked like a water jug on the front of the desk, reminding him that his throat ached.

"Could I have a little water, if you don't mind. I'm feeling kinda dry."

The boss motioned with his hand and the tall man next to him moved forward, took up the jug and filled a glass. He approached and handed it to Jaimie, his still eyes studying him with no particular expression. Jaimie nodded and tasted the water, then drank half of the glass.

"My name's Jaimie, sir, Jaimie Hannen."

'There I go with this "sir" thing again', he thought, but then in his present position, he might as well play it that way for the time being, after all the Colonel had addressed him as 'young man'.

"Hannen..." the Colonel repeated, "Hannen. Where are you from?"

Jaimie finished the water.

"Brooklyn, New York."

The Colonel seemed interested.

"Really. So you are not Liberian, and you don't work for Heywoode?"

"No, I don't. I think I got caught up in something I know nothing about here," Jaimie said.

The Colonel sighed, deeply this time.

"I see... Like I said, I don't make mistakes. But not everyone can

168

say the same, can they Maxwell?"

From the direction of the Colonel's stare, Jaimie figured that Maxwell was the gunman in the suit, the one who had hit him on the head. Maxwell kept quiet under his boss' stare. The Colonel walked back a few steps towards Jaimie, stopped to draw on his cigar.

"What have you done with Tania?" Jaimie asked.

"Oh, she's safe. Don't be concerned."

Colonel Liston had a particular way of speaking, articulating his words carefully, pausing in between as if to consider their effect. He added:

"The issue, I think, is what I am to do about you. As you pointed out so rightly, you have been..." he paused here and used Jaimie's exact terms, "...caught up in something you know nothing about..."

Though the Colonel's tone was light enough, Jaimie was sure that he was a serious man. He thought he'd better make things clear.

"Look, I don't know what the problem is but like I said, Tania's my friend and I wouldn't like anything to happen to her. If you released her, and me, I'm sure you could work things out with her father."

The Colonel was standing in the semi-lit area between the desk and the chair. Jaimie, whose eyes were adjusting to the setting, saw his large face break into a smile for the first time.

"I really wish it was as easy as that, Jerry..."

"Jaimie."

"Yes, Jaimie."

Colonel Liston walked to the front of the desk, sat on it.

"If you don't mind, sir, now that we've agreed I'm not the enemy, could you take that light out of my face?"

The Colonel blew out some smoke. He seemed deep in thought for a moment.

"The light? Oh yes, of course. Maxwell give us some light in here."

Maxwell switched off the lamp and flicked on the neon lighting. The office was sparsely but tastefully furnished, no pictures on the wall but two huge, man-size carved wooden figures stood out against the white back wall, one either side of the desk. Jaimie could see the three men clearly now. From the malevolent stare he threw him, the fat one to his right seemed to bear a grudge about the fight.

169

Maxwell was younger, probably around Jaimie's age, a well-dressed hood with a sneer. The slim and tall man who had served him the water had strong, well-defined dark features. With his short beard and high forehead, the stillness of his face reminded Jaimie of the image of an Egyptian pharaoh in a history book. Colonel Liston had babyish looks, chubby cheeks and well defined eyebrows. Only the deep, groove-like scars in the lower part of his chin belied his gentle appearance.

"What do you know about Tania's father, Jaimie?" the Colonel asked, studying Jaimie closely.

Jaimie shrugged.

"Not much. I fixed his car once, that's how I met him."

'Hmm', the Colonel seemed to be thinking. He asked distractingly:

"And...how long have you known Tania?"

"Not very long, a couple of months..."

"I see," Colonel Liston said, whatever that might mean. He was reflecting on something, slowly rubbing his chin with the back of his hand. His cigar had gone out.

"My name is Liston, Colonel Liston," he declared, pausing to appraise Jaimie with a long look. "You see, Mr Heywoode and I are very old friends. Presently, we are having a little misunderstanding and, uh...and he is being very difficult to reason with. So I thought he might become more..." he thought for a second, "...conciliatory if his daughter could present my position to him." Then he added: "Tania is like my own daughter, I've known her since she was a baby, you know..."

Jaimie nodded. By now, he was getting real curious to know what the whole thing was about. He needed to know for he was now involved in some way, against his will. He was wondering how to put it to him when the Colonel stood up.

"Maxwell, bring the young lady in, will you?"

Maxwell went to the door.

"And Maxwell..."

The man turned to his boss.

"Be nice," the Colonel said simply.

Maxwell nodded and left the office. Colonel Liston was deep in thought.

"I guess you are wondering what this is all about?"

"Right, I am. I didn't expect this kind of excitement in London!"

170

Colonel Liston smiled.

"Life is full of surprises; some good, some bad. Tell me, Jaimie, are you a believer?"

The question caught Jaimie by surprise.

"Sure, I am, but I'm not the church-going type, if that's what you mean."

The big man nodded.

"Then do you believe in retribution?"

Jaimie frowned, unsure of what the Colonel meant by that.

"Retribution, revenge, if you like..."

Jaimie didn't know where the man was going, but he thought about it before saying:

"I guess it depends on what the person did to me in the first place. Sometimes, life takes care of it."

That was the conclusion he had arrived at years before, back in the day. Colonel Liston was looking at him with a curious expression.

"Have you ever been to Africa, Jaimie?" he asked. The man had a stare that could make even a rough and ready veteran like Jaimie a little uncomfortable.

"Not yet, but I'm hoping to, soon."

Just then the office door opened behind Jaimie. The Colonel stood up as Tania appeared followed by Maxwell. Jaimie spun around in his chair. Tania stopped in the middle of the room. Five pairs of male eyes were on her, she focused only on Colonel Liston. Smiling, he walked towards her.

"Tania, my child, I'm so pleased to see you."

Jaimie watched the Colonel give the unsmiling Tania a short hug. She said, in a very cold tone of voice:

"Good evening, uncle."

'Good evening?!' Jaimie couldn't believe what he was hearing. And she was even calling him uncle! What the hell was going on?

"A chair for the young lady," the Colonel said.

The fat guy was the nearest. He grabbed a chair near the wall but the Colonel's gaze informed him that it wasn't suitable. He then picked up an armchair, placed it in front of the desk and drew back to his corner.

"How long has it been? The last time I saw you, you were just a schoolgirl. Look at you! Please, take a seat."

The Colonel seemed genuinely pleased to see Tania, which is

171

more than could be said for her. She sat down, turned to Jaimie.

"Are you OK?"

Jaimie nodded confidently, despite the throbbing bump on his head. Colonel Liston was standing by the desk, smiling at Tania.

"Oh Jaimie's fine. My boys didn't mean to hurt him, they were only trying to obey orders, I'm sure you can understand."

Jaimie thought he heard Maxwell repress a snigger. Tania spoke, polite but visibly very angry. Jaimie had never seen her this cold before.

"No, uncle, I'm not sure I can understand."

Uncle cleared his throat and walked slowly back to his desk.

"I know you're angry about the way I sent for you, and you have a right to be, but there was no other way for me to talk to you. Your father is being very difficult."

"And kidnapping me is going to make things easier?" Tania smirked.

The Colonel sighed, a worried expression on his face.

"Tania, please don't take it like that. I really wish there was another way, my dear, but I have a delicate problem and you are the only person that can help me solve it. I really apologise for the inconvenience."

'Inconvenience' was a nice way to describe Jaimie's throbbing headache.

"Leave us, please," Colonel Liston ordered.

His three men exited the office quietly.

"Jaimie, I'm afraid you'll have to excuse us..."

"Let him stay," Tania said.

It took the Colonel by surprise.

"It might be better if we discuss things in private."

But again she insisted. "Since he was hurt trying to help me, I think I owe him an explanation. Jaimie can stay...if he wishes to."

She turned slowly to Jaimie, her face still set hard, then she faced the Colonel. There was something in that look, Jaimie had felt it, something she meant, he was sure of it.

"Fine, if you say so, my dear."

The Colonel had a way of saying 'my dear' that sounded insincere. But Tania wasn't paying any attention to that, she knew the man too well. Jaimie sensed a peculiar atmosphere between Colonel Liston and Tania, something in the silent conversation of their eye contact.

172

"Like I said, I have a serious misunderstanding with your father. I don't suppose he spoke to you about it?"

Tania looked at him like she was a schoolteacher tired of hearing silly excuses.

"Uncle, you know that not even my mother is privy to his business! He certainly wouldn't talk to me about it. If I'm involved, give me the facts."

Tania was getting a little impatient.

"Hmm, right, the facts. OK. Your father is in possession of certain valuables that don't belong to him and I have come from the States to ask him to return them." Tania frowned.

"Uncle, are you calling my father a thief?"

Colonel Liston held her stare. Unruffled by her tone, he said:

"I knew what your reaction would be, and it pains me to have to speak to you of these things, believe me." He paused. "Your father denies everything, even though I have presented all the evidence to him. You don't know how hurtful it is."

She didn't know and clearly didn't care either.

"So you got me to come here to tell me my father is a thief and a liar, is that it?" she asked icily.

He nodded.

"Tania, the truth hurts me like it will hurt you. Your father took away the *sale*."

Jaimie saw Tania squint.

"What did you say?" she asked.

Behind the desk, the Colonel reached for the lighter, calmly drew at the flame and puffed little round clouds that rose above his head.

"I didn't think you knew," he said kindly. "I realise it's been many years, and life has changed for all of us. All these years..."

Tania stiffened in her chair and asked in a blank voice:

"How do you know?"

"You were still a child when all this happened," the Colonel began, "but in the last weeks before the events, when I realised we would have to leave Liberia, it was arranged that I should take the *sale* out of the country, for safekeeping. Only, the man I sent to get it never returned. He seemed to have run away with it. I discovered he had flown out to the States and I have been trying to find him ever since."

"And what has my father got to do with all this?"

173

The Colonel sighed, shifted his large bulk in the tall armchair.

"Last summer I travelled to Toronto for business and while there I was accosted by a young waitress in a restaurant. I didn't know who she was, but she said she was Liberian and that she remembered me. I asked her name and was very surprised to find out that she was the daughter of that soldier I had sent to get the *sale*. It seemed such a strange coincidence, but when I asked her whether her father was still in the States and if she was in contact with him, she looked at me strangely. She told me her father's body had been found a few days after the coup amongst other corpses. The family claimed it and buried him. That young woman is now employed by me."

Jaimie was trying to follow. The Colonel continued:

"Now, I always found it difficult to accept that that man could have betrayed me, but it's even harder to believe he would have stayed behind to die during the coup. In any case, he died. That means someone travelled out of the country with his papers, in his name, do you follow me?"

She was following, step by step, her hands crossed in her lap.

"But, we all travelled together, don't you remember?"

"Yes, I remember." Colonel Liston nodded. "He was too smart to do the job himself, but only he could have played me out like that. I know now what he is capable of!"

Tania was indignant.

"How could you believe my father would do such a thing? He was your friend!"

For the first time, Colonel Liston appeared to react spontaneously. He stopped, cigar in the air.

"He was my brother." Then he added with an air of infinite sadness: "But didn't Cain kill Abel?"

Jaimie was so totally engrossed by what he was hearing by now that he had all but forgotten his aches. Tania's legal mind was ticking away furiously.

"All your story proves is that someone travelled under your soldier's identity, but not necessarily with the *sale*. And to involve my father in it is pure speculation."

"Love often blinds us, Tania. I'm sorry to have to hurt you."

Composed, Colonel Liston stretched one arm to the telephone on his desk, picked up the receiver.

"Send my guests in," he ordered.

174

Tania threw him an exasperated look. She had all but forgotten about Jaimie for the time being. A light knock at the door and it opened.

"Please, come in," Colonel Liston said.

Jaimie turned to see who the guests were, but it was Tania's reaction that startled him. The expression on her face as she beheld the two men standing by the door was so intense that for a moment Jaimie thought she would faint. She gasped, brought her hands to her face in surprise and stood up. The two newcomers walked in, stopped a little way from where Tania stood. Tall, with his white skullcap and dark brown, wide-sleeved robe, the elderly man in front was a striking sight. Though his eyes were shielded behind dark glasses, his very presence radiated an hypnotic intensity. His younger companion had the same dark, shiny complexion and despite his sober grey suit and 'scholarly' spectacles, resembled the other very much. He smiled at Tania.

"Annalia..." the old man addressed her.

The voice was deep but warm. As the old man stretched his dark and bony hand towards her, Jaimie saw tears falling down Tania's face. She walked up to him, he said a few words and slowly touched her face, from the forehead downwards, his long fingers gently tracing the curves of her features. Then he opened his arms and hugged her, speaking softly. She cried and held him. She then hugged the younger man, who kissed her on both cheeks.

"Take them upstairs," the Colonel told his man Maxwell. "I think they need to talk."

Tania held on to the old man's arm and he led her out.

Jaimie didn't know what to say or what to ask first.

"Life is so unpredictable, Jaimie, don't you think?"

Colonel Liston sounded rather pleased. He leaned back in his armchair and sighed deeply.

"Who are they?" Jaimie asked.

"I know how frustrating it must be for you, all this mystery. But I would rather let Tania explain everything to you," the Colonel said smiling. "For now, I would like to ask you to help me solve this problem."

Jaimie's head was full of unanswered questions but he knew it would have to wait.

"What can I do for you?" he asked.

The Colonel finally disposed of the cigar butt. Out of one of the

175

desk drawers, he pulled a white envelope, placed it on the desk.

"I would like you to deliver this to Mr Heywoode."

"What should I tell him?"

"You can only tell him what you saw; that will be enough. Tell him to give you what I want."

Jaimie took the envelope he was handed.

"You trust me to come back with it?"

Colonel Liston smiled broadly, the smile of a lion to his prey.

"I know you're an honest man."

It sounded patronising, but as he walked around Jaimie's chair, the Colonel added:

"More importantly I know that you wouldn't betray Tania."

Colonel Liston's laugh was short and dry.

CHAPTER TEN

7.53 on the dashboard clock. Jaimie parked near the newsagent's. He ran into the phone booth, fumbled in his pocket for change. It took five rings for the phone to answer.

"Lorraine? Yeah, fine. Where's Junior...? Where...? Alright, I'll call him on his mobile... He hasn't got it with him? What the hell has he got a mobile for if he don't carry the thing? Right, listen carefully. Tell him as soon as he gets in: I want him to get the spare key for my car, at home in the kitchen, and go get the car out of parking in Kensington. Yeah..."

As patiently as he could Jaimie explained to Lorraine where the jeep was parked. He hung up. That was all anyone could do for him right now. He jumped back in the car, drove off fast. At any other time it would have been a kick to test drive the new 450 SEL but tonight Jaimie handled the Mercedes without even thinking about it. He felt...he didn't even know how he felt in fact! 'Freaked out' was probably the nearest feeling. Freaked out and speeding towards the Heywoode residence as the messenger of their daughter's kidnapper. 'What the hell is going down here?' he kept asking, shaking his head. There was silence in the car. The breeze through the lowered window was cool. It could have been a real mellow evening, and then this...crazy situation.

Absent-mindedly he touched the back of his head and winced in pain. Absorbed in analysing the story, he had forgotten about his bump, although not about Maxwell.

"Don't take too long, homeboy, your girlfriend's gonna miss you," Maxwell had smirked as he and the fat soldier had left Jaimie with the car near Hammersmith. Another soldier drove behind them. Jaimie had been blindfolded and had mostly ignored Maxwell's sarcastic remarks.

Jaimie was trying hard to figure out the Colonel. And who were the two men Tania had seemed so shocked to see? And that...Jaimie couldn't recall what the Colonel had called it...thing, what was it and why would Mr Heywoode steal it? All this just from trying to get close to Tania. Talk about falling for the wrong girl! He slowed down and swung a right into the tree-bordered street leading to the Heywoode's cul-de-sac.

Jaimie parked in front of the closed gate and entered the grounds. No guards, no dogs. He walked up to the main entrance and rang the bell. The maid remembered him and opened. He waited in the lounge while she went off to call her boss. The house was really quiet.

"Jaimie!"

He turned towards the far end of the room, surprised; he had expected Tania's father.

"Good evening, Mrs Heywoode."

Jaimie realised how weird his greeting sounded. He could read the anguish in the woman's eyes as she stopped in front of him.

"Please, take a seat," she said, her voice sounding remarkably composed. She sat beside him on the couch. He noticed her fingers were crossed together.

"Is Tania alright?" Mrs Heywoode asked.

Jaimie tried to sound light.

"Oh yeah, she's fine."

There was an embarrassed silence as he wondered just how much the woman knew about the whole thing. Tania's remark to Colonel Liston that her father didn't discuss his business with his wife flashed in his mind. The message was for her husband but Tania was her daughter too. His discomfort was eased by Mr Heywoode's arrival. A grim faced Eddie was shadowing him. Jaimie stood up.

"Jaimie, how are you?"

Mr Heywoode motioned to him to sit back down then sat in the armchair across from him. 'How am I?' Jaimie thought to himself.

"Fine, thank you," he said. Standing behind his boss, Eddie was staring coldly.

"What do they want?" Mrs Heywoode asked.

Though she was as impeccably dressed as always, Tania's mother wasn't her usual assured self. Jaimie noticed the nervous twitch of her mouth.

"I believe it's some kind of thing which..." he started.

He was trying to present the case tactfully, then he remembered the envelope in his shirt pocket. He held out the white paper rectangle to Mr Heywoode.

"Colonel Liston told me to give you that."

Mrs Heywoode looked at the envelope apprehensively, her husband made no move towards it so Jaimie placed it delicately on the coffee table. For a moment they all stared at it in silence.

"He wants me to bring back the item...gave me a phone number to call."

"Give him whatever he wants so he'll let Tania go."

Mrs Heywoode's voice now reflected her anxiety.

Eddie was still staring at the table.

"Should I open it for you, sir?" Jaimie asked finally, as Mr Heywoode glanced once again at him then back to the envelope, considering the options.

"It's alright, I'll do it."

Carefully he picked it up, checked the other side, blank too. Slowly, with the long nail of his thumb, Mr Heywoode tore open the top of the envelope. Just as carefully, he took out the folded sheet of paper within. His wife watched him closely, hands clasped against her chest, very still except for the quiver at the corner of her mouth. Peering over the top of the letter, Jaimie made out a single line of large writing in the middle before Mr Heywoode very quickly folded the sheet, slipped it back inside the envelope, then inside his jacket pocket. No one said anything for a few seconds.

"I'm afraid Colonel Liston made a mistake. I haven't got what he is looking for," Mr Heywoode commented quietly.

Jaimie sighed, not knowing what to say. In his mind he saw Tania's face, stone cold, staring down at the Colonel.

"Go and talk to him; you'll be able to work it out with him. We were like family. Why would he kidnap Tania?"

Mrs Heywoode's words flew out of her heart. The fear she felt for her daughter was real enough.

"He won't hurt her," her husband said. "It's only a way to get at me." He massaged his forehead with his forefinger, concentration showed on his face. "Did Tania talk to the Colonel?" he asked Jaimie.

"Yes, they talked a little. She also said you didn't have what he wants."

Mr Heywoode was about to ask something else when his wife cut in: "What is this thing he is talking about?"

Jaimie shrugged.

"I can't remember what he called it."

"It's just something he's trying to get hold of. He thinks I have it but he's mistaken." Mr Heywoode turned to Jaimie. "Tell him if he doesn't release Tania, we will go to the police."

Mr Heywoode's squint was eloquent enough. But the panic Mrs Heywoode felt was gnawing her.

"Do something. You know enough people. There must be someone with enough influence..." she demanded of her husband.

"It's not as simple as that, you don't understand the way Liston operates."

"I only understand one thing," she stated firmly. "Tania has nothing to do with your business problems. Do whatever you have to but bring me back my child."

Now she sounded upset, clearly angry at her husband.

"I don't know how he can suspect me, we were close back then," Mr Heywoode inhaled deeply.

Jaimie nodded.

"That's what Tania told him, sir, that's when he sent for the guests."

"What guests?"

"I'm sorry, I didn't get to tell you. The Colonel brought in two men, one old and a younger one."

Mrs Heywoode gasped, the look on her face spelled fear.

"What does the old man look like?" Mr Heywoode's voice was uncharacteristically urgent.

"Tall, dark complexion, dressed like a...a Muslim. He wore shades..."

"Glasses?"

"Yeah, dark glasses. Tania cried when she saw him."

"Oh my God!"

Mrs Heywoode sobbed, hands over her face. Jaimie watched her get up and walk hurriedly out of the lounge. Her husband didn't move.

"Tell me, what did Tania say after that?" he asked Jaimie.

"She just left with the two men, then I was let go." He added: "That Colonel Liston looked like he was serious. I mean, I'm a little concerned."

"He is a very serious man, yes, but I'm afraid I can't meet his demands."

Jaimie looked at him.

"Aren't you afraid he'll hurt Tania."

"He's bluffing."

"Bluffing?"

The phone in the hallway rang twice. Jaimie and Mr Heywoode

180

were both thinking alike. He got up, walked out to take the call. Eddie remained, ignoring Jaimie completely. Mr Heywoode came back in, walking slowly, hands behind his back. He didn't sit down, but walked to the windows and stared outside for what seemed to Jaimie like a long time. Then Mr Heywoode turned to him.

"Have you got any idea whereabouts you were taken?" he asked.

"I was blindfolded, but I guess the return journey took about forty minutes."

"I'm sorry you got hurt," Mr Heywoode sat back down.

"I'm sorry I couldn't stop them."

Eddie, for the first time, said something.

"You could have got me shot."

Feeling wrecked as he was, Jaimie wasn't even going to mention being hit on the head. He threw the man a spiteful glance.

"Yeah? I risked my butt to do your job. You couldn't even take care of yourself. Man, what kind of bodyguard are you anyway?"

Eddie stiffened under the insult. Jaimie glared at him, inviting his response. But there wasn't to be one. It was Mr Heywoode's face which drew Jaimie's attention. He followed his stupefied gaze through the bay window, beyond the gate where yellow-orange flames were dancing inside the white Mercedes, lighting the moonless night.

"Fire, fire!" Eddie shouted, not very originally.

Recovered from his initial shock, Mr Heywoode jumped up.

"Get the extinguishers! Call Luke and the others!" he shouted, rushing out.

Jaimie was already moving. Luke arrived with two canisters. Eddie got another one and the other guards rushed in with buckets of water. One of them quickly hooked a garden hose at the front and they managed to get the blaze under control fairly quickly. The weird thing Jaimie noticed was that only the inside of the car was on fire, the leather interior destroyed. The driver's seat he had occupied less than an hour ago was now a smouldering ball. Neighbours came out, alarmed, some still in their night clothes. Somebody must have called the fire brigade because two trucks arrived, sirens blaring and squeezed into the little street. Once they assured themselves that the fire was under control and they had a word with Mr Heywoode, they left. It was the biggest excitement in the neighbourhood for many years. One elderly white lady in a

181

sponge bathrobe and cardigan, grumbled on her way back to her bed:

"That was no fire. During the war, then we had fires!"

It took over an hour after everything was over for the street to get back to its usual peace. Mr Heywoode had his men push the blackened chassis of the Mercedes inside the grounds. Jaimie followed Mr Heywoode back into the lounge. It was only then that the thought hit him:

"I could have fried in that car..."

Mr Heywoode looked up with a grave countenance.

"Sorry, what did you say?"

The more Jaimie thought about it, the more it seemed Colonel Liston had set him up.

"He must have got his boys to rig up a timed device...unless he operated it by remote, but at that kind of range..."

He was talking more to himself than to Mr Heywoode, but the man said cryptically:

"Could be, but there are other ways."

"You still think he's bluffing?" Jaimie asked.

Mr Heywoode didn't answer directly.

"He's known Tania since she was a baby..." Then he added: "but he's crazy enough. Colonel Liston might seem very polished to you, Jaimie, but believe me he is as deadly as you get them."

"Is he really that bad?" Jaimie asked.

Mr Heywoode nodded slowly.

"I'm not sure what kind of people you've mixed with, but Colonel Liston would probably scare the hardest ones."

That sounded unlikely to Jaimie.

"Tania called him 'uncle'. He said you and he were brothers."

Mr Heywoode reflected silently on that.

"We went through a lot together."

"Is he really a Colonel?"

"Yes, in the paratroopers. We served in the same regiment." He added: "Liston is one of those 'old-school' soldiers, you know the type."

Jaimie thought this might be his chance to pick up some info.

"This thing he wants is worth a lot to him?"

There Mr Heywoode put up his guard.

"It's a long story..." He paused. "I'm really sorry you got mixed up in all this."

182

Jaimie shrugged.

"Don't worry about me, I'm OK, but to tell you the truth, I'm kinda lost here. I don't mean to get into your business, but...what is this thing the Colonel is after?"

Mr Heywoode's eyes were fixed on the table in front of him. He was about to speak when the ring of the telephone sounded from the hallway. Mr Heywoode made no move to get up. Jaimie heard Eddie's voice, then the man appeared at the entrance to the lounge. There was a long silent look between him and his boss, then Mr Heywoode nodded slowly and Eddie disappeared. Jaimie was feeling tired and hungry but his mind kept drifting back to Tania. Mr Heywoode sighed deeply, put his glass down and got up. Jaimie watched him disappear into the adjoining room, then return a few minutes later with a black leather briefcase. He placed it delicately on the table, sat back in his chair. There was a pause as Jaimie felt Mr Heywoode's pupils look into his. Then he looked down before asking:

"Do you believe in spirits, Jaimie?"

The question hung in the silence of the large room, Mr Heywoode watching Jaimie's reaction. Jaimie inhaled to clear his head. He'd been through more excitement than he needed, and things weren't getting any lighter! That was an odd question. He recalled Colonel Liston asking the same question. Jaimie shrugged.

"Uh, I come from Brooklyn, sir, so...I'm not really down with that kinda thing..."

Mr Heywoode nodded, thinking to himself for a few more seconds. He seemed unsure how to start.

"Basically, in Africa people believe the reality of everyday life is influenced by spiritual forces. Apart from the spirits of their ancestors, there are various kinds of other forces, all of which can be called upon by certain individuals for various purposes. Do you follow me so far?" Mr Heywoode paused.

"Yeah, I'm with you."

"Right, so, some people have the ability to communicate with particular spirits. Those dealing with divination and healing, called medicine-men or even witch-doctors by Europeans, are in fact diviners and herbalists who function as priests in their communities."

Jaimie was listening keenly. Mr Heywoode continued.

"Then there is another kind of person who practises destructive

183

magic and who is feared and hated."

Jaimie thought about it then asked a question.

"I thought that since Liberia is, I mean, from what I have been told, you're more westernised than other African countries, I didn't think you'd be into that."

Mr Heywoode said gravely: "We are different in terms of our ancestry, that's true. We are the descendants of freed American captives and we live and think more like Americans, like you..." he allowed himself a brief smile. "But in Africa, everything in life is connected to spiritual forces. It doesn't matter what your education is, it is a part of your world."

"So you believe in it?"

Mr Heywoode looked at Jaimie straight.

"If you believe what you see, well I've seen things which made me believe. The object Colonel Liston was speaking of is called a *sale* in Liberia, a spirit. It is believed the life-force of an ancestor lives inside it and it is used as a..." Mr Heywoode searched for the exact word. "...an oracle. It is very old."

Jaimie sat there, taking it in. It sounded heavy.

"So Colonel Liston wants this...*sale* to tell the future?"

Mr Heywoode waited a little before he answered.

"It doesn't belong to him, and he can't use it himself. This is very powerful but only in the right hands."

Jaimie suddenly realised he was pointing to the leather case on the table. He raised his eyebrows.

"This? This is it?"

He saw Mr Heywoode nod gravely.

"The object inside this case is over eight centuries old. It is a venerated object for the people it belongs to."

Jaimie wanted to ask more questions, including how come the said precious object had ended up in Mr Heywoode's residence, but the man seemed to guess he did.

"I think you will find out the rest of the story later." Then he added, very casually considering the serious circumstances: "You're going to need another vehicle to deliver it."

Jaimie was still staring at the case, thinking about what he had just heard about the object inside.

"You want me to carry that?"

Mr Heywoode seemed surprised at the question.

"I believe that is the mission Liston gave you."

184

A cold chill ran down Jaimie's spine, he'd stopped using the word 'mission' the day he got himself released from the army base in Fort Benning.

"Yeah, but I mean, how dangerous is this thing?"

"It's not, you're perfectly safe. Unless you plan on opening the case..."

"Opening it? No sir!"

He noticed Mr Heywoode studying him, then shake his head.

"You know, for a while I suspected you of working for the Colonel."

Jaimie looked shocked.

"That's crazy! What about now?"

"I know you don't."

Jaimie thought about it for a few seconds. The whole story was weird anyway.

"Could I use your phone, I want to check on my car," he asked.

"Sure, go ahead."

Jaimie got to the hallway, called Junior, got Lorraine who said he'd been in and had gone to get the jeep. Jaimie then called the mobile and reached his brother who started to tell Jaimie something, but there was no time for that. Jaimie gave him the Heywoode's address and told him to pick him up urgently. When he came back in the lounge, Mr Heywoode was meditating over a double whisky.

"My car will be here soon. I'm gonna take this thing to the Colonel and everything will be straightened out."

Mr Heywoode looked at him and took a sip.

"Be careful with that man, Jaimie. He's not what he seems to be."

"A lot of people are like that."

Jaimie's remark seemed to touch Mr Heywoode who looked at him strangely but didn't reply. They sat in the quietness of the lounge, not speaking much until the beams of the jeep appeared at the gate. Jaimie got up and under the faraway gaze of Mr Heywoode, took the attache case from the table.

"Tania will be home soon, don't worry," he told him confidently.

Mr Heywoode didn't get up.

"Thanks for your help, Jaimie." He sighed, smiled sadly. "Please, tell Tania that I'm really sorry about everything."

185

Jaimie said he would and left. Near the gate Luke, the giant, and his two dogs, stared silently as he passed them. Junior was going to slide to the passenger seat but Jaimie let him drive. As they turned off the side street, Junior looked at his brother.

"How come you looking so rough, man?"

"It's a long story..."

"What's in the case?"

"Nothing you can eat, Junior."

"Where we going?"

Jaimie stretched wearily.

"Get me to Hammersmith as fast as you can."

"Alright!"

That was all Junior needed to hear. He flashed a couple of cars to overtake them, flouted the speed limit down Cricklewood Broadway. It was almost ten o'clock now and Jaimie felt pangs of hunger pulling at his stomach but he breathed deeply to overcome them. He turned down the volume on The Lench Mob. He wondered how Tania was doing out there. Lots of thoughts raced through his mind, overloaded as it was by the events of the last few hours. He realised Junior was talking to him.

"What you say?"

"You remember Cooler?"

"Cooler...Cooler...right; the kid that gave Richie the shit?"

"Right. Well, he shot a cop last night."

"What?!"

Junior explained he'd learned from his friends that the young dealer had been stopped in a car with two other youths and shot and wounded an officer trying to block his escape. He was on the run.

Jaimie sighed. He had other things on his mind right now but he reflected that another black mother had lost her son. Junior was still speeding, shifting lanes to keep a free run. He glanced in his mirror, slowed down a little and said: "Shit!"

"What's up?"

"I think we're being tailed..."

Jaimie checked. He could see a car behind them swerving in and out, trying to keep up with them. First he thought it might be an unmarked police car and winced. He would have a hard time explaining whatever it was he was carrying in the case. But the car was only two vehicles away and still didn't flash them. 'It could be

186

Colonel Liston's men making sure I don't get lost.' Jaimie thought to himself. But he could see the driver was alone inside the car.

"Try to shake him off," he told Junior.

"Yeah?!"

Jaimie immediately regretted saying that as his brother gassed down and started handling the jeep, his jeep, like he was in a movie. He thought of taking the wheel himself, just in case. Junior lived for opportunities like this and the look of delight on his face showed it. Yet Jaimie had to admit he was good, but so was the other driver. Then something clicked in Jaimie's mind.

"Slow down a little," he told Junior, as he glanced in the side mirror.

"It's the same car!" he muttered to himself. He couldn't read the licence plate but it sure was a brown Granada.

"What?"

"Alright, I want to catch this guy."

"Jaimie man, what's happening?"

There was no time to explain.

"Take a right, don't drive too fast."

Junior obeyed, took the right into a large avenue. The Granada was still behind.

"Get some speed right up to the end, then take a left and stop in the middle of the road, you with me?" Jaimie told his brother.

"Yeah, yeah."

Crazy stuff, that was Junior's style! He put his foot down and sped down the deserted road. The Granada was still on them. The jeep was doing well over 60 mph and Jaimie prayed no car appeared in the opposite direction. Junior geared down for the left turn, took it and braked hard. Jaimie had picked up the claw hammer he kept underneath the passenger seat. He opened his door, jumped out.

"Don't move!" he shouted to Junior as he ran to the sidewalk.

He walked back around the corner, crouching behind a parked car. He saw the lights of the Granada arriving at speed. 'I got you!' Jaimie smirked to himself. After the way he had been outplayed the last time, he was determined to find out who the mysterious pursuer was. 'Just like old times...' he caught himself thinking as the car screeched to a halt. It started to turn. Jaimie came out of hiding, his hammer firmly in his right hand. Quickly, the car started to reverse but an oncoming vehicle blocked its retreat, forcing it to a halt. The other car was flashing its lights. Jaimie ran around the back of the Granada, to the driver's door. Swiftly, he pushed the hammer through the open window and held the metal claws an inch from the driver's nose.

"Freeze or you lose your face!" he growled.

The driver chose the first option, held his arms up above the wheel. Jaimie opened the door and pulled him out. Behind, the other vehicle had started blowing its horn. Ignoring it, Jaimie spun the shocked driver around, spreadeagled him and frisked him. He wasn't about to take any chances. But the man wasn't armed, so he ordered him to turn around to face him. The driver of the other car, growing impatient, had come out and walked to the Granada but when he saw two black men, one with a hammer, he wisely decided to get back to his vehicle. Jaimie hardly heard the car reverse in haste. It turned into the nearest side street. Jaimie studied his captive. He was a young man, casually dressed. He stood there, passively. Junior arrived from the jeep. Jaimie lowered his hammer now. Towering over the smaller man, he growled:

"What's the story, man?"

Half an hour after Jaimie made the call, a black Pontiac Trans Am arrived at the meeting point and Maxwell's smirking face appeared at the window.

"You're late, homeboy!"

Jaimie would have liked to inform him that he was no homeboy of his, but he kept cool and climbed in. In the back seat, the fat soldier sat, looking dumb.

"I think you got something for us," Maxwell said, looking at the leather briefcase.

"You think wrong. This stays with me until we get there," Jaimie retorted coldly.

Maxwell didn't insist. He said:

"You know the game; we got to blindfold you..."

The fat one covered Jaimie's eyes with a bandanna, tying it tightly. Maxwell couldn't resist teasing Jaimie during the trip, but Jaimie paid him no mind. The Granada driver's story kept running in his mind. At first it had sounded totally impossible to believe but as the young man explained it, Jaimie became convinced that it was true. It was too weird, too fantastic to be otherwise. There was only one way to confirm it but first he had to get Tania released.

Junior was freaked out by the whole thing, to him it sounded exciting. Jaimie had him park the jeep near the pick-up point and take a cab. Just as well he didn't agree to let him tail them as he had wanted to; Maxwell was driving the Trans Am like a maniac! Maxwell's annoying noisy rock music tapes on the stereo disturbed Jaimie's meditation. He was glad to get out of the car.

They didn't remove his blindfold until he was inside the house. Colonel Liston was still in his armchair, the collarless printed shirt the only indication that he had left the office at all. Toying with an unlit cigar, he scrutinised Jaimie's face with his predator's eyes. He hardly paid attention to the black case on his desk. Maxwell was standing to Jaimie's left, the fat man to the right, against the wall.

"Please, sit down, Jaimie," Colonel Liston said as if welcoming an old friend.

A leather thong circled his thick neck, like a necklace.

"I got what you wanted," Jaimie told him.

Colonel Liston asked, fixing him with his piercing eyes:

"Did you open the case?"

"That's none of my business," Jaimie told him. "I done my part, now you can let Tania go."

"I think it's love," Maxwell mocked.

Jaimie did his best to ignore him. Wound up as he already was by it all, he would have happily vented his frustration on the guy but there were more important considerations at hand. Leaning back in his chair, his fingers tapping rhythmically on the fat cigar, Colonel Liston glanced at the case.

"Some people take more convincing than others but things have to fall back into place."

"Yeah, and some people play with other's lives," Jaimie remarked. "I didn't like the way you rigged up that car! If something had gone wrong with that bomb, I could have fried..."

Maxwell looked at his boss. The Colonel smiled at Jaimie.

"Bomb? There was no bomb," he said reassuringly. "You were perfectly safe, I am not so callous that I would put your life at risk."

"Yeah? Well, I don't feel safe. And I don't like to be used. You got what you wanted so just release Tania and we'll be gone."

Colonel Liston coughed, reached for the lighter on his desk and lit his cigar. Through a puff of smoke, he said:

"I'm afraid I can't do that just yet..."

Jaimie gave him a cold look. He was starting to lose his patience.

"Listen, I'm getting tired of your little games now."

"Hey, homeboy; watch your mouth or I'm gonna have to straighten you out again!" Maxwell's sneering voice cut in:

Jaimie turned to face him, squinting. He'd had just about enough of this fool.

"You get off my face or I'm gonna wipe the floor with your face, you dog-faced punk!"

Maxwell cringed, glaring at Jaimie like he was about to explode. The fat soldier stood by impassively. Colonel Liston drew another thick puff out of his cigar. Jaimie told him:

"You gotta be short of help to have a clown like this working for you."

To his right, he saw Maxwell bite his lip as his right hand slipped inside his jacket.

"You take that piece out and I'm gonna stick it up your ass," Jaimie warned him, cold as ice.

"Maxwell..." the Colonel called out calmly.

But the man was too angry to even listen to his boss. He pulled out the automatic...

Jaimie was on him before he could even point it. He leapt up, his right hand grabbed Maxwell's wrist firmly, jerking the man towards him so that his face came crashing hard into Jaimie's awaiting left elbow. There was a dull crack and a cry of pain. The fat soldier moved forward but Jaimie had anticipated that too and already twisted Maxwell's arm, wrenching the gun from him. He now stood behind him, his left arm folded around the man's throat. The fat man stopped where he was, eyes fixed on the black muzzle pointing at him. Pretty fast move for a 'retired' man!

Colonel Liston hadn't blinked. His hands were flat on the desk, smoke from the cigar rising upwards. An uneasy silence reigned in the office. After a full minute, Jaimie saw Colonel Liston slowly reach for the phone, pick up the receiver. He didn't say a word but his gaze was on Jaimie all the time. Jaimie was cool, he knew the man wouldn't make any mistakes in such a sensitive situation. He heard him say a few words in a language which sounded like Spanish. The fat man was still frozen on the spot. Maxwell had breathing problems it seemed. Soon after Colonel Liston had replaced the receiver, two little knocks on the door. Then it opened. Tania stepped in and stopped, observed the stand-off with a blank face. Her eyes caught Jaimie's. Even in the circumstances and at that

190

late hour, the woman looked dignified, calm.

"Come in, please. I think we now have what we have been waiting for."

Colonel Liston sounded relaxed. A serious look on her face, Tania walked up to the desk. Jaimie was impressed by her cool demeanour. She looked down at the case on the desk.

"What is going on here?" she asked in an even tone of voice.

"Oh don't concern yourself, dear; everything is fine. Isn't it, Jaimie?" The Colonel sounded almost jovial.

Tania turned to Jaimie again. His right hand had dropped to his side but he knew she'd seen the weapon. He reflected that he had never before seen the expression she now had, her features seemed changed somehow.

"Right, we all understand each other better now," he said.

Releasing his grip around Maxwell's throat, he shoved him forward.

"Take a seat!"

The man obeyed, gasping for air. A little blood trickled from his nose. Calmly, Jaimie deposited the automatic on top of the desk, near the jug of water.

"Now you can verify for yourself whether I told you the truth," Colonel Liston told Tania.

Her eyes turned from Jaimie and came to rest on the briefcase. After a brief glance at the big man behind the desk, Tania delicately took hold of it. She picked it up, turned and walked out as naturally as if she was going to work. Jaimie watched her close the door. Colonel Liston too, pulling a long draw from his cigar.

"You can leave us now," he said simply, looking at his two soldiers in turn. Maxwell was the first out of the door. Jaimie was still standing near the wall.

"Not bad, not bad at all..."

Colonel Liston smiled to him through the smoke.

Though still a little weary, Jaimie relaxed. He wasn't in any real danger after all.

"Have you eaten?" the Colonel asked, incongruously.

Jaimie shook his head.

"I missed dinner with all this excitement," he said coolly.

The Colonel laughed, a deep belly laugh. He got up. Stubbing the rest of his cigar in the ashtray, Colonel Liston told him:

"Our guests have already dined, but I was waiting for you."

Friendly, he led Jaimie out of the office, through a large and beautifully decorated living room where a grand piano stood in the background, black and shiny against wine-coloured drapes. Jaimie was thirsty and while he sipped his soda, the Colonel, a glass of cognac in hand, made idle chat, asking him questions about his army days and such trivia. Then he took him to another room where a table had been set for two. A black man in a white waiter's jacket appeared and deposited two covered dishes before disappearing to fetch some more.

Colonel Liston was a hearty eater, as his girth testified and what was more, he knew about food. Whoever his chef was, he was first class. Jaimie found the smoked fish stew particularly sweet and accepted a second helping.

'This is crazy,' Jaimie reflected as he finished eating. He had been kidnapped after all! Now here he was, sharing a late supper as a guest of his captor, who was insisting he should have some more wine. Wine! In the middle of it all, he wondered how Tania was doing.

Colonel Liston, Jaimie discovered, was an educated man. He knew a little about everything and a lot about diverse topics such as world politics and African history. He also seemed to be an expert zoologist. As they chatted, Jaimie learned fascinating facts about sharks and ants. The Colonel said he wasn't surprised to learn that his guest spent time in the army; something about him, he said. With a groan of satisfaction, Colonel Liston put down his glass.

"How about a cognac?"

"Well, I don't know..."

"Come along, it will help the digestion!"

Jaimie got up and followed his host back to the living room. He felt really full. He hadn't lost track of the circumstances but things often seem less urgent with a full stomach.

"You have a beautiful house," he said, sitting down comfortably.

Colonel Liston came back from the corner bar near the piano.

"Yes, I like it. And this area is so quiet. Do you miss the States?" he asked, handing Jaimie a rather large amount of cognac.

"Only some things, sometimes," Jaimie said.

"It is different, and I find life in America so...intense. Especially New York."

"Do you spend much time there?"

Colonel Liston sat back, his large hand enveloping the bulbous

192

glass.

"Not really. I have a house in Florida, just outside Orlando. Have you ever been there?"

"No, I don't know down there."

"Very good climate, more like back home."

Jaimie sipped a little cognac; first class, and strong. He asked:

"Do you plan on going back home?"

He saw the Colonel's eyes drift away for a very short moment.

"Whenever the situation improves, yes." He looked inside his glass before adding: "I guess I'm homesick."

Jaimie had made a point a few weeks before to read about Tania's country. This was an opportunity to find out something.

"How bad is that civil war down there at the moment? You don't hear much about it nowadays."

The Colonel pulled a face.

"It's not even a civil war anymore, just armed groups of marauders massacring each other." His voice was grave, the words carefully chosen.

"Why can't someone negotiate some peace?" Jaimie asked, hoping he wasn't sounding naive.

"Both the UN and the West African peacekeeping forces have tried, but neither have the resources to deal with the political crisis."

Jaimie was listening, intrigued.

"It's hard to understand the reasons for all these wars in Africa. I mean, all these endless killings over politics."

Colonel swallowed some more cognac.

"Politics is the art of dividing people." He focused on Jaimie as he qualified his statement. "Once you really understand human nature, the psychological make-up of a man, you can manipulate it and channel all his deep-seated fears in one particular direction. It is all about fear."

"Fear?" Jaimie repeated. There was something fascinating about the way the Colonel spoke, the way his mind worked.

"You see, Jaimie, I am a soldier," he continued. "And in order to shape a soldier, you must teach him how to think. Are you following me?"

"Perfectly..."

Colonel Liston nodded, remembering Jaimie's own experience. He went on:

"Now, a man is a very complex entity, possessing a spiritual

193

element, a force which gives him the potential to become...well, almost divine, to lift himself up to spiritual greatness."

Jaimie was taking it in keenly.

"But a man is also subject to base instincts...animal forces which, if not subjugated, can turn him into a...a monster, so to speak." The Colonel paused. "Do you see now how one can successfully appeal to mankind's lower instincts?"

The warmth of the alcohol soothed Jaimie's nerve ends. He was digesting the Colonel's words, realising his first impression of the man had been wrong.

"You're saying the politicians in Africa have turned people one against the other?"

Colonel Liston had a laugh, not deep; just a little disillusioned laugh.

"I am saying that politicians in Africa are no different from anywhere else. They know they only have a certain amount of time to get rich. Between one's own greed and fear of poverty and concepts like integrity and the greater good of your people, the choice is usually easy."

Jaimie nodded, thinking about it. The man made sense. He heard him say, as an aside: "The Europeans might have mastered the art of setting us one against the other in taking over Africa, but believe me, we have learned that skill quite well."

Impressive logic. Jaimie drank a little more liquor. He thought of something. Colonel Liston might be more willing to talk now.

"Can you tell me about this thing in the briefcase?"

"What did Heywoode tell you?" Colonel Liston asked.

"He said it was an oracle." Then he added, aware that he might upset his host: "He said it don't belong to you."

A large grin appeared across the man's large, smooth face. He said nothing, but grinned like a man who's just played an excellent practical joke on his best friend. Jaimie had to press on.

"Is it worth a lot of money?"

The Colonel wasn't grinning now. Serious, he told Jaimie:

"In terms of money, this could have made you fabulously rich, but only a fool would think in those terms. Its real value is in its power."

"You know, I'm still not sure about all this 'spirit' thing." Jaimie shook his head.

Colonel Liston observed him. "What are you not sure of?"

194

Jaimie sighed. It was past midnight and so many things had happened in the last few hours that he wasn't sure of much.

"I mean, I believe in God, right, but I ain't into no ghosts and things like that."

He could feel Colonel Liston's eyes on him, kind of glinting. He seemed to be amused.

"Ghosts?" he repeated, interested. "What about the Holy Ghost?"

Jaimie shrugged:

"Holy Ghost? Well, that's not really the same thing..."

"Hm," Colonel Liston said, nodding. "Tell me, is not a ghost, whether you say it is holy or not, a spirit? Aren't they different words for the same thing?"

Jaimie could feel this thing getting heavy, but his inquisitive mind nudged him on.

"Have you ever read the Bible?" Colonel Liston then asked.

"Yeah, sure..."

"Good, good." He seemed personally pleased to hear that. "Then...would you call Jesus a 'healer'?"

"A healer? Yeah, I would."

Colonel Liston asked again:

"Would you call Jesus a 'magician'?"

Jaimie thought a little longer. The Colonel saw his hesitation.

"I see the word might confuse you. You would agree that Jesus had power over spirits then?"

"Yeah," Jaimie nodded, digging deep into his memory for biblical references. "He drove away evil spirits..."

"Unclean spirits, OK." He looked at Jaimie. "So, you do believe spirits exist," he insisted.

Jaimie could now see his point. Colonel Liston's next remark took him totally by surprise.

"Before you came here, you met someone on the way."

The shock on Jaimie's face must have been obvious. Colonel Liston smiled and finished his glass of cognac. He got up, pointed at Jaimie's half-filled glass.

"Uh, no thank you."

Colonel Liston refilled his glass and returned to his seat. Jaimie still had a questioning look on his face. How did the Colonel know?

"I realise all this is new to you, Jaimie, but through...chance, you've been caught in the middle of something you're not prepared

195

for, although I can see you're a bright young man."

Jaimie wondered if he was being patronised, but then the Colonel sighed deeply. Jaimie observed him closely, trying to recall which American personality he reminded him off.

"I think you have the right to know the truth... The object you asked about is, as you have been told, an oracle. It is a very old and sacred mask which belongs to a family clan from Mali, in west Africa. Have you heard of that country, Jaimie?"

"Mali? Uh, yeah, I read something about it in a black history book. Muslim country, right? It was an empire, I think..."

All his reading time in the correctional facility library hadn't been wasted after all. Jaimie saw Colonel Liston was kind of impressed.

"Right on both counts." He cleared his throat.

"Since you know that much, before Mali was an empire called Gana, which ruled a large territory to the north of the actual country of Ghana. That is where the name comes from."

A pause. The silence, substance of suspense, played its part in titillating Jaimie's awakened curiosity and he was captivated by Colonel Liston's rich, deep tones in the high-ceiling wood-panelled room.

"According to the story, in the tenth century, one of the last kings of Gana took a wife from a country called Wagadou. She belonged to a clan of priestesses who, because of some sort of spiritual kinship with a genie, a spirit, were healers and diviners of great fame."

The Colonel paused. Jaimie nodded to let him know he was still with him and to go on.

"So, after she gave him a son, the king took the daughter of a vanquished king, who was also a powerful sorcerer. His wife told him she had seen bad omens in a dream but he banished her and she returned to her own people with her son. Although he was forewarned by his family and his wise men that it would cause the ruin of the kingdom, the king married the sorcerer's daughter and soon after the empire started to crumble. The queen learned in a vision that on the day of her death, a gold mask of her face would be made. It would serve as a fetish for the protection of their clan. This mask is the object you brought back to me today."

Jaimie's eyes opened wide.

"A gold mask?!"

196

He was looking to the Colonel to elucidate, but masterful as he seemed to be in playing for effects, the man just sat there.

In Jaimie's mind, the story was being cross-referenced with the little bits of information he had already picked up.

"And your guests," he said, "they have something to do with that mask..."

Colonel Liston nodded and took out one of his beloved cigars.

"The old man belongs to the family of that queen. The other one is his son. The mask has been used as an oracle by the priestesses of their clan ever since."

"How? I mean what does the mask do?" Jaimie asked.

That drew another deep sigh from the Colonel.

"The soul of that queen dwells in the mask. She can be consulted at certain times for healing or divination through a specially initiated person, a priestess."

"You mean like a medium?" Jaimie asked again.

Colonel Liston weighed the word carefully.

"Yes, in a way."

"Why did Tania cry when she saw the old man?"

Colonel Liston smiled briefly.

"I think you know the answer to that question, Jaimie," he said almost kindly.

Jaimie frowned.

"It's impossible..."

Colonel Liston gave him just enough time to shift around in his mind things he didn't want to add together. He lit his cigar and stood up.

"I think I shall leave the rest of the story to Tania. Come along, I'd like to show you something."

Jaimie got up and followed, wondering what else this man had in store for him tonight. This had to be the weirdest story of his life. They walked back through the dining room, where the table now stood empty but for a beautiful set of silver candle holders, and into the kitchen where the man who had tended them at the table and another tall bearded man played cards, with the sounds from an old horror movie filtering down from a small TV set above the breakfast bar. They stood up as they noticed him but he motioned them to carry on. Jaimie nodded to the two men who barely acknowledged him. The swing doors at the far end of the kitchen led on to a long, narrow corridor. Colonel Liston was still puffing on his cigar.

197

"Apart from a few modifications which I made, this house is the same as it was in the nineteenth century when it was built," he told Jaimie proudly.

Captivating news. The Colonel continued to the end of the corridor where he stopped in front of what seemed to be the back wall. He turned to his guest.

"This area of the house is restricted. You are a very privileged man, Jaimie."

On the painted brick wall was a little square black box, the size of a cake of soap. Colonel Liston stood to the right of it.

"Please, come and stand here."

Intrigued, Jaimie stood right in front of him as he was told. The Colonel put out his cigar between the thumb and forefinger of his left hand, the ashes dropped at his feet. Then he ran the tip of his right index finger across the top of the black box. Jaimie almost lost his balance as the floor started to move under him. He was standing on a revolving floor. Before he had time to think, both floor and wall had turned 180 degrees and they were in an adjoining room. Jaimie squinted to see where he was and then stepped off the 'merry-go-round'. It was dark until a neon was switched on and he realised he was in a storage cupboard of only a few square feet. Against the wall to the right, a pile of wooden crates.

"Here I am."

Jaimie turned and saw Colonel Liston, a little smile on his face.

"Not again!" Jaimie said.

"Yes, again..."

As he said that, Colonel Liston pressed another button on the wall and they descended into darkness. The neons came on and illuminated what seemed like a pet shop. The Colonel positioned himself in front of the row of cages. Jaimie joined him. All around the room, wire cages of all sizes lined the walls and Jaimie could make out various types of animals. The round-shaped cages hanging from the ceiling contained birds. There were also rabbits, rats, mice and a few other rodents, a tank where a dozen frogs squatted around, and a tall wire drum which Colonel Liston called the 'bat-house'. Jaimie was astonished. He watched the Colonel take a mouse from its cage.

"Do you like animals, Jaimie?"

"Yeah, sure. We used to have a cat when I was a kid."

Colonel Liston toyed with the little white mouse in his grip,

198

caressing the top of its head.

"What did Heywoode tell you about me?"

Jaimie did his best to recollect the man's exact words.

"Well, he said...he called you 'deadly', I believe."

Jaimie's face was almost apologetic, showing he didn't share that viewpoint. Colonel Liston found that rather amusing. He stroked the tiny mouse and sighed.

"I wish you never experience the pain of betrayal, Jaimie," he declared sadly. But he didn't stay sad for long. "Come, let me introduce you to the residents."

'Residents'? Jaimie wondered, following through an opaque glass door at the far end, which took them into another world where large glass tanks adorned the walls. It looked like one long, continuous fish tank with partitions, except that there was no water in the tanks, only vegetation, rocks and tree limbs. The white mouse still in his grasp, Colonel Liston stopped in the centre of the room to check the thermostat dial. The tiny animal in the Colonel's hand squeaked and wiggled.

"Come along, I doubt if you've ever seen any of these."

Through the glass panels, Jaimie could see nothing but small shrubs, sand and stones. An individual thermostat was set from inside the tank. The mouse kept shrieking and Jaimie soon found out the reason for its panic. With his free hand, Colonel Liston used a long prodding stick, to dig around in the tank. Suddenly there was a movement underneath the surface of the sand. After a little more shuffling from the Colonel's stick, the flat head of a long brown snake raised itself, looking their way.

"This is Edgar, he is called an egg eater. This type of snake usually sleeps during the day and searches for birds' eggs at night."

The body of the reptile was covered with wooden-looking, tightly-packed scales. Its eyes were perfect marbles.

"He can swallow an egg twice the size of its head, break it in his mouth and spit out the shell. Isn't it amazing?"

Colonel Liston seemed impressed by it. Jaimie nodded. He felt there were better things he could have been doing than snake-watching. He didn't care much for reptiles. Neither did the mouse. They moved to another part of the 'snake pit'.

"Lucy here, is a milk snake, so called because people wrongly thought they went into cowsheds to suck the milk from cows." Colonel Liston was grinning. "When in fact they are looking for

199

mice."

The mouse still prisoner in Colonel Liston's hand was whimpering faintly. The Colonel continued as if he was giving a seminar.

"A milk snake is harmless to men. Look at his colours," the Colonel pointed out. "Red, black, yellow. If you see red, yellow, black; it's a coral snake, very...deadly."

Amanda lived in the next tank, thin as a finger and green as a vine and that was what she was: a vine snake. Wrapped around two adjoining branches, the animal's triangular head and dark eyes followed them. Jaimie didn't like the look of Amanda.

"A vine snake can lay still in a tree for hours, but when it moves, it's as fast as lightning. It can catch a bird or a lizard in a third of a second. One jab of poison and it's all over. A vine snake kissed me once!"

Before Jaimie could smile at the joke, Colonel Liston rolled up his left sleeve and revealed two black spots against the dark brown skin of his elbow.

"It happened years ago, in the bush in Guinea," he explained. "I was lucky; I was carried to a healer who lived only half a mile away. He saved my life. That is the old man you saw earlier on."

"That's the man who saved you?"

Colonel Liston smiled.

"His name is Cisse. I still owed him a favour. Today I have repaid it."

The Colonel moved towards the back wall where a slice of jungle had been reproduced in a glass tank.

"So now, you have no more problems with Mr Heywoode," Jaimie said, following his train of thought.

In the green glow of the room, the animal wasn't immediately visible. Only after much scrutiny did Jaimie discover that the rope-like loops flopping over the tree limb belonged to one creature. The head was almost invisible under a cluster of leaves.

"It's all down to strategy," Colonel Liston said, stroking the terrified mouse in his grip.

"Strategy?" Jaimie repeated, unsure whether it had anything to do with his question.

"Yes. With Heywoode, I had to use a hunting strategy, just like a snake does to catch his prey. Did you know that snakes sniff out other animals by tasting the air?"

200

Jaimie didn't, plus he still wasn't being told what he wanted to know.

"Jake here is a tree boa, he may look big but he's only a baby."

With his usual skill the Colonel switched topics once more:

"Only Cisse could have convinced Tania. She's the bait, you see."

Jaimie frowned. Under the green glow of the overhead neons, Colonel Liston's shaven skull seemed even smoother.

"OK, now you've got the mask back, you don't need her any more."

A sharp glance from the Colonel.

"The mask belongs to the Cisse; I want what belongs to me..."

"There's something else?!" Jaimie cried out.

Colonel Liston seemed preoccupied with the mouse. In the background, Jake shifted position slightly on the tree limb.

"For fifteen years I have been following a false trail, because I would have suspected anyone but my closest friend. Greed is man's strongest motivation, Jaimie. It is specific to mankind to always crave for more than we need."

It was a little late for a philosophical debate, Jaimie reflected. He was impatient to leave this obsessive man. But the Colonel was otherwise preoccupied. The snake seemed to be moving now, the dark loops on the tail end sliding slowly downwards, its head now semi-erect and the vertical slit in the centre of its eyes visible through the glass.

"Take snakes, for instance. Snakes are honest creatures, you can trust a snake." The Colonel seemed to be addressing the trembling mouse.

'What the hell is he talking about?' Jaimie wondered. He wanted to get back upstairs and outta here! The Colonel was getting freaky.

"Look, I'm sure Tania will be able to talk to her father so that you can get back your property," he offered.

Colonel Liston replied with a chill to his voice.

"My property...is one thing. Then there is the price of betrayal to pay."

The words filled the immediate area around them with an echo. From the Colonel's tone, Jaimie was sure the 'price of betrayal' was too high for any man. He understood now Mr Heywoode's reluctance to meet his old friend. Colonel Liston stopped stroking the mouse.

201

"The wages of sin, as they say."

With that the Colonel slid open a small trap at the front of the tank. The mouse's shrieks grew louder as the Colonel suddenly pushed the reluctant mouse inside the tank and slid the trap shut. Somehow, Jaimie never thought that he would actually do it. He watched in shock as the terrified little animal scratched in vain at the glass pane, trying to find a way out. From his tree limb, Jake, the baby, had seen the move and silently his coils began to stretch as he progressed along the ground. Then the mouse stopped its futile scratching. Jaimie watched, fascinated despite himself. He saw the mouse turn and face its predator for a few, agonising seconds, before taking cover behind the lower part of the tree trunk.

"The law of the jungle..."

Colonel Liston's tenor voice rang like an epitaph.

After Jake, Jaimie had no desire to meet any more snakes. Colonel Liston took him back upstairs but no matter how amicable he sounded, Jaimie now saw him in a different light. Back in the living room the Colonel declared that Tania had agreed to call her father in the morning to arrange a meeting. In the meanwhile, he suggested Jaimie should do like her and get some rest. Even at this late hour, Jaimie would have happily walked home, however long it took. But the Colonel was determined to hang on to Tania as 'bait'. Jaimie had no choice but to accept. A domestic escorted him to a bedroom. Short and dark with a gentle, fatherly face, he glanced at Jaimie as they climbed upstairs. Jaimie tried to engage in conversation but whether the man understood English or not, he simply nodded his head and smiled. At the top of the stairs, the light was dimmed, soft against the dark wood panelling of the hallway. There was a faint fragrance Jaimie thought he recognised in the air. The little man stopped in front of the second door on the left and produced a bunch of keys from his pocket. He tried two before finding the right one, opened and switched the light on. He smiled to Jaimie who gave him a polite little grin back. The man nodded, showing him in. Jaimie entered a large room, his eyes immediately catching sight of the four poster bed with its white lace netting. The sound of the door closing made him turn around. He shouted as he heard the clicking of the key in the lock, but it was too late. "I can't believe this!" he said out loud. He inspected the place quickly. The adjoining bathroom was beautiful with coloured tiles and a thick rug. He went inside to splash cold water on his face.

Refreshed, he flopped on the bed and felt the tension of the manic day seep out of his exhausted body. He wondered where Tania was. If only he could talk to her. He needed to find out what it was Colonel Liston was after now and what she knew about it. And he had to tell her about the incredible story of the man in the Granada. But first he had to get them both out. But how? The door was solid, no escape there. He paced to the window, trying to clear his head and to think of a way out but his mind was feeling sluggish. To think that he had gotten himself in this crazy situation just by trying to get to know Tania better! She sure didn't seem this dangerous. Jaimie sighed, scratched the back of his head. He looked around the room, comfortable but bare of any non-essential accessories. He peered out the window, at the moonless night. By nature, he hated being locked in and the years he'd served had brought an even more acute dislike of confinement, even for short periods of time. He had to find a way out.

He checked out the window. It opened easily. He leant forward to see how high up he was. The ground was about twenty or twenty five feet down. He exhaled in the cool night air. He was confident he could jump down, maybe even find his way out of the grounds safely but then what? He thought about going to the nearest police station, then decided that in all probability, Mr Heywoode didn't want them involved. Also, the Colonel might disappear with Tania before he returned with help. No, he had to get out of Colonel Liston's custody and take Tania with him. But how?

"Damn!"

Jaimie laid down on his back on top of the bed. There had to be a way out! There always was, he told himself. With all the brain work, his body relaxed and a deep longing for sleep won him over.

When he resurfaced some time later, Jaimie couldn't quite recall where he was for a few confusing seconds. Then he recollected everything. He sat on the bed, feeling a little cold. The light was still on but the silence was now filled with the sharp beat of raindrops on the window pane. He continued from where he had left off; 'How do I get outta here?' A burst of lightning flashed outside, then the roar of thunder. Jaimie caught himself counting the seconds, like they used to do as kids in Virginia during the storms. Those early summer holidays in Grandma's old house had been another kind of schooling!

Jaimie got up, stretched. The storm might be just the thing he needed, he reflected. He went into the bathroom to empty his bladder and caught a glimpse of his own rough reflection in the mirror above the sink. That made him decide to shower. Taking off all his clothes, he tried out the water spray, set the temperature and stepped in. The warm water running all over him had a nice feeling and Jaimie felt fatigue being washed away. He massaged his skull slowly, then his face to clear away the remnants of sleep. Outside, thunder kept rolling at regular intervals. Though he would have loved to linger under the water some more, there were things to take care off, urgent things. He dried himself quickly and dressed and inhaled deeply, feeling a surge of adrenaline as he prepared himself mentally for...well, anything.

'I'm outta here; anybody gets in my way, it's on!' he told himself, feeling that old drive rising inside him again. It had been a long time since he last felt this way, ready for action. Now that inner voice was calling him to arms. Suddenly he stopped and listened hard. There really was a voice, a faint cry, a whisper almost. So many weird things had happened recently that he still feared he imagined it. But then he heard it again. It sounded like it was coming from behind the mirror. Climbing on the edge of the tub, he peered into the ventilation shaft near to the ceiling. He could see nothing but darkness inside. Then he put his ear to it and heard clearly the plaintive voice from within, chanting something, or perhaps praying. Either way, there was definitely someone next door. He climbed back down, his brain working rapidly. That voice...the old man with the shades...it had to be him. If he could just get to talk to him, he would know where Tania was. Jaimie tapped the wall a few times and realised it was a stud wall. He went back inside the bedroom and inside the wardrobe found what he was looking for. The metal clothes rail was easy to lift off. Jaimie returned to the bathroom with it. The chanting was still floating through from the other side. Using the clothes rail as a chisel, he knocked the plaster from the edge of the shaft. Underneath the plaster, he found wooden fixtures. The ventilation shaft rested on one thick beam which pulled away easily. The chanting on the other side was now more audible. When he had cleared a large enough hole to slide through, Jaimie sighed contentedly and climbing in, proceeded to crawl over to the other side of the wall. He found himself in the darkened bathroom. Through the door, cracks of light seeped in from the adjoining bedroom from where the chanting was coming. Slowly, Jaimie approached the door, started to open it, carefully.

The dancing shadow of a candle on the opposite wall was dwarfed by the larger one of a man's head and upper body. On one of the two beds, Jaimie could see a sleeping man in his trousers and undershirt. He opened the door wider. The chanting suddenly stopped. Jaimie stepped out of the bathroom as naturally as he could under the circumstances. The old man, clad in a white necklace robe, knelt on a prayer mat which was no more than a strip of carpet, a string of white beads in his right hand and a skullcap on his head, his face turned towards Jaimie.

"I'm sorry to disturb you," Jaimie started uncertainly.

The old man didn't move, but muttered something Jaimie didn't understand. The old man said something again and the sleeping man on the bed stirred, sat up. They were father and son the Colonel had said. The younger man studied Jaimie curiously before getting up.

The old man was perfectly still. Father and son exchanged a few words. Then the young man said very distinctly:

"Please take a seat, Jaimie."

Despite his surprise, Jaimie did as he was told. Meanwhile the old man stood up, still holding his beads. It was when he stretched his hand to steady himself that Jaimie realised. 'He's blind!' he thought. Then he remembered the dark glasses the man was wearing when he'd first seen him earlier on. With his father seated on the bed facing Jaimie, the son rolled the prayer mat and placed it under the bed. Next he poured out some water from a jug on the sidetable and handed his father the glass. Jaimie observed them silently. They were both about the same height as him, though of slimmer build. The son sat on the bed beside his father.

"I'm sorry to disturb you," Jaimie said again.

"It's alright, I'm glad you came," the young man smiled.

He sounded so perfectly American that although Jaimie had been told differently, he still asked:

"Are you from the States?"

The man smiled again. His expression was kind, calm.

"No, but I live there. Oh. I'm sorry," he said apologetically, "my name is Cisse, Mamadou Cisse, and this is my father."

Despite himself Jaimie nodded to the old man who seemed to be chanting softly, fingering his string of beads.

205

"I guess you know who I am," he said.

Mamadou Cisse simply nodded.

"Yes."

"They locked me in next door," Jaimie explained. "I had to tunnel through your bathroom. I was trying to find out what happened to Tania."

"She's next door," Mamadou said very naturally.

"Is she OK?"

"Oh, she's fine."

That was good news. Outside, the thunder and lightning seemed to have ceased and there was a pervading calmness in the air.

"Look, I think Tania should get outta here before morning," Jaimie said. "Colonel Liston is planning on using her to get something from her father again."

Mamadou nodded gravely.

"Yes, I know."

"Well, don't you think we should do something?"

The young man shook his head.

"This is between Colonel Liston and Tania's father, you know."

He sounded too relaxed about it.

"Sure, but Tania..."

"He wouldn't hurt Tania," Mamadou sounded confident.

"Yeah?!" Jaimie winced. "You trust him?"

The old man's deep, quiet voice spoke in its musical mother tongue. The younger man listened then asked something. The old man took a little time before answering his son's question.

"What did Colonel Liston tell you?" Mamadou Cisse asked once his father had spoken.

Jaimie told him what he knew, as far as he understood it.

"He didn't explain to you about Tania?" Mamadou asked.

"No, he left it to her to do that."

Mamadou Cisse nodded, drank a little water then he started:

"Everything the Colonel told you is true. Our family originated from what is now Mali, but emigrated to Guinea sometime during the tenth century. My mother was a healer and priestess of our clan. My father is also a traditional doctor, 'marabout' is the term we use. He saved Colonel Liston's life years ago and followed him back to Liberia. I was born there. The mask which you brought back is an extremely sacred relic which has been passed down through the generations. It contains the spirit of our last queen and has been

206

used by the priestesses of our clan for protection and healing. It is a very powerful fetish."

Mamadou paused.

"I know a lot of this might sound strange to you and you may not believe what I am saying, but I would not lie to you, Jaimie."

Something in the young man before him inspired trust in Jaimie. The father though, seemed lost in a meditation of his own.

"I will now tell you the part that you don't know," Mamadou Cisse declared in his soft tone of voice.

"As she might have told you, Tania was born in England."

Jaimie nodded. He was all ears, guessing he was about to learn the full story.

"She was only a few weeks old when her mother brought her to Liberia. Very soon after, she became ill but all the doctors her parents called were powerless to help. They saw nothing wrong with the baby but she was getting worse all the time. Nothing worked. Her parents were very worried and when the baby fell into a coma, they expected to lose her. At that time, Colonel Liston and her father were in the army together and he told him that he should bring the child to my mother as she was known to be a very good healer. Tania's parents were afraid at first because they didn't know anything about African medicine and believed what the Europeans said about it. But all the doctors had given up on Tania anyway, so Mr Heywoode brought her to our house. My mother took the unconscious baby and retired in her room with her that evening. She stayed inside the whole night, working to save the little child. Tania's father waited outside with my father. My mother didn't come out until the evening of the next day, but when she did Tania's eyes were wide open. My mother had brought her back to life. When Tania's mother saw her child was alive, she fainted. Anyway, afterwards, my mother called Tania's parents to talk to them. She said their child was in fact a returned ancestor and that she had healed her through the spirit of our ancestor-queen, which dwells in the golden mask. She explained that the fetish had shown her that the little child's double, her shadow, was being 'eaten' by a greater force. She had succeeded in winning back Tania's shadow-soul but the spirit demanded in exchange that the child be initiated in our clan as a priestess."

Here, Mamadou Cisse paused, maybe to allow Jaimie a chance to ask questions. He could probably see the astonishment on

207

Jaimie's dumbfounded face.

"I know you must have problems trying to rationalise all this," Mamadou commented kindly, adding: "Everyone connected can confirm what I have just told you."

"What happened after that?" Jaimie asked.

"Well, Tania grew up with her parents until she was five, at which point she started spending a lot of time with us as my mother initiated her in the rituals of her function. She realised quickly that Tania, even at such a young age, was psychic. All she needed was to learn how to utilise her gift. She was only seven when she told my mother the exact date of her departure..."

"What's that?"

"Tania was told in a dream of the date my mother was to die."

Jaimie looked at the young man who had so calmly told him such an unbelievable fact.

"She dreamt the date of your mother's death?"

Mamadou Cisse nodded.

"You see, my mother was my father's second wife. She gave him eight children, I was the youngest. Tania and I are the same age, we grew up together. As a priestess, my mother knew she wouldn't live to old age; that is the way it is. When Tania had the dream, she was afraid of telling her at first, but my mother knew she was hiding something from her. When Tania told her, she thanked her and from then on started to teach her everything she would need to know to succeed her. She died two years after the vision, just as Tania had predicted."

Jaimie could feel the boundaries of his imagination being stretched to their limits. Mamadou wasn't finished yet.

"Tania became the priestess of our clan after that. The spirit of the mask revealed a lot of things to her and she healed many people."

"What do you mean by 'healed'?"

"You see, Jaimie, the functions of a traditional doctor, a 'medicine-man' as it is sometimes called, are multiple. He or she works as a herbalist, curing physical ailments but also as a spiritual healer, removing spells and charms which are very common occurrences in Africa. Also, depending on the personal power of the person, the work involves a certain element of divination."

Jaimie was finding it hard to believe that the attractive young woman he had been chasing was the same psychic person

208

Mamadou was talking about.

"What happened when she left?"

The young man waited a little, as if thinking out his answer.

"Many people knew something was about to happen. I was only a child at the time, but I remember my father telling me we would have to leave Liberia soon. He had made arrangements for Colonel Liston to move the mask out of the country for safety because he knew there was going to be looting. The man Colonel Liston sent for the mask a few days before he was due to leave disappeared. As far as we knew he had absconded to America."

"You left the country at that time?"

Mamadou Cisse shook his head.

"We didn't get out on time. There was so much chaos in and around the capital that we missed the last planes out. It cost my father his eyes."

"Why?"

Softly spoken as ever, the young Cisse explained:

"My father didn't really want to leave Liberia. He had spent many years there and liked the country. He never thought people he had lived amongst for so long and many of whom he had helped, could turn on him. But because of the privileged position of the Afro-Americans, the ethnic population came to hate them and anyone connected with them. When the soldiers of the new government came to our house, my father gave them money and food so they would leave us alone. He'd known some of them for years, but they still took him away. He survived but they took out his eyes... He says it's his punishment for losing the mask."

"What did you do then?"

"We left for Guinea soon after. Later I went to university in France, then to America. I settled down in Houston, Texas, got married and opened a medical practice. That's where Colonel Liston found me last month and told me he knew who had the mask."

"How did Tania take it, I mean, when she found out her father had it all this time?"

"Badly. She can't understand why he did that."

Old Cisse seemed to be listening to their conversation although Jaimie was almost sure he didn't understand English.

"What's going to happen now?" Jaimie asked.

Mamadou shrugged.

209

"What you see now is two old friends whose thirst for riches has turned them into enemies. This has nothing to do with Tania or with us. My father is old, he just wanted to get the mask back for our clan before he dies. He will go back home in two days time, I will go back to Houston."

Jaimie had one more question.

"What is it Colonel Liston wants from Mr Heywoode?"

Mamadou looked at Jaimie.

"A diamond."

"A diamond?" Jaimie repeated.

The young man smiled sadly.

"Colonel Liston is a very rich man. He was Commissioner of Police back then which, if you can imagine, is the ideal position for someone ambitious and ruthless. He was feared by most people. Just before he left, he was one of the major diamond traders in the whole region. According to what he told us, Mr Heywoode, his former associate, double-crossed him and intercepted one of a pair of very rare diamonds which he was expecting."

"Expensive stuff..."

"Very, but that is not what concerns Colonel Liston. These particular stones have a reputation amongst collectors. They are called 'snake eyes.' They are said to bring misfortunes to anyone who doesn't know certain rituals to neutralise their power." Mamadou paused. "You must understand something about Colonel Liston: money doesn't matter to him. His thirst is not for riches, not material ones anyway. Spiritual power is what he craves... Sometimes a man can lose his mind in such a quest."

That last remark hung like a noose in the quietness of the room.

"I wanna get Tania outta here," Jaimie told the young Cisse.

"She said you would do that."

That made Jaimie feel good.

"Do you think she is sleeping?" he asked.

Mamadou shook his head.

"At a time like this, my sister watches and prays."

There was pride in the way he had referred to Tania as his sister. Jaimie realised he must have had a deep love for her.

"Where are we?" he asked.

"I don't know. We haven't been out since arriving last Thursday."

"What can you tell me about the house? Are there any guards

outside?"

Jaimie needed to check his bearings. Fortunately, Mamadou was a sharp-minded person.

"We've been able to tour the property. The main gate is about a hundred yards down." He pointed through the window. "There's a small cabin near to it, like a guardhouse. I think one of Colonel Liston's men lives in there. The gate is locked electronically, it's operated by remote."

"How big is the property?"

"I'd say around a couple of acres. The land slopes down at the back of the house, past an old barn, going all the way to a tree grove further down."

Jaimie listened keenly, trying to map out the place in his mind.

"Is there a gate at the back also?" he asked.

Mamadou shrugged.

"I haven't been over that side, but it's walled all around."

Jaimie nodded.

"Where do the rest of the men sleep?"

Mamadou thought about it quickly.

"The cook and another man sleep in the extension on the right of the house. The American sleeps downstairs, the domestic on the third floor. So does Colonel Liston..."

"Right." Jaimie was figuring out in his mind.

He told Mamadou the plan. Taking another clothes rail from the wardrobe, they both chiselled their way through the plaster board partition wall between the rooms until they forced a large enough hole as Jaimie had previously done. Jaimie climbed through first into adjoining bathroom.

"Come on!" he called to Mamadou who was standing on the other side with a grin.

"You go ahead, I'll wait here."

Jaimie left him and entered into the bedroom next door. Tania was sitting on the bed, her back to him, reading at the light of a candle. Without turning, she said:

"You took your time."

She turned to face him with a smile.

"It's hard work, all this digging through walls!" he answered.

He felt warm inside to see her again and was even more delighted when she got up and hugged him.

"You OK?" he asked, after a moment.

211

She nodded, then sat back on the bed. He sat down beside her.

"I guess you know the whole story by now," she said.

"I'm still a little bit freaked out. We've got to get outta here before morning. Colonel Liston is gonna use you as a bait to get your father."

Her hands were clasped in her lap, her eyes fixed on the yellow flame of the candle.

"I didn't believe him but he was right," she said coldly.

Jaimie sighed, shook his head. He realised she was feeling bitter after finding out about her father. Strangely, something Mr Heywoode had said came back to him. He told her:

"People are not always what they seem to be."

"How could he do a thing like that?"

It was a rhetorical question. Jaimie heard himself saying:

"I guess he had his reasons. You're gonna have to ask him yourself."

Inside his head, a little voice was urging Jaimie to grab Tania by the hand and get out of the house as fast as possible.

"I...I won't be able to trust him anymore, not like before."

The hurt in Tania's voice was real.

"I know it must be a shock, but he didn't do anything to hurt you."

Her face in the low flickering light was stern.

"People suffered because of him. He had no right to deprive Cisse's people of their fetish."

Silence enveloped them for a while. Jaimie could relate to the taste of betrayal Tania was feeling inside her.

"This spirit thing, is it still with you? I mean, how..."

Jaimie still found it hard to deal with what he had learned on a rational level.

"I was only a child at the time. Everything has changed now."

"Mamadou said only you can communicate with the spirit in the mask."

Jaimie studied her closely. Despite all he had heard tonight about her from three different and very serious men, he still couldn't quite believe that the beautiful young woman next to him possessed the powers he had been told about.

"I cannot serve anymore," Tania said sadly.

"Why not?"

"Did Colonel Liston tell you what he is really after?"

"No, but Mamadou said it's a diamond...Was he really a big time trader?"

Tania's face was hard.

"Apparently my father and he were in this together."

"You didn't know, right?"

"As far as I knew, he was into import-export..." she said drily.

Jaimie sighed. It was import-export, true enough. He could imagine what a shock it must be for Tania to learn after all these years about her father's real line of business.

"My father is a murderer, and I am an accessory to it..."

Tania's voice was cold as ice, her words heavy as the final sentence of a hanging judge. Jaimie frowned.

"Yo, don't say things like that. "

"You heard Colonel Liston say that the man he sent for the mask was killed?"

"Yeah, but it doesn't mean your father did it. Anything could have happened..."

Somehow, Jaimie couldn't figure Mr Heywoode as a killer.

"Yes, but the man is dead and my father had the mask."

Admittedly, it looked bad.

"What did Mamadou tell you about this diamond Colonel Liston wants?"

Jaimie checked his memory.

"Only that he's got the matching one. He said they're called 'snake eyes' and they're very valuable."

"The 'snake eyes' were cut out of a very expensive black diamond from Namibia. People in the trade claim that the 'eyes' are possessed of a spirit which brings bad luck to their owner."

"Is it true?" Jaimie asked. By now he was almost getting used to all the weird stuff.

Tania shrugged.

"All those who have owned the 'snake eyes' have either died or become insane."

"Then, if the stones are that dangerous, why does Colonel Liston want them?"

Tania paused before answering.

"It is said that only a man who knows certain rituals can overcome the curse of the 'eyes.' Through them, such a man will become very powerful spiritually."

Jaimie thought about it briefly. Once again, it was all about

213

magic!

"How does Colonel Liston know your father has the diamond?" he asked.

Here, Tania stared at the dancing flame atop the candle. She spoke without looking at Jaimie.

"Colonel Liston is a cunning man. Once he worked out that my father had the mask, he brought in Cisse. He knows I would do anything for him. He also knows that if I had the mask, I would be able to see for myself if my father had the diamond."

Jaimie waited, unwilling to interrupt the flow of inner thoughts he could guess were streaming behind Tania's closed face. She said after a while:

"In the last days before we left Liberia, Colonel Liston had managed to make a deal with a diamond smuggler from Zaire who had the 'snake eyes.' He bought the first one from him and made arrangements for the other. The man was very cautious; he knew some very powerful people were after the stone. So, the meeting was set but when Colonel Liston got there, the smuggler was dead and there was no sign of the stone."

Jaimie nodded. One way or another, the 'snake eyes' had brought ill-luck on the unfortunate smuggler.

"Well, somebody got to him first."

Tania's eyes caught his in the low light.

"My father knew where the man was hiding."

Jaimie waited before he asked:

"How?"

"I told him."

In his mind, Jaimie was making connections. He had all the information and the inescapable conclusion made his remark obvious:

"The mask," he said.

Tania's gaze was once again on the candle.

"I caused this man's death," she said.

Jaimie didn't want her to get too deep into that guilt trip, not now. He needed to get her out; she could deal with that later.

"Look Tania, you were just a child, the fault is not yours." He touched her hand, held it. "If you don't get outta here now, you might not see your father again to ask him about it."

The remark alerted Tania's attention. He told her softly:

"Colonel Liston's got bad intentions."

She read in his eyes that he was serious.

"Can we get out of here?" she asked.

"You bet."

Though he didn't quite know how he was going to do it, Jaimie had been working on it. He got up, her hand still in his. She stood up too.

"I have to say goodbye," she said.

She followed him into the bathroom and through the hole Jaimie and Mamadou had dug in the wall. Old Cisse knew immediately when Tania stepped in. Even in the low light of the single flame, Jaimie noticed the change in the old mans' countenance. She went to speak with him, then called Jaimie over, made him sit on the bed beside the old man. Mamadou replaced the dying candle, darkness receded further. Old Cisse seemed to be lost in thoughts for a time. Then the old man spoke.

"He asks if you pray?" Tania told Jaimie.

"Yeah...I pray."

He wondered how formal praying was meant to be for the old blind man. Tania translated, then she said:

"Give him your hands."

A little apprehensive, Jaimie gently placed his hands in old Cisse's open palms. The man's thumbs felt his fingers, went over the back of his hands then he turned Jaimie's hands over. His long and dry dark fingers examined his palms. Mamadou and Tania were watching silently. Then the old man's hands felt their way up to Jaimie's face. He said something which Tania translated.

"He asks you to forgive him, he says his hands are his eyes now."

Jaimie felt a little weird at first as the old man's fingers traced the curves of his features from his forehead to his chin, but it was such a strong experience, so full of meaning, unlike anything he'd ever experienced before. He could literally feel loving warmth exuding from the old man. Old Cisse finally left his face and said something. Tania looked at Jaimie and laughed.

"He says you look like one of his cousins."

Jaimie smiled. The old man said something more. Tania waited before translating it.

"He says you are an honest man."

Then the blind man spoke again.

"Whatever you did it was out of love for justice," Tania

215

translated.

Hearing that gave Jaimie a little pinch deep inside his stomach. How could this old man know what he did and had been through. Yet that simple statement summed up so much of what his life experience had been that he was speechless. He was still thinking about it when they took their leave. Tania hugged the two men. Jaimie shook hands with them and left the old man fingering his prayer beads. Mamadou went back to Tania's room with them.

Jaimie's plan was simple enough: climb up on the window ledge and slide down the drainpipe. The rain had stopped now and it seemed feasible. Tania wondered if he was serious when he explained it, but she didn't have a better idea. Jaimie went first and made it down without difficulty.

"Come on, it's easy," he whispered, motioning to Tania to get moving.

Mamadou helped her to climb onto the narrow concrete ledge. Jaimie watched as she carefully reached out for the plastic drainpipe. She got hold of it and found a foothold on the bracket. The rest was simple. Mamadou watched them from the window. Tania waved to him before following Jaimie around the side of the house, crouching low to avoid their shadows giving them away in the moonlit night.

"Which way now?" she asked when they reached the back of the house.

Jaimie's eyes were gradually getting accustomed to the darkness. In front of them to the right, the silhouette of a tall tree cut a menacing shadow. Beyond, he could make out a low building next to the boundary wall. This had to be the guardhouse Mamadou had told him about.

"Let's try the back."

Treading as silently as possible on the damp gravel, they walked away from the house into the darkness. Jaimie led the way, careful not to slip on the wet grass as they went. Tania's hand found his as he led her into the unknown.

"Don't move!" Tania whispered suddenly.

She must have had eyes like a cat to have spotted the two dogs a few yards in front of them. Jaimie felt a sharp little pinch at the bottom of his stomach. He would have walked right into them. Tania was standing beside him now, she had let go of his hand.

"Oh shit!" Jaimie mumbled under his breath.

216

Any other dogs would have barked or at least growled, but true to their peculiar nature, the two dobermans seemed frozen motionless, heads slightly tilted, watching the two escapees, waiting. Once he had recovered from the initial shock, Jaimie tried to think of a way out of the unexpected and potentially dangerous situation. He didn't fancy his chances squaring up to just one of them, let alone two. Next to him, Tania stood very still, eyes set on the animals. They seemed to be waiting, and from what he knew about doberman dogs, Jaimie knew they could have them standing here until morning. As long as they didn't move, Jaimie and Tania might be safe. Tania said something but in the rush of thoughts inside his mind, Jaimie didn't catch what it was.

"What?" he whispered, keeping his head straight.

"Kneel down."

Jaimie had heard this time but couldn't believe that was what she said. From the corner of his eye, he saw her lower herself, very slowly, until she was kneeling in the grass. He couldn't think why but he obeyed and did likewise. Still moving in slow motion, Tania stretched out her hands in front of her towards the dogs. Jaimie saw one of them tilt his head to the left some more. He could feel his body tense, ready for the attack he was expecting any moment now. Here he was in the middle of the night, kneeling down in front of two potentially vicious guard dogs. How crazy can you be!

"Stretch out your hands, slowly," he heard Tania say.

What else could he do? Then she started speaking, not to him but to the silent dogs. Her voice, as calm as if she was talking to a friend in her living room, flowed through the dark, gentle, almost cajoling, in a language Jaimie could not understand, but hoped fervently the two dogs were fluent in. As he knelt there, hands outstretched like a mystic, he prepared himself to go down fighting. When the first dog started to move, his heart skipped a beat. Jaimie was no coward but a situation like this would test any man. Tania was still talking to the dogs, as if inviting them to come over. The second dog sauntered lazily over to Jaimie who held his breath.

"Relax, they can smell fear," Tania whispered.

'Relax!' Jaimie thought. Easier said than done. The first dog was gingerly sniffing Tania's fingers and the second dog followed suit on Jaimie. In moments like these Jaimie wished he had read more widely on such creatures. But the dog seemed content enough to brush his wet muzzle against Jaimie's stiff fingers. Not losing sight

217

of his new acquaintance, Jaimie watched as Tania patted the dog lightly on the top of his flat head. The dog seemed to like it so Jaimie decided to do the same. For a long minute that's all they did until Tania finally said:

"It's OK; you can get up now...slowly."

Jaimie was still a little tense, but followed Tania who stood up and started walking casually into the night, a doberman on either side of them. To the right, near the boundary wall, a cluster of trees spread their leafy branches like giants' arms. Above the wall, two lines of barbed wire stretched threateningly, but one of the trees nearest to the brick wall had a limb which stretched over the barbed wire onto the other side. It could have done with being a couple of feet longer, but the thick branch would offer a springboard from where the wall might be jumped.

"What do you think?" Jaimie asked Tania.

She could see what he was thinking. At their feet, the dogs remained silent.

"There doesn't seem to be any other way," she remarked calmly.

Jaimie was amazed at how cool she was being. He explained that to get close enough to the wall, they would have to do a balancing act on the tree limb. One slip would mean disaster. Tania was ready, so leaning his back against the tree trunk for support, he gently hitched her up. She got hold of the branch and pulled herself up with surprising ease.

"You OK?" Jaimie whispered.

"Yes," she replied in equally hushed tones.

Tania progressed cautiously along the limb, until she came to its end. There she balanced precariously above the barbed wire for a moment. She had to make a jump for it. That was the only way. She breathed in a deep sigh and then prepared herself for the jump. Then she did it. She launched herself into the air and a moment later Jaimie heard her land on the other side of the wall with a thud and a muffled cry.

"Tania..." Jaimie called out.

"I'm alright. Come on!"

He smiled with relief. After a last look at his canine companions, he jumped up, reaching for the tree limb and balanced himself as best as he could until he was standing above the barbed wire. It wasn't easy, Tania must have had guts like a trapeze artist!

"Here I come!" he called out as he leapt in the air. He landed

218

with his knees slightly bent and rolled forward as he had been taught in the army.

"Alright, we're out," he told Tania as he got back up.

Colonel Liston's property was situated at the end of a private lane, the back of it bordering on what seemed to be a large park. Jaimie and Tania walked hurriedly along the length of the wall. They turned left into a small street, at the end of which they could see what seemed to be a main road. At this time of night, traffic was sparse and wherever they were, there was little chance of finding a minicab office. They paused briefly on the pavement, not sure which way to go, or whether they were still in London. Jaimie decided they should go left, hoping they would come across a public phone which would give them their location and from where he could call Junior to come and rescue them. They walked for a few hundred yards alongside large houses, most of them without a light in their windows. As they passed a large mansion, Tania said:

"Look! There's a light on the ground floor. Let's ring the bell and ask to use their telephone."

Jaimie looked at her as if she were insane.

"Are you kidding me? Disturbing people in the middle of the night is not a good idea."

"But it's an emergency. We'll just explain the situation."

Jaimie stopped and sighed.

"Get real! In a neighbourhood like this, if they see black people hanging around their house, even in the daytime, they probably call the police...What are you gonna tell them? That you've been kidnapped?"

She looked at him despondently.

"Come on," he said. "We'll work something out."

They walked for another ten minutes without seeing a call box. Then Jaimie's eyes caught the illuminated sign of a Texaco gas station about fifty yards up the road.

"Let's try down there!"

They crossed over and walked into the station where a lone, new Rover stood by one of the pumps. A woman had just finished paying at the window. Though he didn't put much hope on it, Jaimie decided to try something.

"Excuse me..." he started as the middle-aged white lady was getting back to her car.

The woman took a quick glance at them then hurriedly got

inside her vehicle, not even taking the time of hearing him out. She turned on her engine and took off without a second look. Jaimie sighed. He realised they weren't looking too presentable but such a lack of courtesy was still annoying. They walked to the cashier's window where a young Asian man looked up from his newspaper with a puzzled expression.

"How ya doin'?" Jaimie smiled. "Have you got a phone we could use?"

The man shook his head.

"No phone."

Jaimie doubted that somehow.

"Look, it's an emergency. We need to call someone to come and pick us up..."

Another vigorous shake of the head. Jaimie looked at Tania but she said nothing.

"Alright, d'you know where we could find a call box around here?" "I don't know."

It seemed hopeless trying to get help from this man.

"Right...d'you know where we are? What area is this?"

"What area?" The man repeated with a heavy accent. He seemed puzzled by the question.

Jaimie sighed patiently.

"Yes, what area? Here, what area, what is this neighbourhood called?"

"Ah!" the smile on the man's face announced he understood the question now. "Hampton. Here, Hampton..."

"Hampton?!"

"Yes, Hampton." The man nodded affirmatively.

"London; which way to London?" Jaimie asked him.

The man pointed out to the right.

"London."

"London, this way, yeah?"

He seemed sure. Jaimie thanked him and they walked out of the station forecourt.

"Where is Hampton?" he asked Tania as they left the station to get back on the deserted road.

"I'm not sure, south I think..."

That was helpful. Jaimie scanned the road up ahead. If he could find a phone, they were home free. He had a quick thought about Colonel Liston, hoping he was sleeping soundly and hadn't taken it

220

upon himself to check on his guests. Then suddenly up ahead salvation loomed large.

"At last," Tania said. "There has to be a phone there!"

A few minutes later, they entered the grounds of the hospital, as an arriving ambulance screeched to a halt outside casualty. Its doors flung open and a man was carried out on a stretcher by the paramedics. Tania was about to follow inside the swing doors when Jaimie stopped her.

"Wait up, we might just get a ride..."

Jaimie was watching a nurse over by the parking bay to the right of the gates.

"I have to call home," Tania said.

"Come on, let's get my car first," he insisted.

Taking her by the hand he headed for the parked cars. He wasn't sure what he was going to say but there was a chance and he just had to play it. The nurse had just placed her shoulder bag on the back seat of the Volkswagen and was climbing in the driver's seat. Jaimie composed himself.

"Pardon me, Sister," he started, adopting the right tone of voice for what he was about to say, "I'm sorry to trouble you but I was wondering if you would by any chance be driving back towards London?"

The nurse, big built with glasses, looked up.

"You see my wife and I brought in a pregnant friend earlier on who had just started feeling labour pains, and now we're trying to get back home...I'm really sorry..."

The nurse glanced at Tania standing beside.

"How far are you going?" she asked.

"Hammersmith," Jaimie said. "But if you could even drop us off at a taxi station..."

"I live near Hammersmith. Hop in!"

"It's really very kind of you. Thank you very much." Jaimie smiled with relief.

Courteously, he opened the back door to let Tania in first.

Jaimie got in the front and they drove off.

"Did your friend have the baby?" the nurse asked as she steered the Volkswagen onto the main road.

Jaimie knew Tania was unlikely to keep up with the invented story.

"Not yet, but the doctors said it won't be 'til morning."

221

A night time radio show played at low volume on the car stereo.

"Child labour can be a long process," the nurse said. "Is her husband with her?"

Though he felt a little bad about continuing with his lie, Jaimie had to play all the way.

"No...he's out of the country right now. But we called him from the hospital." He added: "He's a soldier, you see."

"Ah, I'm sure he'll be pleased. Is it her first child?"

"Yes, first time.' Jaimie nodded.

He didn't need to look back at Tania for the look on her face.

"Have you got any children yet?" the nurse asked.

Tania saw her look in the mirror.

"No, we don't," she said dryly.

"Not yet," Jaimie added perversely. "We only got married recently."

The nurse smiled knowingly. She and Jaimie kept up the conversation until they got into town. She insisted on dropping them off home. Unfazed, Jaimie picked a street near to where his car was.

"There it is..." he pointed to a terraced house.

The nurse stopped the car. They got out and thanked her, waited until she had driven off to move away from the gate of their supposed home. Tania's face was a mask of disapproval.

"Lying comes awfully easy to you," she told Jaimie.

"Oh, come on," he replied. "We got a ride, didn't we?"

He added, mockingly:

"We actors gotta do what we gotta do..."

The jeep was where he'd left it.

"I have to phone home to let my parents know I'm safe," Tania said as they got out of parking. Jaimie hit the button on his radio until he found a station with a melodic saxophone blowing. Despite the early hour, Hammersmith Broadway already had a regular stream of vehicles.

"There's a call box! Stop!"

Tania was pointing to a BT public phone on the left. Jaimie kept on driving. He said:

"I have to take you somewhere first..."

She turned to him.

"What?"

In his mind, Jaimie was trying to find the best way to explain what he had to do. If he came out with it straight, she would probably think he had lost his mind. With all that she had been through already, he knew Tania was unlikely to take it well but Jaimie had given his word. What he was told sounded incredible at first but no more than the things he had learned at Colonel Liston's house. It would be up to Tania herself to verify the story.

"There's someone you have to meet."

He heard her sigh deeply.

"Look Jaimie, it's four in the morning and I have to get home to reassure my parents. A lot of things have happened since yesterday. I'm tired and I'm sure you are too. Get me home, please, I will be happy to meet your friend some other time."

Once again Jaimie found himself at the centre of things he had nothing to do with.

"Alright, listen to me; I know you don't understand what I'm talking about and if I told you, you'd probably think I was crazy anyway. It's nothing to do with me; it concerns you and it's very important that you should meet this person. Now, I promised I would take you to them so let's just check it out. You gotta hear it for yourself, alright?"

Jaimie stopped talking. He could feel Tania's eyes on him. When he turned to look at her, her face was tense, her eyes staring through the windscreen. Already, the sky was showing lighter shades, announcing the coming dawn. He asked:

"Do you trust me?"

"I do, but..."

"Be cool, baby, we'll be there soon."

It was the first time he had called her 'baby', and maybe it had nothing to do with it but after that Tania simply rested her head against the seat, closed her eyes and asked nothing more.

The directions he'd been given were clear enough and Jaimie found the street he was looking for easily. He parked the jeep in front of number twenty-three. Tania had dozed off.

"Where are we?" she asked, as he switched off the engine.

"Clapham."

He looked in her face, smiled.

"You OK?"

She nodded and stifled a yawn.

"Let's go," he said.

Jaimie rang the bell once, wondering what he was doing at this time of the morning waking people up he didn't even know. Yet everything he had been through in the last twelve hours had been so...insane! Tania was looking at him, her eyes asking the same question. Jaimie rang again, twice. Soon after, the door was unlocked and opened. The young man, the driver of the Granada, stood before them, dressed in pyjama pants and a white undershirt. He had obviously been woken out of his sleep.

"I'm sorry, we've only just made it out," Jaimie told him apologetically.

"It's alright, we were waiting for you. Come in."

He let Jaimie and Tania in, closed the door and led them through to a large living room.

"This is Tania..." Jaimie told the young man.

"Hi, I'm Delroy."

"Good morning," Tania said.

Delroy studied her closely, then said:

"Have a seat. I'll call my uncle."

Jaimie and Tania sat on a three seater couch. Delroy left them. The room gave the impression of a well-lived in place. Family portraits covered much of the wall space, sports trophies stood proudly on the mantel piece and varnished wooden wall unit. A large framed picture of two grinning little girls sat above the television. Jaimie was relaxed on the couch while Tania sat up rather straight on the edge. She was visibly uneasy, wondering why Jaimie had dragged her here. She would have spoken her mind there and then if Delroy hadn't walked back in.

"He won't be long. Can I get you a cup of tea?"

Jaimie looked at Tania first.

"If it's not too much trouble," she said.

Delroy smiled:

"No, no, I'm gonna have one myself. Jaimie?"

"Yes, thank you."

Delroy went out again.

"Have you known him long?" Tania asked, still trying to figure out what was happening.

"Never met him until last night," Jaimie told her.

He could see on her face that she didn't enjoy the suspense. Delroy brought a tray with three tea mugs. They sat drinking the hot drinks, Jaimie engaging in small talk and Delroy all the time observing Tania, as discreetly as he could. He got up pulled back

224

the drapes, the nascent daylight entered the room. A door closed somewhere inside the house, then footsteps came down a flight of stairs. The man who appeared at the living-room door was of medium height, dressed in brown corduroy pants and a white open-necked shirt. The crown of short, nappy grey hair contrasted with the deep hue of his skin. He paused at the door, his gaze hovering for a few, intense seconds on Tania. She and Jaimie got up as one. Jaimie thought he saw a faint smile on the man's face.

"Please, don't get up," he said, his voice low but richly toned.

"Good morning, sir," Jaimie said.

"Yes, good morning," the man nodded curtly.

He walked in and sat in a chair facing the couch. For a little while, no one said anything, the older man's dark eyes shifting slowly from Tania to Jaimie and back. Then Delroy got up.

"I'll get your tea," he said and left the room.

Jaimie cleared his throat.

"We're very sorry to wake you up this early..." he started.

"It's alright, Delroy said you would come," the man said.

His accent clearly indicated a Caribbean origin. Tania seemed even more uneasy now. She could feel the man's eyes on her.

"I am very happy to see you."

The comment from the man was addressed to Tania, but it did nothing to dissipate her nervousness.

"I heard you were involved in some little problems. Is everything alright now?"

"Well...not quite yet," Jaimie answered.

Delroy came back in, placed a smoking mug on the tray on the little wooden table, then left them again.

"I think I should leave you two to talk," Jaimie said.

To Tania's relief, the older man motioned to him to remain seated.

"It is best you stay," he told him warmly. Then he seemed to realise he had not introduced himself.

"My name is Campbell, Stanley Campbell. Delroy is my nephew."

"I'm Jaimie, and this is Tania."

Mr Campbell nodded. He picked up his mug and tasted the tea, careful not to burn himself, kept the mug palmed in his dark, bony hand. His faced showed strong lines around the mouth, thin ones at the corners of his narrow eyes.

225

He looked into Tania's face again.

"I know that you don't know me, so what I am about to tell you is going to be a big shock to you, Tania..." Her name sounded very different spoken by him. "But this is something you have to know, and I have waited many years to meet you."

Tania listened, clearly puzzled. She had regained that composure Jaimie had learned to recognise in her, that almost aristocratic way she had of holding up her head, the impassiveness of her features.

"I was born in Jamaica, in a place called Jericho, in the parish of St James," Mr Campbell told her.

"I came to this country for the first time in 1968. I was a young man then, just twenty-two. At the time I got a job working for British Rail. I settled down in London then I sent for my younger sister, Delroy's mother."

Tania listened politely to Mr Campbell's life story, unaware of the impatient tap of her foot.

"Life in this country at that time was not as hard as now, you could still make a living. Anyway, around 1970, I met a young lady and we started seeing each other, you know. Eventually, we decided to get married and make a life together so we moved in a rented apartment in west London, near Notting Hill. We got married in early '72; it was a very cold January, snowing... At that time, my wife was already expecting. She was still studying but my job wasn't paying too badly so I was earning enough to support us. The baby came a little early, in June."

A bright sun had started to rise outside, gleaming through the window of the quiet room. Jaimie sat still fascinated by the older man's story.

"Well, for the first two days my wife was in the hospital. After work, I visited her and the baby in hospital. You can imagine how happy I was to be a father! The third day, I went there in the afternoon to take them home...I didn't own a car back then but one of my friends drove me down to the hospital, so the baby wouldn't catch cold on the way home..."

Here Mr Campbell paused, took a sip of his tea. He looked up after swallowing.

"So, when I got upstairs to the wards, I find the bed empty. When I asked the nurse, she told me my wife had already left earlier that day. So, I told her it must be a mistake because I am her husband and she was waiting for me to pick her and the baby up. The nurse checked it out with the others and they told me she had left that morning, in a taxi. I couldn't believe it..."

He paused again, then said very calmly, very quietly.

"I never saw my family again."

Then Mr Campbell lifted the mug to his lips, sipped twice, put it back down on the table. He said nothing more for a full minute. The silence in the room was alive with unspoken questions. Jaimie looked at Tania but her eyes were on the grey-haired man in front of her. Her eyes and his met and for the first time she stood his gaze. Whether it was sorrow or the expression of long-accepted bitter irony, Mr Campbell's voice had a deeper ring to it when he said:

"I took some pictures of the baby in the hospital but my wife vanished with the camera..."

The power of the story, soberly told, affected Jaimie. Inside he felt really sorry for the man. For all he had suffered in his own short life, he realised nothing had been quite as cruel as this.

"It must have been really painful for you," Tania said.

These were the first words she had spoken to Mr Campbell. They came out almost unwilled, drawn out from her spontaneous feeling of compassion. Mr Campbell nodded slowly, fixing upon Tania his intense pupils. She wasn't quite ready for what he said next.

"My wife's maiden name was Winfield...Louise Alma Winfield."

Even though Jaimie expected some kind of reaction from Tania, forewarned as he was, the intense expression of shock that took over her face touched him. The mug nearly fell out of her clasped hands. Mr Campbell's eyes were set on her, watching, waiting. Her mouth was half-open, no sounds coming out.

"I have waited twenty three years to tell you that story," Mr Campbell told her simply.

He leaned back in his chair and sighed deeply. Jaimie noticed how sad he looked just then.

"It's not possible..." he heard Tania say finally.

Mr Campbell nodded gravely.

"God is my witness. But only your mother can confirm my story."

A powerful silence floated around the room. Outside, another bright morning was lifting away the remaining mist. In the short time he had known her, Jaimie had never seen Tania in the grip of such powerful emotions as she was experiencing now. He had seen her cry for the first time on seeing old Cisse but her eyes right now were nowhere near ready to shedding tears. The were fixed, stony, lost in a stunned contemplation of the framed portraits on the opposite wall. Mr Campbell's voice cut through the echoing silence.

"After a year, I finally had to face the fact that I would never see my child again, so I quit my job and left England. I went back to my village, back to cultivating the land. The years passed and although I tried to settle down after a while, I never stopped thinking about my baby, never. It was only last year when I came back to London for some medical tests that I saw a photo in a hospital magazine and recognised my wife. She had changed a lot, but it was her. That was the way I found you, Tania..."

She looked at Mr Campbell.

"The brown car..." she said, as if speaking to herself.

"I got Delroy to help me. The doctors said I shouldn't drive any more," he answered.

Tania was under the sway of a deep emotional turmoil, as anyone caught unawares by such a revelation of such magnitude would have been. Jaimie wasn't sure what he should do; whether there was anything anyone could in fact do was unlikely. Given the blow she had suffered the previous night in finding out her father's true colours, Tania's mind was in no state to deal with such sudden and cold facts about her own mother, facts which touched down to the very core of her being. How could Mr Campbell's story be true? For her to consciously accept, rationally, that her mother, whom she loved and knew so well, could have kept such a secret from her, meant a complete crumbling of her world. It just wasn't possible, he had to be mistaken. But how did he know her mother's maiden name? Tania shook her head, as if to force the nightmare to vanish like smokes drifts away. Suddenly, she got up. Her face showed neither anger, nor hurt, not even shock anymore. Rather, Jaimie was surprised to read what he saw as a soft, almost resigned look in her eyes.

"I'm sorry. As you said, this is all a great shock to me...I would like to go home."

Jaimie looked at Mr Campbell, got up.

"I understand..." Mr Campbell got up, a benign smile in his eyes. "All I wanted was for you to know the truth some day. I think

228

it matters still...I am happy God has granted my wish."

Jaimie could feel the pinch of emotion in his own stomach. Tania was maybe about to comment when a woman's voice broke through the charged atmosphere.

"Stanley, you're up already?"

All three gazes switched to the living room door where a short woman in a green dressing gown and white tie-head scarf now stood. Her eyes opened in surprise as she noticed the two visitors. Jaimie saw her squint as she focused on them.

"Jesus Lord!"

Her exclamation caught Jaimie by surprise. He watched her walk up to Tania, staring at her with an awestruck look on her face.

"This is my sister Coleen, Delroy's mother."

The woman seemed to finally remember herself.

"I'm really sorry, good morning," she said, her voice had a high pitch to it, not unpleasant. "I can't believe this!" she exclaimed, unable to tear her gaze from Tania.

"Tania needs to go home now. She have things to attend to..." Mr Campbell told her.

His sister hardly heard him. Tania stood there, visibly uneasy about all this, but Mr Campbell's sister had such a pleasurable smile across her fine features now that she had recovered from the initial shock. Tania was looking deep in the woman's face too now.

"But Stanley, you don't see who she favour?"

Mr Campbell had a genuine smile, the first real smile since they had met. Jaimie caught himself checking Tania, then 'auntie' Coleen, as it might be. There was a definite resemblance especially in the lower part of the face, more obvious with her than with Mr Campbell. He guessed Tania was starting to see it too.

"Wait here, my dear, I soon come," Coleen said, before marching out of the room, the dressing gown flapping around her as she went.

"Excuse my sister, Tania. She doesn't realise you need time..."

His sister was back already, holding something in her right hand which she handed to Tania.

"You look at this picture, tell me what you see..."

The black and white photograph had yellowed with age, but it nevertheless captured Tania's attention for several seconds, before she turned to look at Auntie Coleen then back to the seated person in the photo. Jaimie was trying to peer over Tania's shoulder when

Auntie Coleen said:

"Alright, let your friend see it and tell you if I'm right."

Jaimie took the photo. He could but shake his head in shock. The woman seated outside what looked like a wooden barn wore a long skirt, and a buttoned white blouse for what seemed like a formal snapshot, the kind grandparents liked to take after Sunday church services. Even allowing for the neatly cane-rowed grey hair, the features on the smiling dark face could have been the mould for Tania's own. Jaimie passed the picture back to her.

"This is Miss Bertha, your daddy grandmother and mine..." Auntie Coleen told Tania.

Then she clapped her hands, lifting up her eyes to the living room ceiling in wonder.

"Lord, what a t'ing!" she exclaimed, her deep eyes set on an overwhelmed Tania.

Her emotions couldn't be held back any longer. The short woman stepped up to Tania and hugged her close, as if to feel for herself if she was real. Mr Campbell and Jaimie's eyes met. Jaimie felt the warmth of the older man's expression inside him.

CHAPTER ELEVEN

The six o'clock news bulletin ended. *"Another sunny morning rising over London town..."* the Choice FM DJ said before sending out a couple of dedications on the first few beats of a 'less-bump-more-grind' swingbeat tunes. 'Another sunny morning!' Jaimie shook his head meditatively. The traffic was thick but still progressing, snaking lazily ahead. In the passenger seat, Tania's eyes were closed, her head against the headrest. She hadn't said a word since leaving Clapham. Jaimie could imagine how much turmoil her mind was in right now. How confused would he be if the same thing happened to him, he wondered. Back there, at the Campbell's house, he couldn't help admiring how stoically Tania had taken it all in. Auntie Coleen's embrace was like a magic healing balm. Unlike her brother, she felt no bitterness associated with finding his long lost daughter. She had immediately accepted Tania as a member of the family, and as surprising as it was to Jaimie, Tania soon responded in kind. Talk about overcoming the shock! A kind of female bonding 'vibe' had formed between them. After eating a hearty Jamaican breakfast, it was time to leave.

Once again Jaimie observed the beautiful young woman beside him. This had to be the craziest night of his life, and it wasn't over yet. He sighed, pushed into gear as the light turned green at the intersection.

The first thing Jaimie noticed on turning into the cul-de-sac was a familiar vehicle parked in front of the gate of Heywoode's residence. He frowned.

"What is he doing here?"

Tania opened her eyes.

"Who?" she asked.

Jaimie parked the jeep and they walked through the open gates, up the driveway. Tania was looking around, puzzled.

"Where are the guards? What is going on?"

From the front entrance to their left came a shout:

"Tania!"

Mrs Heywoode was climbing down the steps faster than her usual composed pace, hurrying towards them. Jaimie slowed down a little.

"Thank God!"

Tania was drawn into her mother's embrace. The dark circles under Mrs Heywoode's eyes told of a night spent waiting and worrying. She hugged her daughter as if she thought she had lost her for ever.

"Are you alright? I was so afraid..."

"I'm fine, Mummy, really."

"Hi, Mrs Heywoode," Jaimie called out.

"Jaimie...I was so worried. How are you?"

"I'm fine, thanks."

At the top of the steps, he appeared, dressed in a bright blue track suit, grinning in the early morning sun. Jaimie shook his head.

"What are you doing here?"

"Man, we were so worried about you!"

Junior walked down, behind him Jaimie saw the reason for his brother's grin, smart at this early hour in beige dungarees and black tee shirt.

"Tania! Jaimie! I'm so glad you're back."

Millie ran down to hug her cousin. Jaimie got a hug too.

"I was waiting for your call, like you said..." Junior told him.

"Where is Daddy?" Tania asked her mother.

Mrs Heywoode's face look bemused after the relief of seeing her daughter.

"He...he's gone," she said, not sounding very sure.

"Gone?" Tania exclaimed, "Gone where?"

Right then, all eyes turned towards the front gate where a sleek, dark grey Daimler had just come to a halt. Jaimie didn't have the time to guess as the driver's door opened to reveal Maxwell's unsmiling face. Another black man, suited, with a moustache and glasses climbed out of the big car's front passenger door. Maxwell opened the back door to let his boss step out. Dressed in a pearl grey three-piece suit, black tie and shades, Colonel Liston led the way inside. Mrs Heywoode was rooted on the spot, her cold gaze focused on the approaching bald man. Tania stood by her side, Millie and Junior a little way back. Jaimie felt a fleeting glance as Colonel Liston passed him. He couldn't mistake Maxwell's cold and brief stare though. At close quarters, the third man looked like a typical accountant, very neat, very formal. He looked at no one in particular. Jaimie watched Colonel Liston stop in front of Tania and her mother. The babyish smile opened up his features.

"Louise, my dear, how are you?" he asked, sounding very genuine.

Colonel Liston kissed Mrs Heywoode formally on the cheek.

"Hello, Colonel," she replied rather tersely.

"Tania, good morning," he said.

She nodded, straight-faced.

"Good morning."

Jaimie squinted in the glare of the bright early morning sun. 'Good morning?!!!!' he thought to himself, more than a little surprised.

"Please forgive me for disturbing you at this early hour..." Colonel Liston sounded his usual smooth self, "but I really need to speak with your husband."

As if nothing had happened. Mrs Heywoode looked up at him.

"I'm afraid you're too late. He's gone?"

"Gone?" Colonel Liston repeated.

Mrs Heywoode sighed deeply, told him very coldly:

"He left sometime last night, without explanation." She added: "Maybe you could explain to me what this is really all about?"

Colonel Liston winced from behind his shades. He turned to Tania, who held a defiant stare.

"You are welcome to see for yourself, in case you think..." Mrs Heywoode began.

Colonel Liston shook his head as if such a thought was sacrilegious to him.

"Louise dear, I would never doubt your word, you know that...I'm very sorry about this whole misunderstanding."

"What did you want to see my husband about?"

Watching them, Jaimie had the strong impression that these two people knew each other very well. Politely, Colonel Liston declined to enlighten Mrs Heywoode. He shrugged his massive shoulders, spread his hands sideways a little, in a dismissive gesture.

"Please, don't concern yourself with this, dear. Just a...business transaction. It will wait."

Tania and he exchanged a brief but intense look, then he nodded:

"Well, I won't take any more of your time." He noticed Millie behind her cousin. "Millie! I almost didn't recognise you. How are you?"

"I'm fine, uncle," she replied with a diplomatic smile.

233

"Good," the Colonel said. "Tania, my apologies for the inconvenience I caused you. Louise, take care, my dear."

Colonel Liston turned and started back, his two men followed. He paused for a moment in front of Jaimie.

"I was right about you. You've got something."

The voice was warm enough. Jaimie made a little modest gesture.

"I do my best, sir."

Colonel Liston smiled. Behind him, Maxwell smirked.

"If you ever need a job, look me up, Jaimie."

Jaimie smiled. Colonel Liston turned and went on his way.

"Max, how's it hanging?" Jaimie called out.

Following his boss, Maxwell chose to ignore him.

The Daimler drove off. Jaimie turned to find Tania's eyes fixed on him. He tried to figure out what the look meant. Just then Mrs Heywoode's rather shaken voice said: "Tania, you know what this whole thing is about. Don't you think I should be told?"

Tania turned to her mother, paused.

"You're right, Mummy, you have the right to be told. Why don't we go inside."

Jaimie watched the two women disappear into the house. Just then a sleepy voice called from above:

"Jaimie! Yo, Junior! Hey, what's happening?"

Barechested, squinting against the bright early rays, totally oblivious to the turmoil surrounding his family, Carl had emerged from his slumber. He came down, joined them in the lounge, listened with bewilderment to Jaimie's summing up of the events of the previous night. Junior explained that Millie had called him on his mobile around midnight, after finding her aunt very distressed.

Carl didn't yet know that his father had left. From what Millie told Jaimie, Mr Heywoode had left with Eddie sometime between one and three at night. He had not said goodbye or left a note even to his wife. Carl got some fruit juice from the kitchen and they sat there, chilling out for a while. As an aside, Junior told Jaimie:

"Oh yeah, Cooler's dead."

"What?"

"Yeah; the police found him and arrested him yesterday morning. He died in hospital last night," Junior said soberly.

Jaimie shook his head, still shocked. Though he didn't know the youth personally, the news left him with a bad taste.

234

"Who's Cooler?" Carl asked.

"Some kid from the area," Jaimie said.

Junior looked at his brother.

"Guess where they arrested him?"

Jaimie frowned.

"Down by your friend, that punk dealer..." Junior nodded slowly.

The story was clear cut enough, dirty, pointless and tragic. Tragic because Jaimie knew someone was going to have to do the burying, someone like Cooler's mother.

"He wanted to be a 'G'..." Jaimie sighed.

Carl nodded, as if wise to the facts.

"A what?" Millie had been quietly listening up to now.

"A gangster," Carl explained.

"Is that all they can think about?" she asked, sounding older than her age.

Jaimie sighed and shrugged.

"These days it's all about getting paid. But these kids are usually not around long enough to see pay day."

Laterally, an image slipped into Jaimie's mental frame: a long dark sleek Daimler. He turned to Millie.

"Take your uncle, the Colonel. You could call him the ultimate 'G'..."

Millie looked bemused. Jaimie could tell she wasn't really getting his point.

"Hey, now that you're here, you can listen to my tracks!" Carl jumped up.

Before Jaimie could stop him and explain that he'd had kind of a rough night, the lanky youth was sprinting out and up the stairs for his tapes.

In Tania's upstairs bedroom where she had led her mother, Mrs Heywoode sat on the bed. Standing by the window, Tania was anxious. She had explained to her mother why old Cisse had reappeared in her life so suddenly and what it was Colonel Liston was really after. Incidentally and unavoidably, Tania found herself telling her mother, who had chosen to 'see nothing, hear nothing' for all these years, the real line of 'business' her husband had been engaged in to maintain their highlife. Though the sun bathed the bedroom in sparkling bright sunlight, neither of the two women

235

honoured it with a thought. For each of them, the clear morning marked the end of a phase and the beginning of another. At that precise moment, although different in their respective emotional concerns, they were both alike in their confusion.

"But how could he go away, just like that? Anything could have happened to you!" Mrs Heywoode said.

"I guess he knew Colonel Liston wouldn't hurt me," Tania said calmly.

"That's not the point..."

Mrs Heywoode's fear was turning to anger.

"Look, I'm not angry with daddy," Tania sighed. "His deeds caught up with him, he had to run."

Tania's mother couldn't believe how well she was taking it.

"But what about us? What is going to happen to us?"

"Nothing's going to happen to us. We'll simply carry on, adjust and get on with our lives."

Mrs Heywoode's hands were clasped nervously in the lap of her dress.

"This is absurd," she said, trying to get a grip on herself. "I'm sure your father will call soon." She paused then stated a little more firmly, "I just can't believe he left me like that. I am his wife, I deserve an explanation."

Tania left the window, sat on the other side of the bed.

"Mummy," she said, "I think you're right. I'm sure you'll get a call from him." Tania's hard eyes focused deep into her mother. "But maybe you won't..." She paused, maintaining the visual contact. "Stanley Campbell didn't..."

Mrs Heywoode didn't seem to hear right away. Tania switched her gaze towards the window, then the hesitant question came:

"What did you say?"

Tania didn't turn to her. As if speaking to the fresh air coming in through the open window, she said distinctly:

"I said that Stanley Campbell didn't get an explanation."

There was force in her calm tone of voice. The words penetrated like the stab of a blade through Mrs Heywoode's consciousness, her eyes filled with an icy mist, her hands rose to her face, trembling. By the time Tania turned around, her mother was shaken by convulsive sobs. Tania got up, walked around the bed to the shelf where the line of cuddly toy animals she'd kept since childhood gazed down mutely on the bed. Reaching out, she took hold of

Mitch, the black striped chipmunk who knew all her childhood confidences. Her back to her crying mother on the bed, Tania stroked Mitch's faded fur.

"How could someone do that to a person, Mitch? How could you take a child away from her father?" Tania sighed deeply, feeling the strength of her repressed emotions welling up in her body. She asked:

"Do you think it's right, Mitch, to keep your own child from knowing who they are?" Tania stopped as she could feel her tone of voice rising over the backdrop of her mother's sobbing sounds. She breathed deeply. Still running her fingers over the chipmunk's fur, she asked him again: "Do you think it's right?"

On the bed, Mrs Heywoode was struggling with her breaking heart. Lifting her tear-covered face, she said in a strangled voice:

"You don't know how it was...you don't know."

Tania didn't turn around. Choked by a big sob, Mrs Heywoode swallowed hard before she could continue.

"I was just a young girl, engaged, when I came to London to study. I...I met this man, I lost my mind. My parents kept pressuring me, they threatened me. I ran away...Then my fiance, he came over and found me...I didn't want to go, I had no choice..."

Tania had carefully replaced Mitch on the shelf and turned to face her mother, who was drowned in tears of remorse for yesteryear.

"And that is your explanation?" she asked in a pained, hoarse whisper, before starting out slowly towards the door.

"Tania! What is going to happen now?" her mother called behind her.

Tania turned only to say:

"Now? You're going to take care of your life, and I'm going to take care of mine."

Then she departed.

The two of them leant on the bonnet of the jeep, both looking up to the corner at the other end of the street where Junior's car had just disappeared. Jaimie sincerely hoped Junior was going to drop Millie off and then go to work as he had promised. Inside the house Carl was getting ready, Jaimie having convinced him that today was a schoolday, regardless. Tania was fiddling absentmindedly with the side mirror lost in some inner contemplation. Though he

237

desperately needed a change of clothes, Jaimie felt as rested as if he had slept eight solid hours the previous night. Refreshed, Tania had returned to the lounge to join them refreshed, her hair brushed and neatly tied in a bun. The brown and green patterns of her African print dress stood out against the brightness of the car. Jaimie felt the feeling of relaxation in his limbs. Now that the nervous tension of the night had subsided, his whole body was unwinding. As for talking, well, what was there to say? Each day has its burden, and the previous one had had plenty! Now he was just happy to kick back with Tania for while, suspended in time.

"I wish I had a camera with me," Jaimie said.

"Why?" Tania asked.

"It's a good day."

She smiled faintly.

"What's so good about it?"

"Check it out, there's a lot of good things right here. You're alive, and I'm alive and it's sunny, it's got to be a good day." He added: "And there's gonna be lots more."

Tania turned to face him, gave him a deep look.

"Can I ask you a question?"

"Sure."

"But promise you'll answer honestly..."

"I promise," he nodded.

"You've got to answer totally honestly, right?"

"Right. Ask me the question..."

"Even negative things, you have to tell the truth.." Tania pointed out, index finger in the air.

"OK, ask me..."

"Just be honest..."

"Will you ask me the question!" he sighed in mock frustration.

"Alright..." she was watching him intently. "What do you think of me?"

She saw Jaimie start to smile, frowned.

"You promised..."

"OK, take it easy; I'm gonna answer!" He raised his hands in surrender. All the same he had to smile.

"Why you asking?" he tried.

Tania pulled a menacing frown.

"Alright!" Then he took his time to reflect on it.

"To be totally honest," Jaimie started, standing upright, his hand

238

up in testimony, "and I swear to tell the truth, the whole truth and nothing but the truth..."

Tania waited patiently for Jaimie to finish clowning around.

"OK. This is it," Jaimie leant back against the car, with a sincere look. "I think you're really...fly."

He saw her suspicious frown.

"Is that good?"

"Sure, in fact I think you're the flyest girl I've ever hung out with."

"Really? Why?"

"Why?" he repeated. "Because...because I like hanging out with you, trust me. You're fun, you know."

"Fun!?" she looked at him very surprised now.

"Yeah, I always have a great time with you." He added: "I ain't never been kidnapped before."

"I'm glad you found it funny!"

Jaimie's hand stroked hers, soothingly.

"Come on, it happened for a reason. The main thing is, nobody got hurt...not physically." He had added the last part in acknowledgement of the shock she had been through in the process.

"You're right," Tania nodded.

"Why did you ask me that anyway?" Jaimie said.

"Oh, I wanted to know if you still find me 'stuck-up'."

" 'Stuck-up'?!"

"That's what you said, didn't you?" Tania insisted.

Jaimie gave her the look of a man who had never used the word in his life.

"Me?!..."

She nodded.

"I'm sure, or something to that effect. Anyway, what do you really think now?"

"No man, you're fine." He waited a little. "I'll tell you one thing: I think you're a very adaptable person...And that is one of the best qualities to have."

She gave him a smile for that. Jaimie waited a little. Around them, the morning was sunny and quiet.

"What are you gonna do now?" he asked.

Because their eyes met, Jaimie knew she knew what he was talking about. But she said, very seriously, with an exaggerated yankee accent:

"I'm gonna take the week off!"

Then she laughed lightly. Jaimie laughed too, pushed her playfully on the shoulder, enjoying the humour.

"There, you see, I said you were fun to hang out with!"

She sighed, shook her head.

"I'm not sure what I'm going to do, Jaimie. I'm not even sure if I know who I am anymore."

Jaimie could relate to that in a way.

"I think if you know yourself as a person, the rest will fall into place, you know."

Jaimie wasn't sure if he had heard that somewhere or if he had just made it up, but it sounded so true. He told Tania with a little grin.

"You just have more family than you thought you had. It's all good!"

She nodded.

"You know, while we were in the kitchen, Miss...Auntie Coleen told me my...father is really more sick than he wants to admit." She paused. "He wants me to go to Jamaica with him...He wants to show me my land."

"Alright," Jaimie nodded, happy. "You got land in Jamaica!"

Tania's face turned a little more serious.

"Did Mamadou tell you what I have to do?"

Jaimie tracked back to their conversation.

"Uh-uh, I don't think so. What's that?"

Tania sighed deeply, her face stern, reflecting the seriousness of her frame of mind.

"The mask needs a...servant. Without an initiated priestess, no one can use it. Cisse said I have two choices: either I continue to serve...or I must ask the spirit to choose a new priestess, a child from the clan."

Even in the brightness of the morning, the parallel universe Jaimie had tripped into by accident the previous night was never far.

"Either way, I have to go back with him," Tania sighed apprehensively.

"Man, looks like you're gonna be busy!" Jaimie told her. "I guess you're gonna have to take care of all that, check your priorities, you know what I'm saying?"

Tania gave him one of her deep, searching stares.

240

"D'you want to come along?" she asked.

It didn't quite sink in right away.

"Come along? You mean...to Africa?"

She nodded without breaking the stare.

"Guinea."

"Guinea? What?!" Jaimie's eyes were wide at the thought.

"You want me to go to Guinea with you?"

She waited. Jaimie sighed, nodded.

"Yeah, sure, I'm with it. Alright. Things are happening!"

She smiled at his enthusiasm.

"What about your job?" she asked.

Jaimie gave her a puzzled look, shrugged.

"I'm taking a month off."

He laughed, a relaxed happy laugh.

"You're adaptable too, right?" Tania said.

"Just like you," he nodded confidently. "And anyway," he pointed out seriously, "I couldn't let you run out on me just like that. We're a team now!"

"Are we?" Tania's eyes gave the question its full meaning.

Jaimie drew a little closer to her, stood her gaze.

"We most certainly are...You ain't going no place without me, Miss Heywoode."

She smiled and said simply:

"You're a determined man."

"That's right."

Gently, Jaimie picked up her right hand and brought it to his lips. Tania's surprise showed and she looked away shyly, then back to him. The eye contact was strong, eloquent. Jaimie saw her straighten up and take the one step which still separated them. He didn't move, opened up to let her slender body press lightly against his for that one second. Though furtive as a bird in flight, Jaimie had still felt the kiss. Tania stood in front of him, her hand still in his. Jaimie sighed contentedly, grinning wide. He now knew what he needed to know.

"I'm gonna go home now," he told Tania.

She was watching him and reading him.

"Alright."

"But I'm gonna give you a call. Soon..."

"Soon..."

"Yeah," he nodded. "Most definitely."

241

"OK, have a safe drive home."

Jaimie sat in the driver's seat and with the key in the ignition, turned the engine.

"Get some rest, and be cool. Everything is gonna be alright."

"OK," Tania said smiling.

"Don't worry about a thing..."

He leaned out the window and stole another brief kiss. He sighed with undisguised satisfaction.

"Bye, then..." Tania watched him slip the jeep in gear.

On his radio, the DJ had just finished running a string of commercials. The record that followed stopped Jaimie in his tracks. He forgot what he was about to tell Tania, turned up the volume.

"What have you done to me..." he sang along to Anita Baker's *Body and Soul*.

Tania smiled broadly, gave him a little wave. Reversing, Jaimie turned the wheel and waved back before driving down the cul-de-sac. By the time he drove around the corner, he was singing well above the volume of the song.

The End.

THE
VICTOR HEADLEY
COLLECTION

3 Tuff Novels From The Number One Black Author In The UK:

YARDIE

At Heathrow Airport's busy Immigration desk, a newly arrived Jamaican strolls through with a kilo of top-grade cocaine strapped to his body. And keeps on walking...
By the time the syndicate get to hear about the missing consignment, D. is in business — for himself — as the Front Line's newest don. But D.'s treachery will never be forgotten — or forgiven. The message filters down from the Yardie crime lords to their soldiers on the streets:
Find D. Find the merchandise. And make him pay for his sins...

EXCE$$ – THE SEQUEL TO YARDIE

Things got really hot after D.'s arrest. The police virtually closed down Hackney for business. The posses have had to take stock and regroup. But the shaky truce that followed their turf war, is getting shakier as Sticks, a 9mm 'matic in his waist, dips deeper and deeper into his own supply of crack...

YUSH! –THE FINAL SCORE

The final curtain comes down on the superb Yardie trilogy. An all guns blasting end, worthy of Britain's most popular black writer. If you enjoyed reading it remember to big up the book to your bredrin.

Black Classics

NEW from The X Press-- an exciting collection of the world's great forgotten black classic novels. Many brilliant works of writing lie in dusty corners of libraries across the globe. Now thanks to Britain's foremost publisher of black fiction, you can discover some of these fantastic novels. Over the coming months we will be publishing many more of these masterpieces which every lover of classic fiction will want to collect.

TRADITION by Charles W Chesnutt

In the years after the American Civil War, a small town in the Deep South struggles to come to terms with the new order. Ex-slaves are now respected doctors, lawyers and powerbrokers--And the white residents don't like it one bit! When a black man is wrongly accused of murdering a white woman, the black population, proud and determined, strike back. For a gifted black doctor, the events pose a huge dilemma. Should he take on the mantle of leading the black struggle, or does his first responsibility lie with his wife and children?

THE BLACKER THE BERRY by Wallace Thurman

Emma Lou was born black. Too black for her own comfort and that of her social-climbing wannabe family. Resented by those closest to her, she runs from her small hometown to Los Angeles and then to Harlem of the 1920's, seeking her identity and an escape from the pressures of the black community. She drifts from one loveless relationship to another in the search for herself and a place in society where prejudice towards her comes not only from whites, but from her own race!

IOLA by Frances E.W. Harper

The beautiful Iola Leroy is duped into slavery after the death of her father but manages to snatch her freedom back and start the long search for the mother whom she was separated from on the slave trader's block. She rejects the advances of a white man, who offers to relieve her from the "burden of blackness" by marrying her and eventually finds love and pride in her race.

THE CONJURE MAN DIES by Rudolph Fisher

Originally published in 1932, *The Conjure Man Dies* is the first known mystery novel written by an African-American. Rudolph Fisher, one of the principal writers of the Harlem Renaissance, weaves an intricate story of a native African king, who after receiving a degree from Harvard settles into Harlem of the 1930's. He becomes a fortune teller or 'Conjure Man' and quickly becomes a much talked about local figure. When the old man is found dead the rumours start spreading. Things are made even more confusing when he turns up very much alive!

THE AUTOBIOGRAPHY OF AN EX-COLORED MAN
by James Weldon Johnson

Until his school teacher points out to him in no uncertain terms that he's a "nigger", the anonymous narrator of *The Autobiography of an Ex-Colored Man*, believed that his fair skin granted him the privileges of his white class mates.

The realisation of what life holds for him is at first devastating, but as he grows into adulthood, he discovers a pride in his blackness and the noble race from which he is descended. However a disturbing family secret is soon to shake up his world.

THE HOUSE BEHIND THE CEDARS
by Charles W. Chesnutt

A few years after the American Civil War, two siblings, Rena and John Walden, 'pass' for white in the Deep South as their only means of obtaining a share of the American dream.

With a change of name and a fictitious biography, John starts a new life. But for Rena, the deception poses a bigger dilemma when she meets and falls in love with a wealthy young white man.

Can love transcend racial barriers, or will the dashing George Tryon reject her the moment he discovers her black roots?

Three more forgotten greats of black writing will be available from November 10th 1995. Check out: *A Love Supreme* by **Pauline Hopkins,** *The Walls Of Jericho* **by Rudolph Fisher and** *The President's Daughter* **by William Wells Brown.** Ask for details in any good bookshop. Only from The X Press.